The EVERYTHING
Get Published Book
2ND EDITION

Dear Reader;

Broadly speaking, there are two kinds of writers—those who want to write, and those who want to have written. The first group consists of people who would like to be published someday, but, even if that never happens, they'll continue to write because writing is as much a part of their lives as breathing. The second group tends to be more business-like, wanting at least recognition and perhaps the fame and fortune that comes along with being a bestselling author.

There's nothing wrong with either approach. Writing can be a reward in itself, but there are few thrills that compare with seeing your name in print, associated with the words that you wrote, whether it's in your local newspaper, a national magazine, a popular blog, or on the cover of a book. And when someone actually pays you for what you've written, well, that's like having an extra scoop of ice cream on your cone.

Our goal in this book is to expand your knowledge of publishing in general and to introduce you to the myriad of opportunities to see your words in print. As writers ourselves, we treasure every tiny thrill of suc-cess in our quest for publication, and we hope you will find and savor the same pleasures on your journey.

Meg Schneider

Barbara Doyen

The EVERYTHING® Series

Editorial

Publishing Director	Gary M. Krebs
Director of Product Development	Paula Munier
Associate Managing Editor	Laura M. Daly
Associate Copy Chief	Brett Palana-Shanahan
Acquisitions Editor	Gina Chaimanis
Development Editor	Jessica LaPointe
Associate Production Editor	Casey Ebert

Production

Director of Manufacturing	Susan Beale
Associate Director of Production	Michelle Roy Kelly
Cover Design	Paul Beatrice
	Matt LeBlanc
	Erick DaCosta
Design and Layout	Colleen Cunningham
	Sorae Lee
	Jennifer Oliveira
Series Cover Artist	Barry Littmann

Visit the entire Everything® Series at *www.everything.com*

THE
EVERYTHING®
GET PUBLISHED BOOK

2ND EDITION

All you need to know to
become a successful author

Meg Schneider and Barbara Doyen

Adams Media
Avon, Massachusetts

For writers everywhere, we offer these tools to help you in your pursuit of publication. May success attend your quest!

An Everything® Series Book.
Everything® and everything.com® are registered trademarks of F+W Publications, Inc.

Published by Adams Media, an F+W Publications Company
57 Littlefield Street, Avon, MA 02322 U.S.A.
www.adamsmedia.com

ISBN 13: 978-1-59337-567-6
ISBN 10: 1-59337-567-0
Printed in the United States of America.

J   I   H   G   F   E   D   C   B

Library of Congress Cataloging-in-Publication Data
is available from publisher

This publication is designed to provide accurate and authoritative information with regard to the subject matter covered. It is sold with the understanding that the publisher is not engaged in rendering legal, accounting, or other professional advice. If legal advice or other expert assistance is required, the services of a competent professional person should be sought.

—From a *Declaration of Principles* jointly adopted by a Committee of the American Bar Association and a Committee of Publishers and Associations

Many of the designations used by manufacturers and sellers to distinguish their products are claimed as trademarks. Where those designations appear in this book and Adams Media was aware of a trademark claim, the designations have been printed with initial capital letters.

This book is available at quantity discounts for bulk purchases.
For information, please call 1-800-289-0963.

Contents

Acknowledgments

The authors wish to thank the many people who have shaped their love of words over the years: those who taught us the joys of reading, those who encouraged us to do what we love, and those who inspire us to keep reaching for our dreams. With this volume, we hope we are able to pay a little back to those people and pay a little forward for our readers.

Top Ten Things You Should Know about Getting Published

1. Writers today have more opportunities than ever before to get published in traditional and virtual media, and more opportunity means more demand for good writers.

2. The difference between a rejection and a contract often lies in the quality of your market research, not necessarily in the quality of your writing.

3. The maxims "Think like an editor" and "Write to the market" are code for putting the reader first.

4. The fierce competition in publishing is really an opportunity to learn and motivation to improve.

5. Submission guidelines are your friends; your work stands the best chance of getting noticed when you follow them.

6. Constructive criticism should be cherished. It can make you a more effective writer and increase your chances of getting published.

7. In traditional book publishing, look for a good agent before you try to approach editors on your own.

8. Building solid, respectful working relationships with editors will help your career more than writing the perfect query will.

9. A healthy skepticism is your best protection against scams and the unscrupulous.

10. Getting published is the gravy. The real joy is in the writing, and no one can ever deny you that.

Introduction

▶ THERE ALWAYS HAS BEEN a peculiar romance about writers and writing. The process itself is mysterious, even sometimes to those who do it for a hobby or for a living; it has been compared with giving birth, and it has been described as a form of madness. Most writers don't like to delve too deeply into the mystery of writing. They fear that the magic will evaporate and leave only the wispy, dreamlike memory of the excitement they feel when the perfect combination of words bubbles up from their inner wells. Madness it may be, and laborious, and inexplicable. It doesn't matter. It's what we do.

But that's only part of the romance. The true seduction of writing is the idea that somebody, somewhere, someday will read what we write and be touched, informed, and entertained by it. And, when that happens, we achieve a sort of demigod status, even if only for a fleeting moment. That is the glory of getting published, not just the first time, but every time.

How to get published also is a major mystery for many writers. Countless aspiring authors of every genre find themselves flummoxed and befuddled by a steady stream of standard rejection slips and wonder if there is some dark conspiracy at work to keep their words out of the reading public's hands. It's easy to believe in such a theory when you don't know the inner workings of magazine and book publishers. For ninety-nine out of 100 hopeful writers, the unpalatable truth is that mere talent and great ideas are not enough to pierce the natural and strong sales resistance in today's publishing market. You need a platform to stand on, a track record to prove your ability, and a thorough familiarity with the needs and wants of your readers and the editors who select content for them. There is precious little romance about the publishing business, and writers who want to build a career for themselves doing what they love to do must learn to balance the sentimental glamour of the process with the more prosaic realities of the industry.

That's the bad news. The good news is that there are more opportunities for new writers to break into the business than ever before. Depending on where your interests and talents lie, you might pursue landing bylined feature assignments from national consumer magazines or having your short stories or poems published in small but high-quality literary magazines. You might write exclusively for the innumerable e-zines available on the Web. You might contribute to newsletters for hobbyists, or financial analysts, or chiefs of police. Or you might write press releases and copy for a corporation's quarterly or annual report.

Most books about getting published focus primarily on getting books published, because, for most writers, seeing one's name on the spine of a bona fide book is the holy grail. But there are many avenues to getting published, and any of them can lead to a busy and profitable writing career. Chances are good that they'll even lead to your own holy grail, if having a book published is your ambition. And, like most things in life, chances are you'll take a few unplanned detours during your quest.

chapter 1

The Wide World of Publishing

Aspiring writers sometimes focus their energies on the big prizes in publishing and overlook a multitude of opportunities to hone their skills and build their portfolios. Dreaming big is a good thing, and striving for your goals is laudable. But don't shortchange yourself by limiting your options. Even if your ultimate objective is getting your book published, there are lots of other opportunities for you to make a name for yourself—and some extra money—with your writing.

Newspapers

Your local newspaper can be a great training ground for developing your freelance career. Aside from the opportunity to hone your writing skills and learn how to work with an editor, it's a good place to develop story ideas for other markets. A story about an innovative new business in your community might be of interest (with the proper slant) to a larger newspaper, a regional magazine, or a trade journal, and, through the story for the local paper, you've already done some of the research and developed some sources.

Opinion Pages

Letters to the editor and guest opinion essays are excellent openings for beginning writers. You won't get paid for them, but you will get authorship credit, and these short pieces are valuable exercises because they force you to tighten and clarify your writing. Most local newspapers have a limit of 250 words for letters to the editors, and perhaps 600 to 800 words for guest essays. You don't have room for excessive exposition here; you have to make the most effective use of your limited space.

FACT

It's harder to get your letter to the editor or opinion piece published by larger newspapers. The *New York Times*, for example, receives thousands of letters each week, and only a very select few ever get published. Those that do are generally quite short—100 words or fewer.

Some newspapers have policies limiting how many times you can have a letter or opinion piece published. They might publish a letter from you only once every thirty days, for example. Longer pieces will be published even less often, unless the paper asks you to write a regular column. If that happens, you might well be offered a small honorarium for your contribution, and you may be asked to commit to writing your column for six months or a year.

Weekly newspapers and small dailies often are more open to accepting regular columns from contributing writers (that is, writers who aren't on the newspaper's staff). Pay for your services will be minimal, but a well-written and well-read column can be a springboard to other writing opportunities.

Food, Entertainment, and Travel

Medium- and large-circulation newspapers usually have sections devoted to food, entertainment, travel, and other special interests, such as hobbies or games. Often these newspapers accept articles from freelancers for these sections, especially if they don't have staff reporters who are interested or available to cover these beats. Again, pay usually is low, but you generally get a byline and clips to add to your portfolio.

For food sections, you might be able to review new restaurants, interview chefs in your area, or even write a feature on unusual items for the barbecue or cool new kitchen gadgets. Entertainment sections usually cover such things as movies and concerts but also extend to articles on exhibits and lectures at area art and science museums, festivals, and maybe even architecture and local history. Travel sections usually use wire services such as AP or Reuters for major domestic and international destinations, but there may be opportunities for you to highlight local attractions.

Become a Stringer

Occasional submissions to your local newspaper can turn into a regular freelance gig for you. Stringers, as they are known in the business, are basically on-call reporters who are assigned articles when the regular staff of reporters is too busy to do them. Depending on your newspaper's coverage area, it may need stringers to cover high school sports, graduations, or other events where there are too many things for one person to cover. Some newspapers have general-assignment stringers who aren't limited to any one beat or particular area of coverage. Some have stringers who cover only sports, business, or other specific beats. Pay rates for stringers vary widely and may be based on so much per article or column inch, or on hours worked.

Magazines

As exciting and gratifying as it is to see your byline in *Cosmo* or *GQ*, the truth is that these large markets are highly competitive and almost always out of reach for beginners. However, there are hundreds of smaller magazines, many of which welcome new writers. Pay rates and circulations often are lower than with the big national magazines, but a solid track record with them can help open doors down the road.

Trade Journals

Virtually every sector of business has its own magazine, and very often there are several magazines covering various aspects of a particular industry. These highly focused magazines are known as trade journals, and they have very specialized needs for very specialized readerships. *Northeast Export*, for example, covers New England's international trade community. The *Chief of Police* magazine is targeted to the command ranks of law enforcement agencies. There are hundreds more; *Writer's Market* devotes nearly 150 pages just to paying trade journal markets.

ESSENTIAL

One of the easiest ways to break into the trade journals is to examine the magazines in your own profession, or that of someone close to you, such as a parent, spouse, or friend. As with any potential market, study several issues of a journal to get a feel for the kinds of information it publishes and the writing style.

Trade journals are always looking for well-written articles that meet the needs of their readers, and they are generally open to beginning writers, as long as you can supply appropriate material. This doesn't mean you have to be an expert, or even a practitioner, in the field, but you do have to be able to write for a knowledgeable reader. If you have lots of good ideas for a trade area that interests you, you can make a respectable income while you build your collection of clips.

Consumer Magazines

Most people think of the big national magazines that you see at supermarket checkouts and bookstores when they think of consumer magazines. As noted earlier, these can be hard to break into. But there are hundreds of smaller consumer magazines. Some of them have a general-interest slant, but many of them fill narrower niches, such as rock-climbing, star-gazing, gourmet cooking, or home decorating. If you have a hobby, chances are there's a consumer magazine that could be interested in your material.

Starting out with small consumer magazines can give you the credentials you'll probably need to break into the larger publications. Even so, when you're first starting to approach the big magazines, you have a better chance of breaking in with shorter pieces. The big national magazines generally reserve their main features for established writers, but they also usually have departments that are open to newcomers.

The Internet

The Internet has given rise to a whole new world of potential markets for writers. Every Web site must have content, and Web site operators often need writers to supply that content. If you connect with the right place and know how to write effectively for the Web, you can command respectable fees for your work.

Writing for the Web

According to various studies, Internet users are an impatient bunch. They are willing to wait an average of eight seconds for a Web page to load; if it takes longer, they give up and go somewhere else. They generally like small nuggets of information and tend to shy away from text-heavy pages that scroll on forever. If they can't find what they're looking for within a few seconds on a given page, they try another site.

Most of these issues can be resolved in the design of a Web page. But an effective design requires effective structure in the content. Long pieces generally should be broken into sections to allow for easier navigation. Links to additional information often need to be imbedded in the text. Writers need to think about the keywords users will search for to find what they want.

ALERT!

Whenever you post your writings on the Web, whether it's through an e-zine, a blog, or on your own site, it counts as publication. If you post an essay about your cat, for example, you can't sell first serial rights to that same essay to *Cat Fancy* magazine; the best you can offer is second serial rights.

Writing for the Web can be a challenge, especially for writers who aren't accustomed to thinking about space limitations. It requires tightly focused text, an understanding of how readers will use the site, and insight into what readers want and need. If you can master these elements, you can make a name for yourself creating content for any number of businesses and organizations that need a continual supply of fresh material for their sites.

"Guide" Sites

Becoming an expert guide on sites like About.com can provide a big boost for your writing career. It gives you a platform for marketing magazine articles and book proposals, especially if your articles and book ideas are related to your guide topic. Writing regularly for these sites helps you sharpen your skills, and many such sites pay respectable fees to their guides.

The field is fairly competitive, and the more well-known guide sites have a fairly rigorous screening process for hiring guides. These sites also require you to commit your time to research and writing, because you'll be expected to provide regular updates to your page. However, as in any aspect of publishing, there are other ways to break in. For example, Amazon.com allows you to put together a virtual reference library on a topic you're interested in. You won't get paid for this, but you will draw in other readers who share your interest, and a comprehensive resource list under your name helps establish you as an expert on your topic.

Things to Consider

If you get a contract to write Web site content, go over the provisions carefully. It's reasonable for the site owner to prohibit you from putting material you've written for the Web site into a book. However, the contract should not prohibit you from writing any print books on any topic related to the content you create for the site. Such a requirement is overly broad and even unnecessary, since the target markets for Web sites and print books usually are significantly different.

Your contract also might bar you from providing any articles, on any topic, to competing Web sites unless you get prior approval from the site you're contracting with. This also is a reasonable demand, but, again, make sure it isn't too broad. If you've contracted with a food Web site, you should be free to contribute articles to time-management Web sites, for example.

Articles you write for Web sites often are work-for-hire arrangements. That means you get paid for what you write, but the site owner keeps all rights to the article; you can't sell reprint rights, for example. This usually isn't of too much concern, because most publications aren't interested in printing something that already has appeared on the Internet to a global audience.

Payment for Web content might be calculated in the form of a flat fee or, more often, as a percentage of advertising revenue based on page viewership. Some writers don't like the percentage arrangement because they don't get paid up front for their work. In practice, though, this payment method is like receiving royalties on a book; the more people read your work, the more money you make. Site operators like it because they don't pay for content no one reads, and the onus is on the author to provide interesting, relevant, and useful material on a continual basis.

Commercial Opportunities

Businesses and nonprofit organizations need a variety of written materials to support their missions, and they often look to outside agencies or independent contractors to produce these materials for them. The people who write these materials don't usually get a byline, but they are well paid for their skills, and they get nice finished pieces for their portfolios.

Corporate Communications

Businesses may hire you to write annual or quarterly reports for investors, press releases about new products or services, a history of the company, speeches for executives to deliver at stockholder meetings or other events, content for their Web sites, or copy for brochures. Large businesses usually hire professional advertising or public relations agencies to handle these projects, or they may have their own in-house departments. Smaller businesses, which may not be able to afford the retainers agencies charge and may not have the time or expertise to create their own materials, often are delighted to find an individual willing to do the work for a reasonable fee. Nonprofits often have the same financial and expertise restrictions of small businesses. And, many times, these clients are willing to hire writers with little or no experience for these assignments.

QUESTION?

How should I establish my fees for corporate and nonprofit projects?
Some writers will do these projects for a flat fee, while others prefer to charge an hourly rate, which can range from $25 to $150 or more. An hourly rate ensures you get paid for additional work if your client asks for substantial changes.

A freelance writer who can effectively communicate an organization's message in a variety of media can make good money and build a reputation for himself. You should be able to write in the client's voice, master the key points the client wants to make, and understand the market the client is trying to reach.

Advertising

Small businesses and nonprofits often can use help writing advertising copy as well. If you can craft an effective message for direct mail campaigns, print or electronic advertising, and even flyers, you have an opportunity to sell those skills to establishments that just don't have the time or resources to do it themselves. A flair for phrasing is important here, as is an ability to persuade your audience to take action.

Newsletters

Writing a weekly, monthly, or quarterly newsletter can give you a steady income and, over time, expertise on a particular topic. Many companies, even smaller ones, have a regular newsletter for employees; some even have one for their vendors or customers who have signed up on a mailing list. If you have even a basic desktop publishing program on your computer, you can offer your design services as well as your writing talents.

Like any other publication, newsletters usually have a specific mission and a specific audience. An employee newsletter, for instance, is likely to focus on company policies, benefit information, training opportunities, and the like. A newsletter for vendors might include requests for proposals or bids on a company project or discuss how a vendor's product helps the company succeed. One aimed at customers likely will highlight special offers, new products or services, and the company's philosophy.

ESSENTIAL

E-zines, or online newsletters, make the cost of producing your own newsletter negligible and allow you to reach a much broader audience, which helps you build a platform for other publishing opportunities. Writing an e-zine for stay-at-home mothers with 5,000 subscribers is a hefty credential for the article you want to sell to *Parenting* magazine.

Working on newsletters can help you advance your writing career, particularly if you're trying to sell articles or books that relate to your newsletter focus. If you can't find one that suits your future goals, consider starting your own and build a subscriber base. It can be as broadly or as narrowly tailored as you like, but it should be about something that interests you because you'll be writing about it a lot. Potential topics include hobbies, charitable or political causes, or social issues.

Books

Book publishing is widely seen as the pinnacle of writing success, and there is fierce competition to be one of the "chosen:" a bona fide book author. Even experienced writers with killer clips sometimes have a hard time landing that first book contract. But, like every other market in publishing, there are opportunities for talented writers who do their homework and match their work with the right market.

Adult Fiction

Seventy percent of all books sold in the United States every year are books for adults, and fiction for adults accounts for 50 percent of the American book market. Little wonder, then, that so many aspiring writers dream of being the next Amy Tan, Dan Brown, Stephen King, or Danielle Steel. Besides, fiction is where your imagination and creativity have free rein; for many writers, the fun is in fiction.

Unfortunately, adult fiction is one of the most difficult book markets for new writers to break into, partly because there is so much competition. That doesn't mean there's no room for new talent. On the contrary, agents and editors are always looking for well-written stories with strong characterization and plots that will captivate readers. But if you don't have all those elements in your manuscript, it's difficult to get your fiction noticed.

Researching potential markets is absolutely essential for marketing your novel. If you're writing romances, pay attention to what romance publishers require. Many of them insist that any explicit sex or violence take place offstage; some won't consider interracial or interfaith characters; some don't want any stories that involve infidelity or premarital sex.

FACT

The number one complaint from agents and editors is that they receive material that is not appropriate for them. Study the guidelines in the print directories and online to find out whether an element in your story excludes it from a particular market. If it does, don't waste your time—or the agent's or editor's—by submitting it.

New fiction authors almost always have to have their manuscripts completed before they begin marketing. So many agents and editors have been burned by hopeful writers who can't complete an entire novel that no one will take the risk any more. You may even be required to finish the manuscript before getting a contract for your second or third novel.

When it is time to market your novel, you need to have a clear idea of who your target readers are. Agents and editors are never impressed by claims that "everyone" will want to read your book. You don't have to provide hard numbers in your marketing package, but you do have to give an agent or editor an idea of where your book will fit on a bookstore shelf. Do this by identifying the genre of your novel and, if appropriate, published authors whose works are similar to yours. You shouldn't claim to be the next Amy Tan, but you can describe your novel as an Italian-American *Joy Luck Club*.

Adult Nonfiction

Fiction writers sometimes turn up their noses at nonfiction opportunities because nonfiction is not what they want to write. But nonfiction is easier for unpublished authors to break into, and a nonfiction book credit is helpful when you market your novel, because you are no longer an untried writer. The main question agents and editors have about new authors is whether they're capable of completing book-length work. Even though styles and demands are different in fiction and nonfiction, the fact that you've been published marks you as a professional book author.

Another advantage to nonfiction is that you don't have to write the entire manuscript in order to make a sale. Most nonfiction sales are made on the basis of a proposal, which describes both your book and the market for it. (See Chapter 8 for more details on book proposals.) If you can find a niche to be filled and craft a well-written, well-targeted proposal, you have a good chance of landing a contract.

Children's Books

The children's book market is, in many ways, even more competitive than the adult markets. Publishers receive tons of queries and manuscripts for children's books, both fiction and nonfiction, but only a select few ever make it into print. The good news is that the children's market holds great opportunities for talented writers who know how to write for this demanding readership.

Children's book publishers usually define readers by age groups, progressing in stages from infants and toddlers to teens and young adults. There's plenty of room for both fiction and nonfiction in the children's market. Advances and royalty rates tend to be lower than for adult fiction and nonfiction, but children's books often stay in print longer, and children often become loyal, lifelong fans of their favorite authors.

chapter 2
Planning Your Career

Luck and talent play important roles in most writers' careers, but there are other, more prosaic things you can do to help launch your career and maintain its momentum. Creating a plan has the distinct advantage of helping you avoid disappointment by keeping your goals realistic and giving you a concrete way to measure your progress. Whether your ambition is to become a bestselling author or just to make a little extra money with your writing, putting some practical thought into your dreams will help you realize them.

Tools of the Trade

As in any profession, writers need the proper tools to do their work. You may like to write your stories or articles in longhand on a legal pad, or you might like the hefty clacking of the keys of a manual typewriter. But when it comes time to submit your work to agents and editors, you need the equipment that will make you look like a pro.

Computers and the Internet

A handful of professional writers still cling to the old-fashioned typewriter. But the proliferation of relatively inexpensive home computers and cheap Internet access has made such equipment the industry standard for publishing these days. Indeed, so many publishers—of newspapers, magazines, and books—now prefer to receive assigned material electronically that you put yourself at an unnecessary disadvantage if you don't have a home computer and an e-mail account.

Your personal computer doesn't have to be fancy. You need a good word-processing program, a good-quality printer, and a reliable Internet Service Provider, or ISP. The industry standard for word-processing software is Microsoft Word, although some publishers will accept material in other formats. Word is not typically included in the software bundles for most home computers, so you may have to purchase the program separately or upgrade the software package when you buy your computer.

FACT

Incompatible word-processing programs can result in formatting errors and, often, simply lines of gibberish. If you aren't using Microsoft Word, you may have to convert your material to a text-only file when you submit it. This ensures the recipient will be able to open and read the file, regardless of which program either of you is using.

Ink-jet and laser printers deliver a quality hard copy of your material, and they also are fairly inexpensive. Unless you plan to use it for other things, you don't need a color printer. The only acceptable design for submitting your writing is to use black ink on white paper. It is the easiest combination to read and the most professional. Colored inks and papers—even for your letterhead—are hard on the eyes and will immediately brand you as an amateur in the eyes of agents and editors.

Likewise, your ISP doesn't have to have all the expensive bells and whistles. You need a reliable way to send and receive e-mail and to do Web-based research when warranted. Some ISPs put limits on the size of e-mail attachments, as well as on the amount of server space you have for archiving e-mail, so take that into account when selecting a service.

Office Supplies

Most agents and editors judge materials based on the content, and not necessarily on the way they are presented and packaged. But presentation and packaging can reinforce your image as a professional—or as an amateur. And, in the highly competitive arena of publishing, aspiring writers need every edge they can get.

Start giving yourself that edge by selecting good-quality supplies. Use a 20-pound, white typing paper with some rag or linen content for all your submissions, even your letterhead. For query submissions, use a good-quality, white number 10 business envelope; enclose the same kind of envelope, folded in thirds and paper-clipped to your query letter, as your SASE. For submissions of more than five pages, use a 9×12 or 10×14 manila mailer; again, enclose the same kind of envelope, folded in half, as your SASE.

Always print all of your materials—queries, cover letters, proposals, and manuscripts—on one side of the page only. Printing on two sides may save you a few pennies on paper, but it will annoy the agent or editor and make it more difficult for him to read your submission.

Most word-processing programs have a mailing label function, and your submission will look most professional if you use typed address labels. If you must handwrite addresses, use block letters to ensure readability. Remember to include your own address on your SASE.

Aside from mailing labels, your own handwriting should appear only on the signature line of your query or cover letter. Always sign in pen, never pencil, and use black or blue ink for a professional look. Avoid red ink; studies have shown that people react negatively to red, whether on graded tests in school or in your signature. Other colored inks, like green, purple, or pink, may look whimsical and fun, but they are not appropriate for professional communications.

Your Reference Library

Every writer needs her own reference library. In addition to a good dictionary, a good thesaurus, and a good style guide to resolve grammar and punctuation questions, your library should include an up-to-date directory of potential markets. It may also include inspirational books about the writing life and how-to guides like this one, as well as general references like encyclopedias.

Other titles in your library will depend on what type of writing you do or want to do. If you're mainly writing historical fiction, a guide to the latest scientific discoveries probably won't be of much use to you. On the other hand, a book describing everyday life in the 1800s might be indispensable. No matter what your genre, there are countless books available that can be of enormous help in developing your career.

Finally, your personal reference library should include writer's guidelines and sample issues of the publications you hope to break into. Many magazines include their guidelines on their Web sites, and most will send you a hard copy in exchange for your SASE. Sample issues usually can be ordered for a small fee.

Setting Goals

Many aspiring writers talk about what they will do "someday," trusting in luck and inspiration to fulfill their dreams. If you're serious about a writing career, though, you'll benefit from setting realistic short- and long-term goals. The more specific your goals are, the easier it is to identify steps you can take to achieve them, and the more control you have over the direction and progression of your career.

Selecting a Specialty

Especially in fiction, new writers benefit from specializing in one genre. Having several sci-fi short stories published helps give you a platform for marketing your sci-fi novel. And it will be easier to find a publisher for your second novel if it's the same genre as your first; staying with one genre helps build a fan base among readers, and your second book will be more attractive to a publisher if you already have that fan base to tap into.

This doesn't mean you can't jump from one genre to another. But, in most cases, that jump is better delayed until after your second or even third novel is published. Besides, the more experience you gain in getting stories or novels of one genre published, the more confident you will be when it's time to try something different.

FACT

Fiction writers can benefit from adding nonfiction pieces to their clip files. Nonfiction is easier for new writers to break into, giving you those all-important published credits. You also can strengthen your fiction platform if your nonfiction clips are related to your fiction—if your nonfiction is on new scientific discoveries, for example, and your short story is sci-fi.

Nonfiction writers generally don't have the same restrictions on category, but, like fiction writers, they can get typecast for certain assignments. If your clip file mainly consists of profiles of sports figures, for instance, you might have trouble convincing an editor that you're qualified to write an article about global warming. Some writers get a reputation for delivering quality feature-length articles, and editors are loath to waste these writers' talents on shorter, newsy pieces. That said, it generally is easier for nonfiction writers to get a variety of assignments, giving you a more well-rounded portfolio.

Time Management

Many new writers have difficulty finding the time to focus on their writing. Other obligations—family, your regular job, social engagements, and so on—eat up so much of the day, and so much of your mental energy, that there often isn't any to spare for the creative process. Then, too, beginning writers often don't know where to start work on their project, so they just never get around to it. Here are some tips that other writers have found useful; experiment with them to find a solution that works for you.

- **Make a standing appointment with yourself.** Set aside a block of time (ideally the same time every day) for writing and schedule other obligations around that time.
- **Write at different times of the day.** Experimenting with the time of day can help you discover when you're at your most creative and productive.
- **Set up a place to write.** Even if it's just a corner of the living room, a dedicated place to do your writing can help you focus.
- **Limit your writing time.** This may sound counterintuitive, but having too much time can interfere with getting down to work.
- **Set a goal for each day's or each week's work.** Personal deadlines for finishing a chapter, a character bio, a synopsis, or needed research can help keep you motivated and on track.

The challenge for most new writers is making writing a priority among all the other priorities in your life. At the beginning of your career, before you break into the larger markets and begin to see a substantial return on your investment of time and energy, it's all too easy to let your writing slip into hobby status. But that initial investment is essential if your goal is to become a professional writer.

Juggling Projects

Professional writers are masters at juggling various projects, and they almost always have several projects going at once, in various stages of development. There are several advantages to this, not the least of which is the fact that, when you have a second project to work on, you're less likely to obsess over the fate of your first project. There are always new ideas to pursue, which can be a great comfort when one of your ideas doesn't go anywhere.

Set up a system to keep track of ideas as they occur to you. It doesn't have to be elaborate; it can be as simple as a set of index cards on which you jot notes about potential stories or articles. If you can make notes about ideas when they occur, then file them away safely, these new ideas are less likely to distract you from your current project.

Writing projects have four main stages of development: the thinking-up stage, the research stage, the query stage, and the writing stage. Ideally, you should have one project in each of these phases at any given time. As soon as you send out a query for one idea, begin doing the research for one of your other ideas. This keeps you busy while you're waiting to hear back on your first query. Once you get a sale, you'll have the full cycle going—writing for the sale, querying your next idea, researching markets or information for a third idea, and dreaming up fourth, fifth, and sixth ideas.

Writing for Free

When you're just starting out, you may find that the only markets open to you are ones that pay little or nothing to their contributors. But these markets can help you build the foundation for a more lucrative career. They also can help you build a platform (see Chapter 3 for more on this), which makes you more salable to bigger markets.

Many publications invite readers to contribute ideas, and most have a letter-to-the-editor feature. For example, *Sew News* has a column of tips provided by readers; if their tip is used, they receive a token gift, such as a free subscription. *Better Homes and Gardens* has a letters department; if your letter is published, you do not get any pay, but you can claim contributor's credit in the magazine.

Newspapers, of course, have active letters-to-the-editor sections. The bigger the newspaper, the more difficult it is to get your letter printed. However, if you've had two dozen letters to the editor printed in the *New York Times* or the *Los Angeles Times*, that could impress an agent or editor. It even could lead to an invitation to write a longer op-ed piece for pay.

FACT

Shorter usually is better for letters to the editor, especially for large publications. Speak your mind in a maximum of 150 words, and you'll increase the odds of getting your letter published. Op-ed pieces, also called guest editorials, usually can run between 400 and 800 words, depending on the publication.

Most of the nonpaying markets are small-circulation newspapers and magazines. For some small book publishers, too, you might have to work without an advance, but you should get royalties from sales of your book. A handful of Web sites pay their contributors, but most don't, and the ones that do, like the major publications, are more difficult for newcomers to break into.

The key benefit to you with nonpaying markets is credit, credit, credit. If you don't get a byline, and you don't get paid, then you'll be doing the work for the love of it. There's nothing wrong with that, if that's what you choose. But, for the career-minded writer, the real value of these markets is the opportunity to build your clip file and to use these credits as a springboard to bigger things.

Getting Paid

As you gain experience, you'll move into paying markets, and these, too, typically follow a progression from smaller fees to larger ones. Depending on the type of market, your fee might be based on so much per word, so much per printed page, or a flat fee. Flat fees often are quite small, but not always; *Reader's Digest*, for example, pays a flat fee of $300 for its "Life in These United States," "Humor in Uniform," and "All in a Day's Work" features, which run 100 words or fewer. That works out to $3 or more a word— a very good pay rate for writers. Sometimes it's easier to assess the fairness of the pay by converting it to an hourly rate. Twenty-five cents a word may sound like a respectable rate on its face, but if the research is going to take a great deal of time, the pay may not be worth the effort. Balance these factors and others in choosing your projects.

The bigger your portfolio gets, the more leverage you'll have to negotiate better pay rates—and the more confidence you'll have in asking for more money. Remember that the pay rates listed in market directories like *Writer's Market* often are just averages. You might be offered less money than the listing indicates, especially if you're an unknown. On the flip side, you might be offered more if you've proven yourself as a reliable contributor.

Get It in Writing

Writers' Web sites are teeming with horror stories of writers who received assignments and whose work was published, but who never received payment. Having a written agreement is no guarantee that you will get paid, but a publication willing to put the assignment and the fee in writing is more likely to be on the up-and-up. Most professional writers refuse to do any work without a contract.

Especially for magazines, contracts can be quite short and simple. At some publications, the contract consists of a few lines on the back of the payment check; endorsing the check also executes the contract. (Chapter 12 goes into more detail about the many elements in a publishing contract.) It should spell out the nature of the assignment—or the title of an already-written article or short story—as well as the fee to be paid and when the writer can expect payment, such as "on acceptance" or "on publication." Because magazines usually have lead times of several months, and because your article or story might get pushed back for a number of reasons, getting paid "on acceptance" is the better option for you.

ALERT!

Some writers advocate sending an invoice when you submit articles that have been assigned. If you have a contract for the article, an invoice generally is unnecessary. However, if the arrangements have been made by telephone or e-mail, an invoice that describes the piece and the agreed-upon payment can be a good backup for your records.

Saying No

Payment for your articles or short stories should be commensurate with the quality of your clips and the work involved in the current project. If you're like most writers, you may start out working for little or no pay, but once you've paid your dues with smaller markets, you should be able to garner bigger earnings. And once you've written an article or two at twenty-five or fifty cents a word, you should have enough confidence to turn down the markets that only pay ten cents a word, or to insist on an increase in payment.

Writers who stick with it generally grow beyond the small markets that gave them their start, in terms of both profile and pay. You might still do occasional work for a small magazine once you've managed to break into larger markets, and that's fine. But those occasions probably will become rarer as your career builds and the value others place on your work grows.

Collecting Credentials

Just as your per-word rate should increase as you gain more experience as a published writer, your credential file should follow a natural progression from smaller to larger markets. Little pieces in little markets lead to bigger pieces in those same markets, which lead to small pieces in larger markets, and they in turn lead to longer pieces in the big markets.

ESSENTIAL

Be open to working with the editor at your local newspaper. Especially if you have no formal journalism training, you might have much to learn about how newspaper stories are constructed. A good working relationship with your editor is more likely to lead to additional assignments, as well as a more impressive clip file.

The easiest places for most rookie writers to break in usually are in their own backyards. Check out freelance opportunities with your local newspaper or with regional magazines. Local business journals, entertainment magazines, and the like can provide excellent opportunities for beginners.

And clips from these kinds of publications can help open doors at larger newspapers and magazines.

Don't neglect trade journals in your quest to capture clips. Company or individual profiles, new products, discoveries in medicine or other sciences—these are just a few likely areas for potential articles. Pay rates in the trades vary widely; in some cases, getting a published credit may be more important than how much you get paid, but some of these journals pay very well for well-researched, well-written articles.

The high-profile national magazines are the most difficult for newcomers to crack, but even these usually offer some opportunities. Think small when you're approaching these markets, at least at first. Feature-length pieces almost always are reserved for staff writers or for freelancers who have a track record with the editor or the publication. But most magazines have departments at the front or back of the "book" (the industry term for the magazine) that are open to new writers. These pieces usually are shorter and often don't pay as much as features, but they are an excellent way to build a reputation with a particular magazine.

Image and Attitude

Most agents and editors consider an unknown, unpublished writer to be a liability. They generally have to spend more time with new writers, explaining procedures, making suggestions for improving a manuscript, and, sometimes, offering encouragement and hand-holding when writers succumb to feelings of inadequacy. This time investment may not seem worthwhile when the agent or editor doesn't even know whether the writer is capable of delivering quality material on time, which is why so many of them—especially at larger agencies and publishing houses—deal exclusively with established writers. Because of this, your image and attitude are key elements in determining how successful you'll be in breaking into new markets.

Image

No matter where you are in your writing career, your image can help or hinder your progress. If you come across as professional in all your communications with agents and editors, they will be more inclined to work with you when you submit something that meets their needs. If you come across as unprofessional, chances are you'll sabotage any potential working relationship, even if your material is exactly what the agent or editor is looking for.

Your professional image starts on paper. As discussed earlier, presentation and packaging help reinforce your image. The following elements also play a role in defining your image on paper:

- **Contact information.** Include your name and address (including zip code), as well as your telephone number (including area code) and e-mail address on all correspondence.
- **Recipient's name and address.** Double-check name spellings and titles and use courtesy titles (Mr. or Ms.) in all correspondence. If you don't know the gender of the recipient, use the full name (e.g., Dear J.C. Smith).
- **Proofreading.** A query or proposal dotted with errors in spelling, punctuation, and grammar project an amateur image. Use the spell-check function on your computer and give all material a final read-through before you send it.
- **Margins.** Every page should have one-inch margins all around. The first page of a manuscript and the first page of a new chapter each should have a three-inch top margin.
- **SASE.** This is essential if you want a reply. Always affix the correct postage and make sure the SASE is addressed to you, with the agent's or editor's name and address in the upper left corner.

Be open to working with the editor at your local newspaper. Especially if you have no formal journalism training, you might have much to learn about how newspaper stories are constructed. A good working relationship with your editor is more likely to lead to additional assignments, as well as a more impressive clip file.

Neatness counts in publishing, if only because of the enormous volume of submissions agents and editors have to deal with every day. A professional-looking submission is only the beginning—your material still has to be appropriate for the market—but it does help create a favorable impression in the mind of the reader.

Attitude

Professionalism is more than getting paid for what you write. It involves your general comportment in dealing with agents and editors. Your attitude—how you respond to criticism, how you handle rejection, and how well you respect an agent's or editor's time and expertise—is an integral part of your image as a professional writer.

You don't have to agree with or implement every suggestion an agent or editor makes. However, remember that the agent or editor has, most likely, years of experience in the field, and knows what the market demands. Make an effort to see the issue from the other's point of view.

When you receive criticism on your writing, it almost always is intended to help you improve the piece and make it more salable. Agents offer criticisms based on their knowledge and experience with the book markets, and editors offer criticisms based on what their readers want and need. Writers who argue with even the most constructive suggestions earn themselves black marks with publishing pros. Whether you decide to act on the suggestions or not—and that is always your decision—it behooves you to learn how to listen to and weigh criticism as objectively as you can. (See Chapter 11 for more on coping with criticism.)

In addition, you must develop a professional attitude toward rejection. No writer likes rejection, but everyone who submits his material is bound to run into it sooner or later. (See Chapter 9 for more on handling rejection.) Arguing with a rejection is not only futile, it is the act of an amateur. Don't kid yourself into thinking that an angry note or phone call to the agent or editor who rejected your work will fade into dim memory. Like bad smells, unprofessional responses can linger for a very long time, contaminating your chances of getting a yes in the future.

Professionalism also means respecting the agent's or editor's time. When you're submitting queries, expect to wait at least the time listed in the market directories for a response, and don't pressure an agent or editor for a more rapid reply. When you're working on an assignment, limit phone calls and e-mails to essential communications, and keep them as short as possible. Do not expect an agent or editor to be at your beck and call; she has dozens of other claims on her attention, and your particular issue may be far down on the list of her priorities. If you have something urgent to discuss, send a brief e-mail and, if necessary, ask to set up a time for a phone call.

Establishing Your Reputation

Like most of us, agents and editors prefer to avoid working with difficult people. And, again like most of us, they tend to share war stories about difficult people. It's extraordinarily easy for writers to get a poor reputation in publishing circles. All it takes is one nasty response to a rejection, a temper tantrum on the telephone, or failure to deliver what you promise when you promise to have it done.

You begin building your reputation when you query an agent or editor. A well-written, well-researched, well-targeted query—sent via the method he prefers and containing all the necessary information—projects a professional image. Willingness to work with the agent or editor to fine-tune your idea so it better fits the needs of the market reinforces that image. Delivering a manuscript that lives up to the vision of the initial query and any tailoring done along the way, and delivering it to deadline (or even before your deadline) further defines you as a professional.

Publishing is, in essence, a small network; agents and editors talk to each other. And, these days, editors move around quite a bit. The writer who gives an editor a hard time today likely will be remembered a year from now, when the editor has moved on to a bigger magazine with more responsibility. Likewise, today's agent's assistant may be setting up her own agency in a year or two; she may be seeking clients, but may not be interested in the writer who hollered at her over the phone about a rejection.

The Rules of the Game

New writers can get frustrated by what seem like arcane and foolish rules for breaking into the publishing world. Indeed, from the outside, publishing can seem like a closed circle, admitting only a select few for indeterminate reasons. But the rules that govern the publishing world actually are intended to benefit both writers and the people who make the decisions about what makes it into print.

Submission Guidelines

Agents and editors receive a mind-boggling amount of material every day. Some of it arrives by regular mail, some by delivery services like UPS or FedEx, and an astounding amount by e-mail. And this is just the material from hopeful new writers; it doesn't even count the vast amount of material from established clients and freelancers. Agents and editors establish submission guidelines to cope with the ever-growing mountain of material on their desks.

ALERT!

Treat e-mail addresses as the privilege that they are, and don't share them with anyone unless you have the agent's or editor's permission to do so. Most agents and editors still prefer to receive queries and other preliminary submissions by regular mail and reserve e-mail for active projects.

The best thing new writers can do for themselves is follow the submission guidelines listed in the market directories. Doing so demonstrates your respect for the agent's or editor's time and marks you as a professional. Other ways of approach might look like shortcuts, but really they are unnecessary detours.

Match Your Material

If a market doesn't accept personal profiles or humor, you waste your time and theirs by submitting personal profiles and humor. Take the time to research the markets before you send out queries and match your material to markets that are looking for what you write. Publishing can be a maddeningly slow business anyway; don't slow it down further by aiming in the wrong direction.

chapter 3

Building a Platform

As the costs of publishing continue to escalate and competition continues to intensify, many publishers—especially book publishers—are demanding that their authors have strong platforms from which to launch a new title. Even magazine editors prefer to work with known writers, because established writers tend to require less hand-holding and training than rookies. Don't get too discouraged, though. There are many ways to build a platform for yourself that will make you more attractive and more salable to all kinds of publishing markets.

Teaching

Teaching is an excellent way to be regarded as an expert on a topic, and that expertise adds substantial heft to your credentials when it's time to pursue getting published. And, depending on where you live and what kind of venues are available to you, you might not have to go through the rigors of getting a teaching certificate or license.

Community Colleges

Community colleges and even some K–12 school districts often have adult or community education programs. These usually don't count as college credits. They are often aimed at personal development and enrichment, with courses in subjects like gardening, auto maintenance, foreign languages, crafts, personal finance, and the like.

Because these classes aren't offered for credit, the requirements for instructors usually are less stringent. If you can come up with a proposal for a class that's likely to appeal to a good number of people and demonstrate some expertise in the topic you're proposing, you might be able to get a gig teaching a for-fun class.

Community education classes usually are scheduled for evenings and weekends to allow the greatest number of working adults to take advantage of them. That means you can teach these courses on the side while still holding down your regular job—and while pursuing your writing.

Another advantage to these types of courses is that you can structure them to suit you. You can craft a one-day seminar-type class and schedule it for a Saturday, for example, or you can design it as a continuing course, meeting for, say, two or three hours on Tuesday evenings for three weeks. Contact your college or school district to find out what their instructor requirements, scheduling preferences, and course needs are.

Interim Courses

Some two- and four-year colleges offer intensive courses between regular semesters; these often are scheduled in January, between the holidays and the beginning of the regular spring semester. Students take one course for two or three weeks, spending several hours a day in this one class. These classes often are given for college credit, so the standards for instruction may be more rigorous. But if you have the right credentials for the course (which are not necessarily the same credentials you need for getting published), interim teaching assignments might provide opportunities for you to bolster your platform.

Online Courses

More and more colleges are turning to the Internet to teach students. It's more convenient for many students, especially adults who are returning to college and have to fit their class work into an already full schedule, and it's often more convenient for instructors, who can do their work and be available for their students without being tied to an office. Sometimes, colleges will hire people with real-life experience in the subject being taught to conduct these online classes; they don't necessarily impose the same requirements for these types of courses as they do on regular faculty positions.

FACT

Even after you've been published, teaching can help bolster your platform. The more published credits you have in a given topic, the more attractive colleges will find you as an instructor. You also might be able to use your published clips, whether articles or books, as teaching aids for your course.

Whatever teaching option you pursue, it's always best if you can relate the topic you're teaching to the topic you want to write about. If you want to write about fine dining, for example, the best courses for you to teach might be ones on gourmet cooking, or wine selection, or preparing an elegant dinner party at home.

Combining courses and your writing topics can help you get established as a writer, and once you have some clips, it will be easier for you to branch out into other topics and genres.

Conferences and Seminars

If you can't teach through traditional channels, consider getting involved in conferences and seminars. Some cities have speakers' bureaus, which act as a kind of broker to link audiences and presenters. Check with your local chamber of commerce to see if there's such an organization in your area. You also can arrange your own seminars, if you're willing to put in the work. Choose a topic in which you are both interested and well-versed; people who attend conferences and seminars expect to learn something new and useful.

Conference Opportunities

If you have a particular area of expertise—and by that, we mean something more than a hobby—you might be able to give presentations at professional conferences. You can participate in panel discussions, serve as facilitator of a break-out session, or even deliver a keynote speech. The best place to search for such opportunities is through professional associations. If you're a member of the Public Relations Society of America (PRSA), for instance, contact the head of your chapter to find out what kind of conferences are scheduled and what presentations you might be suited to offer.

QUESTION?

How can I use conferences and seminars to promote my writing?
After your presentation, lots of folks will want to talk to you one-on-one. Be sure to exchange business cards; if one of the attendees would be an impressive endorser for your book proposal, you'll have a unique opening to get it.

Even if you aren't a member of an organization, you might be a good candidate for offering a presentation. Maybe a local PRSA conference would be interested in hearing from a television or newspaper reporter about effective ways to pitch stories to the media. If your expertise is in database management, maybe members of your local or state American Medical Association chapter could use your information to improve their record-keeping. Look for ways that your area of expertise can be made useful to specific, targeted audiences.

DIY Seminars

If professional conferences aren't the best fit for you, you might want to explore offering your own seminars. Again, select a topic that you're familiar with and interested in, and make sure your seminar offers value for the attendees. "How To" topics usually generate the most interest: How to Maximize Your Investments, How to Get Started in Real Estate, How to Write a Business Plan, How to Home School Your Children, etc. As we noted in the teaching section, it's best for your writing career if you can design a seminar related to the topic you want to write about.

Conferences and seminars give you a platform for your related writing topic because they show that you know the market for your topic and the needs of your audience or readership. In addition, writers who have a track record of public speaking are considered more promotable, especially by book publishers.

Whole books have been written about effectively planning and marketing seminars, and we don't have enough space to go into a great deal of detail here. But there are some essential things to keep in mind if you decide to pursue this option:

- **Offering value.** Figure out what you want attendees to take away from your seminar, both in terms of knowledge and skills and in terms of tangible items, like workbooks or other materials.
- **Selecting a location.** Hotel meeting rooms are common locales for seminars, but you might get a better deal by using facilities at your local library, school, church, or municipal building.
- **Selecting a date.** Saturdays are popular days for workshops and seminars, because more working people are able to attend. However, weekends often are packed with family activities and obligations, so evenings might be better for short seminars.
- **Setting a price.** Research has shown that people who pay to attend seminars are more likely to show up on the day and more interested in the material presented. Set a price that fairly compensates you for your time and expertise but still provides value for the audience.
- **Marketing your seminar.** There are many ways to publicize your seminar; do some research to find out which methods would be

most effective in reaching your target audience. Remember that your response rate may be as low as one per 1,000, so plan your marketing budget wisely.

Also consider finding partners for your seminar. If you're using your local library, for instance, maybe you can publicize your seminar in the library's newsletter to members. Maybe the chamber of commerce will waive its usual room rental fee in exchange for a set number of free tickets to give to its members. One of the beauties of do-it-yourself seminars is that you can be as creative as you like in pursuing opportunities, and, at the same time, adding a plank to your platform.

Making the Most of It

Whether you plug into conferences sponsored by someone else or design and promote your own, use these opportunities to sell your work as well as yourself. If you've had a book published, get permission from the conference sponsor to sell your book at the back of the meeting room. If you aren't getting paid for your participation (or if you aren't being paid very much), you should be able to negotiate a deal where you keep the profits— the difference between the wholesale and retail price—on books sold at the conference. If your fee for speaking or presenting is fairly high, the sponsor may want to keep the profits from book sales. That's not necessarily a bad deal; people who buy the book at the conference are highly desirable readers, and they are likely to pass on information about the conference, you, and your work to their friends and colleagues.

You can arrange to sign your books at conferences, but you shouldn't be the one to collect the money for back-of-room sales or announce that the books are available for purchase. Attendees generally don't like to feel that they've been set up for a sales pitch, and you'll come across as more of a shill than a respected authority if you're collecting money for your own book. If the conference organizer can't provide someone else to handle the actual transactions, recruit a friend or relative to do it for you.

Another way to handle the book issue is to include it in the cost of attending the conference or seminar. This can add perceived value for potential attendees, and it's nice to be able to say that 100 percent of the people who attend your events go away with a copy of your book in their hands. You can do something similar even if you don't have a book published yet; make good-quality copies of articles that you've written or that have quoted you on the topic of your presentation, and distribute these as hand-outs to attendees. This helps reinforce your profile in the minds of potential readers, who might become avid readers of future articles by and about you and maybe even eager purchasers of the book you're shopping to publishers.

At any public appearance, your attitude will either reinforce or destroy your image. Smile at your audience and the people who are purchasing your book; offer a quick hello; make eye contact. Even if you're tired and feeling cranky, pretend you're having a good time. You can drop the act when you're out of the public eye.

Stay in Touch

People who have attended one of your presentations might be interested in others, which helps raise your profile and build your platform. Invite attendees to sign up for a newsletter (e-mail or snail mail) to keep them posted about upcoming events. Then use this mailing list to stay in touch with people who are already interested in you and your topic. A regular newsletter offering free and useful information has value for the person who receives it, and you can use it to help market your next conference or seminar, as well as your writing.

Speaking Engagements

As with marketing your writing, the key to successful marketing of your services as a speaker is matching your material with an audience's needs. This takes some research and legwork, of course. But it can pay off by raising your profile, which in turn makes you more attractive to agents and editors.

Of course, the reverse is also true. Building your visibility by getting your articles published can lead to requests for speeches and other personal appearances, requests for other articles, and maybe even interest from a book publisher. Once you get on the publishing and speaking ride, success in one area often leads to demand in the other.

In the past, book publishers have shown the most interest in authors who also are accomplished public speakers. But magazine publishers love having their regular contributors do speaking engagements, too; it's a good way to attract potential new subscribers, or to boost sales for a particular issue. If you're giving a conference or seminar to people who fit the magazine's target readership profile, the magazine may work out a way to provide copies to attendees in hopes of getting new subscribers.

Magazine editors have come to covet authors with strong platforms as much as book editors do. With subscriber bases declining and competition with other media continually on the rise, magazine editors and publishers are always looking for ways to boost their own profiles, even if it's a one-shot deal. Stephen King's name on the cover of a magazine for an article he contributed might not generate new subscribers, but it will boost that issue's sales considerably. King fans who are not particularly interested in the publication will buy it just for his article, thus boosting that month's revenues.

Start Small

A speech doesn't have to be a major event. It can be as simple as a presentation to a Boy Scout troop or as extravagant as a keynote address to a state or national convention. When you're just beginning, though, it's best to aim at smaller targets and smaller audiences. The more experience you gain with these events, the more confident you'll be when it's time to address a larger crowd.

So what do you talk about to these smaller groups? Your regular profession is a good place to start. Schools and youth organizations often have career days or fairs and are always looking for people to discuss the basics of their jobs, what it takes to prepare for a career in a specific field, and so on. Many civic, business, and social organizations also offer special lunch programs, with guest speakers, for their members. A ten- or fifteen-minute speech usually is ample for these kinds of engagements.

Another advantage to this route is that it helps you build contacts and expand your network. This in turn can lead to more speaking engagements, which helps raise your profile, and that helps convince publishing professionals that you're a viable candidate for getting your work in print. Besides, public speaking opens up a whole range of possible article ideas. You can combine your own experience with expert information about such things as stage fright, answering awkward questions, preparation, and proper attire to craft compelling essays or articles for all kinds of magazine markets. If you get proficient enough, you might even get a good book idea out of your experience.

FACT

Book authors especially can benefit from getting on the lecture circuit. Studies indicate that as many as three of every ten conference attendees will buy the speaker's book at the event—a great way to boost sales while solidifying your platform for future projects.

Other Kinds of Speaking

There are other ways to reach audiences with the spoken word. Check out your local radio and television stations and see if they accept commentary from the public. Some television stations permit viewers to respond to editorials, for example, or to submit their own. Some radio stations do the same, and some, especially those with an all-news or all-talk format, encourage listeners to submit essays on a variety of topics—sort of the oral equivalent of the letter to the editor or guest editorial.

Investigate locally produced talk shows, too. If you've built a reputation in your community as an expert on a particular topic, you might be able to land a spot as a guest on one of these local shows. One way to approach these opportunities is to call or e-mail the host or producer with a suggestion for covering your topic.

Web Sites and Blogs

The Internet offers a plethora of opportunities to raise your profile, if you know how to use it. Personal Web sites usually aren't the most effective way to reach large potential readerships; there are so many of them that it's real work to make yours stand out so surfers can find you. However, there are other Internet routes that can provide important support as you build your platform.

The Right Kind of Site

Design your Web site around what you want to write. That doesn't mean you should use your site to post your unpublished works; for one thing, posting on the Internet counts as publication, and potential publishers will be indifferent at best when you ask them to pay you for something that already has been made available to the world. Use your Web site to connect what you want to write with people who will want to read what you write. If your goal is to write fantasy stories, for instance, you might design a Web site for fans of established fantasy authors. If you can pack your site with fun and interesting information, you have a good chance of developing a strong following. Then, when you sell your first fantasy short story or novel, you can use the Web site to alert your visitors; you have a built-in conduit to help promote your own work.

Adding the Opt-In

With so many Web sites, many users are relying on RSS feeds to keep them updated on the topics and sites they care about. RSS is an acronym for Rich Site Summary, also known as Really Simple Syndication. It includes an opt-in feature, where site visitors sign up to have updates sent directly to their e-mail inboxes. RSS also makes it easy to share your site content with other sites, and your content gets listed in directories of RSS feeds—all of which can help expand the reach of your site.

Blogs

Short for Web log, a blog is an online journal. It can be on a single topic, like Our Daily Bread, or on broader subjects, like International News. It can have a single author or several regular contributors. It can be limited to the author's or contributors' postings, or it can be an interactive forum where readers can post replies and comments of their own. The key ingredient for any blog is fresh content. Most of the successful and popular blogs are updated every day, and many of them are updated several times a day. Blog readers get impatient when content isn't updated regularly, and, for them, a promising blog can go stale in just a day or two. That's one of the main drawbacks to blogging, especially for people who are juggling work and home life and trying to launch a writing career at the same time.

On the other hand, the most popular blogs boast devoted followings, and that makes this another tool you can use to build your platform. Especially in book publishing, agents and editors like to see evidence of a strong potential readership and effective ways to reach that readership. A popular blog related to your book topic gives you a unique avenue for marketing your work to interested readers.

Podcasting

Podcasting—the ability to broadcast audio from the Web—is still in its infancy, but, if it attains the same popularity as other Web-based functions, it could become a valuable new tool for promoting yourself and your work. Imagine hosting your own weekly radio show on the Internet, with the potential of reaching listeners around the world instantly and cheaply. You still have to figure out how to make sure your virtual audience can find you; like other Web-based opportunities, there's a lot of clutter to cut through. But, if podcasting takes off the way fan sites, blogs, and other Internet functions have, it might become another de rigueur element for writers to add to their marketing strategies.

Honors and Awards

Another way to build your platform is by playing up any honors or awards you receive. Everybody loves a winner, and these kinds of credentials almost automatically enhance your standing as an expert. Granted, an employee of the year award won't necessarily help you sell your action/adventure novel, but it might help you land more speaking gigs at professional conferences, and it might help you promote your magazine article on how to deal with a difficult boss.

The main message of any award or honor, regardless of whether it relates directly to your writing, is that others have recognized your talent and hard work. It's human nature to want to learn from people who are so recognized. Your job, then, is to figure out how best to combine any honors or awards you have with opportunities to boost your platform.

Writing Awards

Where your writing career is concerned, writing awards are huge boosts to your attractiveness and salability. Such awards (as long as they are legitimate) provide an independent validation of your talent and ability—a sort of generic third-party endorsement. Opportunities to add these credentials to your bio abound in contests sponsored by all kinds of magazines, Web sites, businesses, and other establishments. Many market directories, including *Writer's Market*, devote entire sections to such contests.

ALERT!

Be careful in choosing which writing contests to enter; many of them are simply scams designed to separate hopeful writers from their hard-earned cash. Entry fees should be minimal, publication should not depend on your payment, and the sponsor should be a company you've heard of or can check out easily.

If you've never been published, you might want to start your contest-entering on a local level and build from there. Local newspapers sometimes run contests for holiday stories or other themes, for example. Starting with smaller contests can give you additional confidence to enter larger ones where you'll likely face stiffer competition.

Non-Writing Awards

Awards for things other than your writing might help boost your writing career, too, particularly if you can relate the award to the topic you're writing about. An award for most creative Christmas yard display might help you sell an article about holiday decorating. Winning a karaoke contest might convince an editor to publish your essay about overcoming fear. This is another good argument for not limiting your activities to writing. Other experiences and experiments not only enrich and inform your writing; they can provide great help in launching and sustaining your writing career.

Becoming an Expert

If you select a specialty for your writing, you can at the same time build a name for yourself as an expert. The more published credits you have in, say, home-based businesses, the more attractive you are to the media, conference organizers, and even the legal professions as a knowledgeable source on the topic. The more recognition you get for your expertise, the easier it will be to sell your articles on the topic, and the more published clips you have, the easier it will be for you to branch out into other areas of writing.

There are all kinds of opportunities to develop and exploit such expertise, many of them discussed here and more discussed in Chapter 14. Choose your subject well; if you decide to take advantage of these opportunities, you'll be spending a lot of time writing, reading, and talking about it. Make sure your topic isn't one you'll get bored with quickly. If you're worried about that, pick a couple of topics, and split your time between them.

Build relationships with the media. Keep a separate Rolodex of any media contacts you make and keep in touch with those reporters and editors occasionally by providing them with new material. If you don't have new material of your own to provide, make suggestions for stories that aren't related to your projects. Being generous with ideas that don't directly benefit you helps build trust between you and a reporter or editor, and that trust pays off when you do have something of your own you want to cover.

Investing in professional relationships with the media, conference organizers, and others also gives you opportunities to borrow another's platform. An article about your latest speech in the local newspaper is more effective in building awareness than an ad covering the same material. Having your book available at a seminar sponsored by a professional association adds more credibility to your book than hawking it from your own Web site. A recommendation on a popular fiction blog to check out the short story you just had published is more compelling to readers than an announcement you send out yourself via e-mail. Being able to use other platforms like this isn't just efficient; it's an essential part of elevating your own platform.

Most beginning writers don't have many ways to set themselves apart from the passel of other writers anxious to get published. As hard as it is to break into the industry, you owe it to yourself to explore every possible avenue for convincing agents and editors to take a chance on you. Start building your platform at the beginning of your career, and it will serve you well even after you've established yourself as a professional writer.

chapter 4
Finding Your Market

Market research in publishing is a bit of a chicken-or-egg conundrum: Which comes first, the idea or the market? Some writers come up with ideas for articles, short stories, or books, and then look around for someone to publish their idea. Others study the market directories first, tabulating topics that agents and editors have included in their listings, and then try to write what they believe the market wants. Most successful writers do both and, through practice and experience, they learn to do both nearly simultaneously.

4

Matching Ideas and Audiences

New writers often make the mistake of thinking everyone will want to read their work. Pros know that a claim of universal appeal really is an admission that the writer doesn't know who her audience is. Without a clear idea of your readership, you're unlikely to find a buyer for your work, no matter how well-written it is.

How People Read

To start gaining insight into your potential readers, try thinking about how people read a daily newspaper. Nearly all major newspapers are divided into several sections—there may be one for local news, one for national and world news, one for sports, one for business, and one for lifestyle or recreation. No matter how big the newspaper's circulation is, it is highly unlikely that every subscriber reads every page of the newspaper every day. The reason newspapers separate the different categories of information is so their readers can more easily find the articles they actually want to read.

FACT

Fiction writers also benefit from imagining a single reader as a representative of their audience. As you write, pretend you're telling your story to one person; think of what questions the listener might ask, and when those questions should be answered to maximize suspense without causing confusion. This can help you handle pacing and plot points.

Magazine and book publishers work on the same principle. This is why magazines often are divided into "departments" or other sections and why book publishers—especially the major conglomerates—create imprint lines with narrower audiences. Consider Penguin Putnam, for example. This huge publishing house has twenty-one imprints in the United States, each focusing on specific types of books. The Sentinel imprint, one of its newest lines, publishes exclusively conservative titles such as Ronald Kessler's

A Matter of Character: Inside the White House of George W. Bush. A book by a liberal author, or with a liberal slant, has no chance of being accepted at Sentinel, because Sentinel's readership is not liberal.

Even bestselling books don't appeal to everybody; they just appeal to an awful lot of people. You shouldn't try to appeal to everybody, either; if Michael Crichton and Agatha Christie can't do it, there's no reason to waste your energy trying. Instead, get in the habit of imagining a single reader who represents a composite of your audience. What are his interests? What kind of job does he have? What's his family life like? What does he like to do on a Saturday night? Most important, what does he already know about your topic, and what can you tell him about it that will be new, interesting, and useful?

Who Needs Your Project?

Writers are continually admonished to "write for the market." But what is the market? Instead of thinking about which newspapers, magazines, and book publishers might be interested in your work, look past those markets to the readers they serve. That's the real market you should be aiming for, because those readers will be the end users of your product. When you come up with a project that serves the needs of a specific section of the reading public, selling your work becomes much easier; all you have to do is find the publication that targets those same readers.

Consider this book as an example of this approach. The readers of the *Everything* series generally are novices in the topics covered by the series. They need a grounding in the basics, plus enough detail to be thoroughly familiar with the topic, and resources for adding to their store of knowledge. *Everything* books are not meant to appeal to experts, so they're short on jargon and long on translating technical things into plain English. The information in *Everything* books is meant to be useful, practical, educational, and entertaining.

For many writers, especially those who are doing freelance assignments for publications, the readers you want to reach will change with each piece you do. Your tone, structure, angle, and vocabulary will differ depending on whether you're writing a story about Java script for a computer trade journal or one about effective Web page design for home-based businesses.

Studying Potential Markets

Agents and editors are always urging writers to study the markets they want to write for. One of the most irritating aspects of their jobs is the inordinate amount of time they spend opening queries and proposals that aren't right for them. With all the information available to you from a plethora of sources, there is no reason not to do your research before you begin marketing your work. Besides, the better you know the market, the fewer rejections you're apt to get—simply because you won't be sending inappropriate material.

Directory Listings

Market directories like *Writer's Market* provide essential information about what various publications and book publishers are looking for. Just as important, these listings also often include things the market is not interested in. *Antique and Collectables Newsmagazine*'s listing, for example, clearly states that it is not interested in opinion pieces, religious articles, or exposés. *Listen Magazine*'s listing notes that it has been flooded with pitches about drunk driving and recommends that hopeful writers consider different topics. *Family Circle* magazine's listing shows that it is not interested in fiction or poetry.

ESSENTIAL

Many professional writers advise making a list of five to ten potential markets for your idea, then prioritizing those markets based on your research. The markets that are looking for your topic or slant on an article go at the top of your list. Read the listings and match the market's needs with your idea.

All these listings are clear and direct, in black and white. Yet, the editors at these magazines still spend hours each week responding to pitches for exactly the wrong kind of writing. Editors get frustrated because they have to spend time on these submissions, which they can ill afford and which they would much rather spend reading submissions that are right for them. Writers get frustrated because they collect a whole bunch of rejections, most likely form letters, and never really understand why no one likes their ideas.

To be fair, it's also frustrating when you come up with a great idea for a story and think you've got a perfectly matching market, and then find, when you read the listing for that market, that it isn't interested in the type of idea you just came up with. Unfortunately, that goes with the territory. The only thing you can do is keep reading through the market listings, looking for one that is a good fit with your idea and is open to it.

Read the Publication

There is no substitute for reading the publication you hope to break into. You don't have to be a subscriber, but you should be able to identify—and replicate—the style and tone of various articles. Pay attention to how features are structured. Do they emphasize expert sources, or are they more "real people" oriented? Do they contain a lot of pithy quotes, or are the articles more narrative in nature? Does every feature have a sidebar?

Look at smaller pieces in the publication, too. These often are excellent break-in points for new writers, and a series of small pieces can lead to bigger assignments. Departments sometimes have different editorial voices than the main articles, so pay attention to style and tone here, too.

Thinking like an Editor

Editors have to think about stories that serve the needs of their readers. Writers who learn to think like editors—who get beyond the giddy imaginings of seeing their bylines in a major publication and focus on serving the readers—are more likely to come up with ideas that editors will appreciate. Remember that, as a writer, you are providing a service; readers, not editors, are your ultimate consumers.

Spotting Trends

Cashing in on trends is tricky because the publishing process takes so long. By the time you've done your research and sent off your query, the latest fad could already be on its way out. This is true for magazines and books, less so for newspapers, which publish daily or weekly and so can be more timely in their coverage. Still, magazine and book publishers do like trendy topics, as long as the trend still has "legs"—that is, it's likely to continue long enough to make running a story or printing a book worthwhile. When you're considering a trend topic, keep the actual publishing schedule in mind:

- **Researching and polishing your idea:** one to two weeks for a magazine story; one to two months for a book proposal
- **Response time from a potential market:** one to three months for most magazines; up to six months for agents and book publishers, depending on what material you send
- **Writing time:** four to six weeks for a magazine article; six months or more for a book
- **Publication date:** one to six months after you've turned your story in for a magazine; six to eighteen months for a book

Unfortunately, the realities of the publishing business make a lot of "trend" stories worthless to magazine and book publishers, and therefore not nearly as valuable to you. As noted, you might have better luck pitching such stories to newspapers, which have much quicker turnaround times.

FACT

The death of a trend sometimes can be a good story idea, too. Maybe the resurgence of natural farming is part of the demise of big corporate farms, which have been the trend for many years now. Connecting these two things in a sensible, accurate story could be the story idea that gets a resounding yes from an editor.

How can you tell if a trend has legs? It's part research and part good instincts. Be on the alert for similar stories that crop up in the news media. If you hear a story on NPR about organic gardening one day, then read an Associated Press article in your local newspaper a week later about hormone-free livestock, and a few days later see a television news magazine piece about so-called "green" pesticides and herbicides, you might be looking at a growing trend toward more natural agricultural practices. You'll probably have to act quickly to get a salable story idea out of this, because, unfortunately, you aren't the only one looking for trends, and no publisher wants to be second in covering a hot topic.

Adding Value

Whenever you come up with an idea, think of ways to make it most interesting and useful to the reader. Editors tend to think in terms of packages, or how the proposed idea will look once it's printed. Adding the appropriate package elements to your pitch can help an editor visualize how your idea fits in with her needs.

For magazine articles, think in terms of sidebars and graphic elements. Sidebars are short pieces that are related to the main story; common sidebar themes are checklists, mini bios or profiles of people quoted in the main piece, and little-known facts about the main topic. Study publications to see how they use sidebars and get a feel for average length. Graphic elements include photos, illustrations, and charts.

QUESTION?

Do I have to provide my own photos and graphics?
No. Many magazines purchase these from freelancers, but nearly all of them prefer to deal with professional photographers and graphic designers. Most writers just provide suggestions for photos, illustrations, and charts.

For book proposals, "adding value" might include these elements, too. But, often, agents and editors see more value in things like endorsements from celebrities or well-known experts on your book topic, or having one of these celebrities or experts write a foreword for your book. Another way of adding value to your pitch is to highlight your credentials and platform to show why you are the right person to write your book. (See Chapters 2 and 3 for more on building credentials and platforms.)

Finding Voids

Beginning writers often feel that all the really good ideas have been taken, and they doubt their own abilities to come up with anything fresh. After you've been seriously pursuing your writing for a while, though, you'll find that the real difficulty is having too many ideas clamoring for your attention. It takes some practice to learn which ideas have real potential and which need to simmer a little longer, but that ability comes to most writers eventually.

Starting the Search

When all is said and done, the basics are still the most reliable ways to generate ideas for articles, short stories, novels, and nonfiction books. Examine what you know, what you've experienced, what you like, and what you'd like to learn more about. Make a list of these things, and then make a list of questions about each item. Those questions can lead to great ideas, if only because they prompt you to think about familiar topics in new ways.

Say you like cheesecake. Do you know anything about its history? Who invented it and when? How have the taste and texture changed over the years? When did it become a chic dessert, with all sorts of different flavors and sauces? Is there such a thing as a cheesecake hall of fame, or maybe a cheesecake tour, similar to wine tours? Did it fall out of favor during the low-carb craze? Is it making a comeback? Just a handful of questions can open the door to all kinds of possibilities.

Read as much as you can from as many different sources as you can. News stories can spark great ideas for fiction and nonfiction, especially if you get into the habit of asking yourself "what if" questions when you read. What if the self-replicating robots you read about just kept replicating themselves forever, not out of any weird mechanical consciousness but just because that's what they're programmed to do? What if Pope Benedict XVI had been from South America instead of Europe? What if the identity of Watergate's Deep Throat had been revealed while Richard Nixon was still alive? Again, just asking questions can generate more ideas than you could possibly write about.

Looking for Holes

The key to finding—and therefore being able to fill—a void is figuring out what has been overlooked by others. Look for perspectives that haven't been explored. If you want to write about getting organized, find out whether anything has been done on the effectiveness of services that come to your home and clean out your closets. Do those closets stay organized after a month, three months, a year? Or do they provide only a temporary respite to the chronically disorganized? Has anyone covered the cheerfully disorganized, or how to forgive yourself for being disorganized? How about the psychological aspects of being organized versus being disorganized?

Keep an eye out for stories that don't reflect your experience or opinion. If you don't fit the mold assumed by a particular article or book, it's a good bet that other people don't fit it, either. It's also a good bet that you've just stumbled across an ignored perspective.

The same can be done for nearly any topic. There are forests of articles and books on career planning, for example; are there any aimed at people who enjoy the jobs they have and don't necessarily want to move up the corporate ladder? Is there any advice out there for people who supervise these employees about how to keep them motivated and engaged? Maybe this is a hole waiting to be filled.

Check Out the Competition

The Internet has made it easier than ever to find out what else has been written on your topic. Sites like Findarticles.com continually troll the Web and archive articles from a multitude of publications. You can search articles by keyword and publications by topic, and many of the articles are free.

Use online booksellers like Amazon.com and BarnesandNoble.com to get information about in-print and upcoming books. You can find out the publisher, the format, and often even the table of contents or excerpts of competing books—information that will help you identify both potential publishers and the weak spots in the competition.

Findarticles.com also provides a portal to a broad spectrum of useful statistical information sites, such as the Statistics of Income bulletin from the IRS and the Uniform Crime Bulletin from the FBI. If you're not sure where to look for information and a Google search doesn't turn up what you want, sites like this provide useful alternative searches.

Establishing an Angle

As we've shown, the mere fact that somebody else has beaten you to your topic doesn't mean you don't have a good idea. All it means is that you have to do a little more work to establish your angle. The techniques described here will help you develop the habit of thinking beyond what already has been done. You might even be surprised at how quickly you become adept at finding new approaches to not-so-new ideas.

Finding the Right Market

You've made your list of topics, asked your questions, researched what other people have written, and identified a good angle for your idea. Now you have to match that angle with potential markets, and that goes back to reading the directory listings and studying the publications. (This is why we started out with the chicken-or-the-egg question. Experienced writers travel this same circle many times over, and they usually get to the point where it doesn't really matter where they start, because they'll cover all of the same ground in any case.)

FACT

Market directories often include profiles of publishers' readers, especially for magazines. This should be a standard part of your research activity, even if you're planning to write a book. Magazines that target the same readers you want to reach with your book can help you demonstrate a market for your book and help you further refine your angle.

Remember, too, that your ultimate responsibility, whatever you're writing, is to serve your readers. That means honing your angle to make it a near-perfect match with the market. So, if your story is about the employee who is content to do her job, does it well, and isn't interested in a promotion, and your target readers are human resource managers, your angle might have to incorporate a discussion of the value of keeping these employees as well as creative incentives to retain them.

What about Fiction?

Much of the information we've presented here applies largely to nonfiction. But fiction writers also have many of the same considerations, and many of the techniques for generating nonfiction ideas can be just as effective in creating plots and characters for fiction. Also, fiction writers have the same need to understand and meet the needs of their readers. Fans of specific genres expect certain things from their authors, for instance, and that means the editors who purchase fiction will look for those things, too. Writers of children's stories have to be especially aware of vocabulary and tone to ensure they are appropriate for the targeted age group.

In marketing your fiction, it also is helpful to know what has been done before. Book editors want to know where a novel will fit on a bookstore shelf, so it's useful if you can compare your story or style with a well-known author's. If you say that your mystery is reminiscent of Dorothy Sayers or Ellery Queen, a prospective agent or editor will know just what style of mystery you've written.

ALERT!

Be careful of your phrasing when you compare your work with another author's. If you call yourself the next John LeCarré or Ernest Hemingway, you'll probably turn off the agent or editor you're trying to impress. Say instead that your style is like Hemingway's, or that your story is similar to a LeCarré novel.

Finding out what others have done in fiction also is a good way to research potential markets for your short story or novel. Check out published books in your genre at your local bookstore or library and make note of which publishers are putting out your kind of novel. Check the acknowledgments in these books, too. Authors who single out their agents or editors in the acknowledgments have had a good experience working with these people, and these could be good leads for you. As always, double-check any information you glean here with the various directories to find out how to approach these agents and publishers.

Planning Ahead

Especially when you're approaching magazines, it's important to keep in mind the strange time schedules involved. You might be motivated to write a Christmas story in November, but that's far too late for most magazines. With lead times of two to six months, most magazines will have their holiday issues laid out by August and put to bed by October. It's a little like working a graveyard shift, because the timing is nearly the opposite of what most people experience; you end up thinking about summer activities when everybody else is busy having their furnaces checked for winter.

ESSENTIAL

You must study a potential magazine market so you can get a feel for the tone and slant of the articles and better tailor your idea. If you've never read a given magazine, you have no way of knowing how the editor likes to structure articles or what style of writing she prefers, and that means your submission is nothing more than a shot in the dark.

Make use of editorial calendars when they're available. Some magazines put these on their Web sites, and some include them in their writer's guidelines. Editorial calendars will tell you what special themes the magazine is planning for the next several issues, as well as deadlines for copy. Some even include deadlines for queries for special themed issues. Calendars may be quarterly, semiannual, or, more typically, yearly.

Again, directory listings are a good resource for finding out lead times. Monthly magazines usually have the longest lead times, and weeklies usually have the shortest. That doesn't necessarily mean your article will make it into print any faster with a weekly magazine. Most publications have a hefty backlog of material waiting to be published, including the slush pile of possible articles that haven't been accepted or rejected yet.

Expanding Your Options

Nearly every writer has run into this problem at one time or another: You've got way more information than you can use for your article, and you're having a hard time deciding what to leave out. As agonizing as it can be to make the hard cuts, this actually could be turned into a bonus for you.

New writers sometimes think that shorter pieces are easier to write than longer ones. Actually, the reverse is true. It can be difficult to squeeze all the pertinent information you need into 1,200 words. It's even harder to do it in 800 words. You have to be very good at your craft to crack the small openings in major publications.

One possible solution to this problem is to turn your article idea into a package by using the excess information for sidebars. Another possibility is to divide your information into two or more standalone story ideas; one could be for a general audience, for example, and another for readers who are more expert on the topic, perhaps a trade journal. With the proper research and refining, you could get two or more articles for two or more non-competing markets—in effect doubling the return on your investment of time and energy.

The great thing about researching markets and ideas is that there is always a new angle waiting to be discovered, and it isn't as hard as it may seem. If you keep an open mind in considering ideas and markets, you'll soon find that you, like the seasoned professionals, are able to separate good ideas from bad ones and decide which ones deserve a closer examination.

chapter 5

Working with an Agent

New writers dreaming of a fat advance from Random House or HarperCollins for their mainstream novel or shocking tell-all can feel like they've hit a brick wall when they discover that some publishers—especially the conglomerates—won't even look at a query unless it comes from an agent. The truth is, there are circumstances when you do not need an agent to sell your work, and there are circumstances when having an agent is not only a good business decision for you, but nearly indispensable for your writing career.

Do You Need an Agent?

Whether you need an agent depends in large part on where you are in your writing career and what you're trying to sell. If your main focus is selling features or short stories to magazines, you don't need an agent, and, in fact, you wouldn't be able to find a reputable agent to represent this kind of work because the commissions would be too small. You also usually don't need an agent to represent your children's books, and you may not need one for your adult fiction or nonfiction books, depending on which publishers you hope to interest.

FACT

Advances and royalties tend to be low for children's books, which is why most agents don't handle them; it isn't worth their time when they can't expect much of a commission. Publishers of children's books understand this and are happy to deal directly with authors.

For the Big Players

If your aim is to land a contract with one of the major publishing houses, you probably will need an agent to represent your work. About 80 percent of the books these conglomerates publish are purchased through agents. Some of the largest houses won't even consider submissions from unagented writers; when they get manuscripts directly from the author, the author usually gets a short note in reply advising him to get an agent.

The advantage to the big publishers in dealing only with agents is that agents know what editors are looking for and won't submit work that isn't salable. The agent's reputation, and therefore his ability to succeed as an agent, rides on submitting only the best—not just in terms of ideas, but also in terms of presentation and research—to only those editors who are appropriate for the project. The publisher saves enormous time and expense by allowing agents to do the work of sifting through submissions to find the real gems.

The advantage to you as a writer is that the agent has the contacts, experience, and information to market your book idea to the proper people. Good agents stay informed of which editor is in charge of which topics or lines at which publishing house, and they often get tips from editors about what kind of material they're looking for. When you have an agent, you're putting his expertise to work for you.

Mid-Sized Publishers

Smaller publishers don't have the clout of the major houses, and they don't usually have the resources to offer enormous advances or extensive marketing campaigns. On the other hand, these houses tend to be more open to new authors than the big multinational firms. Although these publishers, like any business, always are on the lookout for commercial successes, they also tend to be more interested than the big houses in titles that won't necessarily capture a huge readership or debut at number one on the bestseller lists, such as literary fiction or niche nonfiction.

Publishing directories such as *Writer's Market* usually indicate whether a publisher accepts submissions directly from writers or whether they accept only agented submissions. If you're undecided about whether to get an agent, first look up the publishers you're most interested in and see what their requirements are.

Many of the mid-sized publishers will work with unagented writers, but, like the big houses, they prefer to work with agents. The reasons are the same: Agents know what editors are looking for, weed out the unworkable, and are familiar with the ins and outs of publishing. An agent also should be able to negotiate a better advance and more favorable terms with the mid-sized publisher than you could on your own.

Small Presses

Many small presses will work directly with authors, and some even prefer not to deal with agents. Likewise, many agents prefer not to deal with small presses because they generally are unable to offer even the average advances of their mid-sized competitors. A good agent will seek out the best advance for her authors, and the small presses know they can't compete with bigger houses. By the same token, agents often relegate the small houses to the bottom of their contact lists, going to them only if and when larger houses pass on a project.

The same goes for university presses. They typically offer minimal advances, and sometimes none at all, which makes them unattractive to agents. As a result, they are open to unagented writers, and many university presses have expanded their catalogs to include titles with a broader, mass-market appeal rather than strictly academic ones.

What an Agent Does

In its simplest form, an agent's job consists of matching supply and demand, with writers supplying the goods and publishers determining whether there's a demand for the goods. A good agent keeps up on industry news and keeps up her contacts; when she has a good relationship with an editor at one publisher, she'll keep that relationship on a solid footing when the editor moves to another publisher, even if the new publisher is one the agent hasn't dealt with before.

An agent usually has a two- or three-stage marketing plan for the projects she represents. Her goal is to find a publisher that will be both enthusiastic about and appropriate for the project and one that will offer the best terms for the author. If the first choices on her list pass, she'll move on to the second-tier choices.

A typical agent's day will be spent largely on the phone and the computer, dealing with editors and clients. In a single phone call or e-mail exchange with an editor, he may negotiate a contract, pitch new projects the editor might be interested in, and discuss problems with a writer's text or deadline. In talking with a client, he might discuss feedback he has received on the author's latest proposal, help the author overcome some difficulty on a manuscript, and talk about publicity opportunities. The agent is a master juggler, continually shifting gears to make sure the highest priorities get taken care of first while keeping the rest of his to-do list from falling through the cracks. The unexpected can always change an agent's daily plan, but her main priorities usually fall in the following order:

1. **New contracts.** After the negotiating is finished, the publisher sends a contract to the agent. The agent reviews this to make sure everything covered in the negotiations is reflected in the written document, then forwards it to the author for his or her signature. This is almost always the agent's first priority, barring some unforeseen glitch.
2. **Publishers' payments.** When the contract is signed by the author and publisher, the publisher returns a copy of it (called the "executed contract" when all parties have signed) and the first advance payment to the agent. The agent deposits the publisher's check and writes a new one to the author, minus the agent's commission.
3. **Negotiating contracts.** After taking care of finalized deals and payments, the agent concentrates on negotiating the details on pending contract offers. Each contract is different because each publisher and each author have their own needs; the publisher may want a "next-book" clause, while the author may have to be free to do a collaboration with someone else for a different publisher. It can take a lot of time to get the details just right for every contract.
4. **Marketing other projects.** After she handles all the contracts, payments, and pending offers, the agent can focus on pitching projects to editors. She may do this in the same phone call to the editor she's negotiating a contract with, if that editor would be appropriate for the new project, or she may write separate query letters or e-mails to editors on her marketing list.

Only after all these priorities have been taken care of (and assuming no emergencies arise) will an agent start reading through the piles of new submissions from prospective clients. Very often, an agent doesn't have time to do this until the end of the business day; sometimes he will put new submissions aside until the weekend so he can get more pressing business done during the week. This is why it takes so long for agents to respond to queries and proposals. They simply don't have time to get to them any sooner.

What to Look for in an Agent

You want an agent because she has expertise and contacts in the publishing industry. You also want one who is reputable and honest in her business dealings, and who has a good track record of sales to royalty-paying publishers. Finally, you want an agent who is reasonably enthusiastic about you and your project.

Specialization

Few, if any, agents handle every type of book on the market these days. The publishing business is highly competitive and changes rapidly, making it virtually impossible for any single agent to keep up with trends and currents in every single book category. Like the publishing houses they sell to, agents tend to specialize, sometimes in specific genres like romance and women's fiction, or in broader categories like adult nonfiction.

This tendency toward specialization is good for you as a writer. First, it makes it easier for you to find an agent who is familiar with the market and publishing climate for your type of book and who has contacts with publishers who could be interested in your project. Second, an agent who has placed several similar books with publishers likely is respected by the editors he deals with, and that respect will rub off on the editor's perception of you and your work when the agent submits it.

Fair Dealing

Reputable agents make their money by selling clients' books to publishers. They do not charge up-front fees for anything—not for reading your submission, offering critiques, marketing your work, drawing up the author-agent agreement, or anything else. If an agent asks you to pay for anything before offering to represent you, the odds are good that you're being scammed.

The Association of Author's Representatives (AAR) sets codes of conduct for literary agents. This code expressly prohibits up-front fees and requires agents to have separate business and personal accounts so that clients' funds don't get mixed in with the agent's personal money. The AAR also prohibits members from participating in any sort of kickback scheme, such as referring potential clients to an editing service or a self-publisher in which the agent has a financial interest.

Not all reputable agents are members of the AAR, for a variety of reasons. Some may not have met the sales requirements to join (the AAR requires new members to have sold ten titles in the past eighteen months), while others may feel that the expense of joining outweighs the benefits of being a member. However, reputable agents who are not members generally follow the AAR's ethical standards.

Track Record

The ultimate test of a successful agent is sales to royalty-paying publishers. Sometimes you'll find a list of recent titles an agent has sold in the major directories, but most agents won't discuss specific sales with anyone except the client and the publisher to whom the book was sold. When you're seeking representation, you'll have to be satisfied with more general information. An agent should be willing to tell you how many titles he has sold in the past year or whether one of the books he represented was a bestseller, for example, but he should not discuss details of any sales, such as the advance the author received.

FACT

New agents aren't necessarily new to the publishing industry. Sometimes editors will leave the publisher side of the business and set themselves up as agents, and they usually have enough knowledge of the business and enough contacts to make good agents. Other new agents might have worked as assistants to established agents for several years before striking out on their own.

According to the AAR, new agents—who, often, are most open to representing first-time authors—should begin making sales in six to twelve months. An agent who has been in business two years and has yet to sell a manuscript may not be either inept or unconnected, but these circumstances don't bode well for your project. Look for an agent who has a strong record of sales for titles that are similar to yours.

Enthusiasm

When you get a positive response from an agent, it means she thinks your work has a reasonable chance of getting a publisher's attention. Very likely, she'll have some ideas for improving your manuscript or proposal to make it more attractive and salable. She may even suggest a new slant that will really make it stand out. But a good agent won't go overboard with visions of success. Publishing is a volatile and vicarious business, and this month's hot book market could be equally as cold next month. No one, not even the most experienced agent, can predict the next bestseller or the story that will earn millions in movie rights. Be wary of agents who promise you the moon; it probably means they don't have their feet on the ground.

By the same token, an agent who reminds you of Eeyore in the Winnie the Pooh stories probably isn't going to be the most effective representative for you, either. Pessimism, like optimism, is infectious. An agent who sounds glum when he's pitching your project to an editor is unlikely to score a request for the proposal, much less a sale.

Finding the Right Agent

You've got a list of reputable, experienced agents, ones who are well-respected, open to new clients, and with whom you think you would feel comfortable doing business. But, as important as those qualities are, they don't necessarily mean these agents are right for you or your work. A big part of finding the right agent is matching your material to an agent's specialty. An agent who focuses on fiction is likely to be of little help in marketing your how-to book for beginning cabinet-makers, even if you could capture her interest.

Some literary agencies will accept new writers only if they are referred by existing clients, and it's a waste of your time and energy to try to "sneak" into these agencies. Instead, concentrate your energies on the many agents who are ever on the lookout for talented writers with promising book ideas.

Directories

There are several reliable directories that list agents and what they're looking for. Writer's Digest *Guide to Literary Agents* is readily available at major bookstores and is updated regularly. You also can check out the AAR's online directory of agents at ✎*www.writers.net/agents.html*.

Another excellent resource is *Literary Marketplace*, known as the LMP. Although the price of the LMP makes it an impractical purchase for most beginning writers, good-sized public libraries usually have the latest print edition in their reference sections. LMP now has an online database, and you can get access to parts of it for free, although you do have to register. LMP also recently introduced a one-week paid subscription, which gives you access to all of the LMP features online for about $20. This can be cost-effective if you consolidate searches for agents and publishers, both of which are available through LMP, or if you plan to do your research at times when your public library is closed.

ALERT!

Print directories usually list agents' telephone numbers and may even include fax numbers and e-mail addresses. This is not an invitation for you to call the agent to pitch your project, or to fax your entire proposal or manuscript to him. Read and follow the submission guidelines in the listing.

The value of these directories is that they spell out such things as how the agent prefers to be contacted—regular mail, e-mail, etc.—as well as what they accept from prospective clients. Some ask for queries only and will return, unopened, unsolicited proposals and manuscripts. Others specify a synopsis and the first three chapters for novels, or an overview and a sample chapter for nonfiction. Very often, these directories also will list what a particular agent will not consider or does not want; some will accept simultaneous submissions, for example, and some won't.

On the Bookshelf

Another way to match an agent with your material is to visit your local bookseller and check out the acknowledgments pages in books that are similar to yours. You can reasonably assume that authors who include their agents in the acknowledgments have a good relationship with their agent and are pleased with their agent's representation. The fact that the author has written a book similar to yours shows that the agent handles your kind of material. If you use this method to gather potential agents' names, you can then check out their listings in the print directories to find out how best to approach them.

Author-Agent Agreements

Agents make money by convincing publishers to buy their clients' books. To be effective, an agent has to have the exclusive right to market your book. Otherwise, any given editor could be getting pitched for the same project from multiple sources, and you can imagine the chaos that would result. Some agents forego formal agreements until your work is sold, but this can be risky for both of you. Without a written contract, the agent has no way of knowing whether he's the only one marketing your book; if you decide to look for another agent, you have no way of knowing that the first agent isn't still pitching your project; and, if a dispute arises over the agent's commission or expenses, you have no written document to resolve the issue.

A written agreement, spelling out the terms and obligations for each of you, really is the best way to protect your interests and the agent's. It should be signed before the agent does anything in the way of presenting your work to his contacts, and each of you should have a signed copy for your files.

Scope of Representation

The meat of the author-agent agreement is the scope of representation. Often, you give the agent the exclusive right to represent all of your book-length work, regardless of the format and no matter where potential publishers might be located. Agents who offer these kinds of agreements are looking to build a relationship with new writers, with the expectation that the partnership will be lucrative for both of you over the long term. Indeed, agents (and publishers) often don't expect to make a lot of money right away with new writers; substantial profits are more likely to come from second, third, fourth or even fifth books. An author-agent agreement that covers all your work, then, can be taken as an expression of faith in your future success.

Note that the agent is only interested in book-length work. It is exceedingly rare for agents to handle short stories, magazine articles, or poetry. For one thing, you don't need an agent to submit these pieces to appropriate publishers. For another, the agent's commission on these pieces would be far too small to justify spending his time marketing them.

Many agents offer short-term, one-book contracts with new authors. This gives both of you a chance to see how you work together without locking you into a long-term relationship. If things go well and you decide you want to continue the partnership, you can consider a more comprehensive agreement.

In some circumstances, you might want to give an agent exclusive rights to only one specific project. It might be appropriate if, for example, you have one agent for your nonfiction books and need someone with expertise in marketing your adventure novel. In that case, your agreements with each agent must include explicit definitions of what the agent is entitled to represent.

Duration of the Contract

Most author-agent agreements are in force for one to two years, although some offer six-month contracts. Initial contracts usually cannot be terminated for a set period—six to twelve months on a one- or two-year contract, for example. This gives the agent time to market your work without fear that her right to represent you will be arbitrarily pulled. Some agents may require you to sign a new contract when the old one expires, but often there is simply a clause in the contract that allows for automatic renewal. Likewise, there usually is a provision that allows either party to terminate the contract—after the initial no-termination period—with one to three months' written notice to the other.

Agent's Commission

Any agency contract must spell out the agent's commission on sales. The industry standard is 15 percent for domestic sales and 20 to 25 percent for foreign sales. There may be higher commissions specified for things like movie rights, too. These higher commissions are warranted because such sales usually involve hiring a subagent—one based in the foreign country where your book is being marketed, or one who specializes in movie options and rights—and your agent's commission will have to be split with the subagent.

How Payments Are Handled

The author-agent agreement also describes how payments from publishers are handled. The agent will be authorized to accept all payments from publishers, including advances and royalty payments, on your behalf, which means that the publisher's check will be made out to the agent, not to you. The agent then writes you a check for those payments, minus the agent's commission. The agreement also may specify that the agent must forward payment to you within so many days after the check from the publisher clears the agent's bank.

Other Provisions

Most agreements include a "warranties and representations" clause, in which you promise that the work your agent is representing is your own. This is virtually the same clause you'll find in most publisher contracts and is designed to protect the agent against representing plagiarized works. There also may be a "hold-harmless" provision, in which the agent is protected from any liability if your work is plagiarized or otherwise violates someone's civil, privacy, or intellectual property rights. (See Chapter 10 for more on the issue of plagiarism.)

ALERT!

Some Internet writing sites encourage writers to post completed works or works in progress for review and comments from other writers. You may get valuable feedback this way, but remember that placing your work on the Internet counts as publication, and you'll have to disclose this to agents and editors who might be interested.

Agreements also usually include a guarantee that you own the work. That is, you are promising the agent that you haven't sold any rights in the work anywhere else or turned over future earnings to someone else. If you have sold some rights (e.g., your novel is based on the same plot as a short story you had published, or a chapter of your book originally appeared as a feature article in a magazine) or turned over future earnings (to satisfy a debt or as part of a divorce decree, for instance), be sure to inform the agent of this before you sign any representation agreement. Full disclosure at the beginning of your relationship will avert lots of potential problems later on.

Building a Professional Relationship

Some writers expect agents to be a combination of writing coach, cheerleader, psychologist, and best friend. In fact, sometimes an agent is all those things for her clients. But the author-agent relationship is essentially a business partnership. An agent's job is to sell her clients' work to publishers. Your job is to write material that publishers will be interested in. You and your agent may like each other personally. You might even end up being friends. But, if that friendship arises, it will grow from a sound professional relationship, based on realistic expectations of what your agent can, should, and will do for you.

Decide whether you want an agent before you begin marketing your book. An agent is less likely to be interested in representing you if you approach him only after a dozen editors have turned you down, because it's going to be hard for that agent to sell a manuscript that has already been rejected by editors he might want to contact.

Respect the Agent's Time

Agents are busy people, and business hours are overflowing with a long list of tasks that need to get done as soon as possible. Unnecessary interruptions that eat into the agent's precious and limited time are annoying and can sabotage your relationship. Most questions can be handled through e-mail, which is less intrusive than a phone call and often more convenient for the agent, since e-mail can be sent anytime. If you absolutely have to talk to your agent, write her a quick e-mail asking for a phone date and telling her, succinctly, what you need to discuss. When you do call her, always ask if she has time to talk with you, and be understanding if the answer is no. She may be in the middle of negotiations or some other critical task, and the hard truth is that, sometimes, you are not her highest priority.

Respect the Agent's Knowledge

One of the reasons you sought an agent is because you wanted to take advantage of his expertise in publishing. When he gives you advice on how to polish your proposal or work with your editor or pursue publicity opportunities, he is sharing his hard-earned knowledge of the business with you. That doesn't mean you have to do everything your agent recommends or be afraid to ask questions. But do recognize that your agent's goal is to help you succeed—success for you means success for him, remember—and listen graciously to your agent's point of view.

FACT

If an agent gives you constructive feedback on your project before you've signed with her and you decide to make the suggested changes, be sure to give her first crack at your proposal after you've done so. She's obviously interested, and she has given you free advice on how to improve your work. In exchange, you should give her another chance to represent you.

If you're a first-time book author, your agent is not just an invaluable guide and ally in the publishing world; she's something of a visionary. She has taken on the responsibility of helping launch your career, with no guarantee that she will ever be compensated for her time, access, or expertise. Understanding and respecting your agent's contribution to your career is a critical component of a successful and professional relationship. After all, you are embarking on a business partnership, which, with the proper care, will reward both of you, monetarily and otherwise.

chapter 6

Magazine Markets

Magazine writing can provide both a steppingstone for your career and a respectable income, which is why so many writers devote so much of their time to researching and querying magazines. Editors need a steady stream of material to fill their nonadvertising pages, and, because the regular staff at most magazines is small, they rely on freelancers to provide articles, columns, and fillers. Competition is stiff because there are more writers than there are markets. But, if you do your homework, you can stand out from the crowd.

Types of Magazines

As we mentioned in Chapter 1, there are two broad categories of magazines for nonfiction: trade journals and consumer magazines. For fiction and what is known as "literary nonfiction," there is a third category: little, or literary, magazines. The "littles" usually are high-prestige, low-paying markets, sometimes paying only in contributor copies. Depending on their focus, they may accept fiction, poetry, and narrowly defined pieces of nonfiction like essays. The writing style tends to be more formal than in other types of magazines, with a distinct artistic flavor.

Magazines run the gamut in terms of willingness to work with new writers and pay rates. If you're just starting your career, your chances of breaking in usually will be better with the smaller-circulation publications. As your clip file expands, so will your opportunities for seeing your byline in the bigger magazines.

FACT

To find out how open a magazine is to new writers, check out the one- or two-sentence author bios in a recent issue. How many of them list credentials similar to yours? How many have a long string of published credits, maybe even books? Your chances of breaking in probably are slimmer if you're competing mainly with already-published writers.

You'll find hundreds of trade, consumer, and literary magazines listed in the market directories. More are cropping up every day, but be alert for problems when approaching a new publication. Many of them fail within months for lack of ad revenue or other financial support, and even those that hang on might run into difficulties paying their contributors. We're not saying you should avoid new markets, just that you should go into them with your eyes open.

For all categories of magazines, pay rates vary from little or nothing to quite respectable fees. Established writers with impressive clips garner the highest rates. Writers who are just starting out or who are new to the market will earn less for their work until they build a reputation with the editor. New writers often have to be content with short items to establish a track record, but those who perform well on such assignments have a good chance of breaking into the feature-length action.

How Magazine Publishing Works

The thing most writers need to understand about magazine publishing is the enormous lead times involved. Monthly magazines usually are working three to six months in advance; quarterlies may be working six to nine months ahead. Weeklies have shorter lead times, but they also usually have regular staff writers and generally don't provide as many opportunities for the newcomer or freelancer.

It's important to know this because any story ideas you have that are pegged to events or seasons have to be planned and submitted far ahead of time. If you want to do something about Father's Day or summer weekend getaways, for example, you probably will have to have your idea solidified and ready to send out in query form no later than February, while holiday craft or cooking ideas need to be in the editor's hands by midsummer.

Editorial Calendars

Many magazines try to help writers (and advertisers, who also are keenly interested in reaching the right audience at the right time) with their planning by issuing editorial calendars that spell out main topics or themes for upcoming issues, as well as advertising and copy deadlines. Some magazines even include query deadlines for specific issues. Calendars often are available on the magazine's Web site and may be included in the submission guidelines; they also may indicate special or extra editions, such as *Sports Illustrated*'s annual swimsuit issue.

Savvy writers make a practice of collecting and updating editorial calendars for their target publications. It's an easy way to remind yourself to think ahead, and it can act as a tickler when you're feeling stuck and idea-less. It's also helpful when you're trying to break into new markets, because it gives you important clues as to what the editors will be looking for and when.

Timing the Timeless

Timeless stories are ones that don't have a particular news peg to hang on. Many interview and profile pieces, for instance, can be published at any time. The disadvantage for you is that timeless articles are all too easy to push off the table of contents in favor of stories with more immediate appeal, thus delaying publication and the addition of another clip to your file. Another thing to consider: Editors generally prefer stories that have some sense of immediacy, because readers generally prefer them, too.

You can earn high marks for freshness by adding an element of timeliness to perennial stories. You might tie a story about sales of hybrid cars to the annual Earth Day observance, for example, or you might take the standby New Year's Resolution piece and adapt it for students in September as New School Year Resolutions.

It takes a little creativity and extra work to add timeliness to essentially timeless stories, but it can be done. Editors are more likely to snap up interviews or profiles when the subject is about to hit a milestone of some sort—releasing a new movie, say, or facing his third ballot for entry into the Baseball Hall of Fame. The added news value makes the story more compelling for editors and for readers.

Cultivate Patience

As long as the lead times are, most writers feel that the response times from magazines are even longer. It doesn't seem to make sense, at least to eager writers, that editors take weeks or months to respond to a simple query. In fact, because of the way most magazines handle submissions, it's a little surprising that it doesn't take longer.

ESSENTIAL

For nonfiction articles, write a query that describes your idea and demonstrates that you know the subject and have access to experts. For fiction, magazine editors generally prefer to see a complete manuscript. Because of the volume of submissions they receive, editors often don't reply to fiction submissions unless they want to publish the story.

Here's what happens when you send in your query—assuming that you've sent it to the right person. The editor in charge of screening submissions usually separates them into two piles. The first pile (and, by far, the largest) is the rejection pile for material that doesn't fit the magazine's needs. In most cases, rejections will get the fastest responses—assuming you've included your SASE.

The second pile is for the "maybes," material the editor likes. But, at most magazines, this editor doesn't have the final decision on whether to purchase an article. Instead, she'll schedule a story conference with her boss (the managing editor, executive editor, or editor in chief); that conference also may include other editors and staff. Just arranging the conference can be a challenge because unanticipated crises, special projects, business travel, and vacations all have to be worked around. So, that conference might not even take place until several weeks after the editor has read your query.

QUESTION?

What if my idea is on hold at a magazine?
You can wait on the magazine to decide whether and when to assign or publish your material, or you can withdraw it and shop it to other markets. Always let the editor know what you intend to do; she'll be peeved if you offer it elsewhere without telling her.

When the conference does take place, your idea will be discussed, and one of three things will happen: The boss will reject it; the boss will accept it, and the editor will make a note to herself to call you to discuss payment, length, and so on; or the boss will say "maybe," in which case you should (but won't always) receive a note or e-mail from the editor letting you know that your idea is on hold.

Spotting Break-In Opportunities

Different types of magazines offer different openings for writers to exploit. The standard advice, and the usual path for beginning writers, is to look for short assignments, prove yourself to an editor with those, and then start pushing for bigger articles and more pay. It also helps if you can think like an editor—especially if you understand his needs and concerns.

Think Cover Blurb

Whatever your idea is, try to envision it on the cover of the magazine you're targeting. A bold headline and deck—the copy under the headline that gives a little more information about the story—are designed to catch the reader's eye and interest. Editors spend hours on the cover blurbs for each issue because strong blurbs can spur single-copy sales at the newsstand or supermarket checkout. If you can come up with a good head and deck for your idea, you've not only got the hook for your query, you've got a good chance of making an editor take notice.

A rule of thumb in magazine publishing is that, if you've seen a story in one publication, you're probably too late to cash in on a trend of similar stories. By the time another magazine could purchase and publish a similar article, the trend will be over.

Go Against the Flow

Controversy sells. Challenge conventional wisdom, and present facts and expert opinions to expose a nontraditional view. Editors at many magazines like these pieces because they get people talking. Readers respond to them because they expect to learn something new.

Offer Many Dimensions

A well-rounded article idea explores more than one facet of the story, and editors like to see depth in their major features. You can add dimensions and layers to almost any topic, often through the use of sidebars or other package elements (another thing editors like to see). A story on summer grilling might include a sidebar about unusual items to grill, like foie gras, for example, or one on the conflicting evidence about whether eating charcoal-grilled foods is good for you.

Studying the Publication

Virtually every magazine listing in every market directory implores writers to study the publication, but few give you any concrete advice on what to look for. Aside from seeing what topics a publication covers and what articles have been published recently, studying a publication means getting a feel for its style, tone, and editorial preferences. Analyzing the content can transport you into an editor's head, if you know what to look for. For every magazine you study, ask yourself these questions:

- **What categories do the feature articles fall into?** Are they mainly "how-to" or service articles? Does the magazine include a lot of profiles or interviews with celebrities or other people of interest? Is the focus on self-help, showing the reader how to accomplish a goal or task?
- **What is the editorial format?** Does each issue include a profile, an essay, a service article, and an investigative piece? Is each issue themed, so that all the articles are on a related topic? Or is the magazine divided into departments, with a main feature in its health, relationships, food, and recreation departments?
- **What is the style for most of the articles?** Is the writing chatty and conversational? Objective and more formal? Do the articles infuse humor into the topic, or are they more matter-of-fact?
- **Do the articles have common structural elements?** Is the emphasis on expert research and opinion, or does the magazine prefer more first-person or man-on-the-street reporting?
- **What other elements are tied into the articles?** Does each main piece include one or two sidebars? Are there photos or illustrations with each piece? Does the magazine use pull quotes to emphasize certain points?

It isn't enough to know what a given magazine covers and who its readers are. If you hope to land an assignment, you also have to know how to present your idea so that it fits the editor's style and taste. You might have a great idea for a first-person travel piece, but if the magazine you're targeting never uses first-person material, you're headed for a rejection. Likewise, submitting a query for a celebrity profile to a magazine that doesn't use them is a waste of time and energy. Use your critical thinking skills on the material in your target magazine to figure out what's likely to hook an editor.

Studying the Readership

Successful magazines have clearly defined profiles of their target readership that cover everything from simple demographic data (age, income, education level, church membership, and so on) to things like purchasing behavior, hobbies and interests, and career aspirations. Everything that appears in the publication, from feature articles and columns right down to the tiny classified ads at the back of the book, is carefully crafted to appeal to one or more aspects of that reader profile. The best idea in the world will be answered with a resounding no if it doesn't serve the needs of a magazine's subscriber base. Yet, amazingly, novice writers sometimes focus so hard on impressing editors that they neglect to study the real market for their work: the reader.

ESSENTIAL

If you can, get hold of the magazine's media or advertiser kit. This will include useful information about the magazine's readers, which will help you further refine your article's slant. Sometimes you can find these kits, or at least request them, on the magazine's Web site. Such kits often include a sample issue of the magazine, too.

How do you learn who a magazine's readers are? The market directories are a good place to start. The listings often include a brief description of magazines' target readers—working mothers, teenage girls, college-educated technophobes, gaming industry managers, etc. But to really gain an understanding of your potential readership, you have to study more than just the articles in the magazine.

Look at the Ads

Ads don't make it into magazines by accident. They are placed because the advertiser thinks the magazine's readership matches the product's target consumer. They have to; advertising is expensive, and companies can't afford to throw away money by going after the wrong kind of potential buyer. You probably won't find Harley-Davidson advertising in an issue of *Redbook*, and you probably won't find Pantene advertising in an issue of *Field & Stream*.

The ads, therefore, can give you quite a bit of insight into the mind of your potential reader. If there isn't any liquor advertising, for example, readers probably won't be interested in an article about the resurgence of martini parties. And that means the editor won't be interested, either.

Read the Letters

Many magazines print letters from their readers, and you can glean some interesting information from studying these. What stories or articles prompted readers to write in? What touched a chord with them? Do controversial articles or those with a strong human interest element get the most reaction? What do readers tend to criticize? What do they want more of? Even if you haven't read the articles referred to, the letters can provide valuable clues about what readers want and expect from their publication.

Submission Guidelines

The ins and outs of magazine publishing are a mystery to most writers, and especially to beginners, who don't understand why it takes so long for editors to respond to even the briefest queries. It's really a simple matter of logistics. The editor you query has dozens of other responsibilities on top of reading and responding to ideas for future articles, and, no matter how well organized the editor is, those other responsibilities will infringe on her schedule for getting things done.

This is why editors develop submission guidelines for hopeful writers. Experienced editors develop a sort of sixth sense about what's right and what's wrong for their magazines. For most of them, especially in dealing with nonfiction, a query letter is the only tool they need to make a yes-or-no decision. They also have their own preferences for receiving submissions. Many editors take submissions home to read in the evenings or on weekends, so it's more convenient for them to receive hard copies via regular mail. Also, many of them dislike having their e-mail inboxes clogged with material from unknown writers; they might accept assigned material electronically, but they may not want to have to print out a bunch of e-mail queries.

For fillers and other very short nonfiction pieces, you can include the completed manuscript with a cover letter. But, unless you're writing an article on spec, don't do the work of writing the piece until you get a green light from the editor. For magazines that accept fiction and poetry, many editors want to skip the query stage and see the completed piece. Again, the submission guidelines will tell you how the editor wants to receive material.

ALERT!

Just like book editors and agents, magazine editors get annoyed when writers sidestep the submission guidelines. Don't send a complete manuscript unless it's requested, and don't send e-mail queries if the guidelines specify snail mail only. Following the guidelines is an easy way to promote a good first impression.

Crafting Your Query

For both book and magazine ideas, the most important piece of writing you'll do is the query letter. For one thing, it's an essential sales tool; ideas gain traction or slide into oblivion based on the query. But, even more important, your query is the only piece of writing that an editor is certain to read. Impress her with your initial letter, and you improve your chances of breaking into print because, even if one idea doesn't go anywhere, editors get a good impression of you from a well-crafted query.

There are lots of books about how to write good query letters, but be careful about copying styles, structures, or formats from these books. Magazine editors get thousands of copycat queries a year lifted directly from such sources, and still most ideas get rejected. Your query letter needs to be inspired by your own ideas and your own words. It also needs to be to the point.

Be Brief

A good query letter is tight. Unless you're pitching a particularly complex idea—and there are very few magazines who are interested in lengthy, complex articles from freelancers—your query letter should fit on one 8½ × 11 page. The first paragraph is your hook; the second paragraph fleshes out your idea and specifies the length and any other elements, like sidebars and photos. In the third paragraph, give a short summary of your qualifications to write the piece. Close with an appreciation of the editor's time and a call to action: "Thank you for your time and consideration. I look forward to hearing from you." (Sample queries are located in Appendix B.)

Make sure your complete contact information is in your query—name, mailing address including zip code, telephone number including area code, and e-mail address—and always include a SASE so the editor can respond. Editors don't call with rejections; the only way you'll know that you've been turned down is if you include the SASE.

Be Enthusiastic

Enthusiasm is contagious, even from a page of typescript, and so is boredom. Don't fill your query with a lot of hype, but do imbue it with a sense of your own excitement about the idea you're pitching. Editors can tell if you're really interested in the topic or if you're just hoping to get an assignment so you can pay some bills. Not surprisingly, they prefer to work with writers who have some genuine enthusiasm for their assignments.

Accepting Assignments

When an editor says yes to your query, he'll most likely call you to talk about it. This conversation should cover essentials like word count, the due date, and payment arrangements. You also should talk about the scope of the assignment. Does the editor want sidebars? How many people do you need to interview? Are there other sources the editor wants you to include? Does the editor want to adjust the slant or make sure your article covers certain information? Getting all these things ironed out in the initial phone call can save a lot of aggravation for both of you later on.

FACT

As a new writer, you can't expect to get the top pay rate; yours may be significantly lower until you prove yourself to the editor. Remember, too, that the rates listed in market directories are only ballpark figures. Some writers get less than the minimum listed, and some established writers get significantly more.

It's also a good idea to clarify the magazine's pay policies. Will you get paid on acceptance, or not until the piece is published? How soon after you turn in your work (or after it's published) can you expect a check? If the editor later decides she can't use your article, will you get a kill fee?

Selling and Reselling

The most effective queries are tailored to a specific magazine's readership. If you're thinking that dozens of markets will be interested in your idea, that's a good sign that you haven't refined your slant properly. Ideas that are too broad or vague usually don't appeal to magazine editors, and, in this super-competitive business, no editor wants to publish what every other magazine is publishing.

That said, it is possible to take one idea and break it into viable pieces for two or more potential markets, as long as you make sure the readerships of your intended markets don't overlap. Very few magazines these days are interested in buying simultaneous rights unless the other publications are practically unrelated to their own. A select few will purchase reprint rights, but, even then, you'll probably have to look for non-competing publications. Don't fool yourself into thinking that every one of your target markets will be satisfied with, or even interested in, a rehash of material that you've already had published elsewhere.

The only way to determine whether you can sell the same article twice is to scour the market listings and submission guidelines. Don't waste your time or energy pitching reprint or simultaneous rights to markets that don't accept them. Instead, focus on refining your idea for one or two specific markets.

Working with the Editor

Successful magazine writing is all about good customer service. You have two customers to keep in mind when you're crafting ideas and writing for a magazine. The first customer is the magazine's reader. You need to provide informative, entertaining material that the reader will find useful and interesting. But the editor you're working with also is your customer, and giving her good service means she'll come back to you for more.

Keep Your Promises

The world is full of unreliable writers who never seem to make their deadlines, who misspell names or get their facts wrong, who space off important elements of their projects, or who decide somewhere in the middle to change focus without warning. Editors don't need any more writers like this, and they do their best to avoid working with them. They do need writers they can count on, and this is why they tend to go back to their stables of tried-and-trusted, established writers instead of taking a chance on a newbie.

It's easier to negotiate a more reasonable deadline at the beginning of the deal than it is to convince an editor to change it later. Be realistic about how much time you need to complete a project. If an editor suggests a deadline that isn't workable for you, talk about your concerns and see if you can compromise.

Whenever you have an article assigned or an idea accepted, you are making a series of implicit promises to the editor. You promise to turn in your material by your deadline. You promise to provide accurate information and clean copy on an agreed-upon topic with an agreed-upon slant. You promise to be available to help with any issues that might arise during the editing process. If you don't keep your promises, your chances of getting another assignment from this editor grow dim.

Be Responsive

Answer your phone and reply to e-mails. Don't assume that a message from an editor can wait. He is unimaginably busy, and if he takes the time to try to contact you, it's because he needs something. Even if it's something minor, the sooner you can help him clear it off his to-do list, the better. Responding promptly to questions, suggestions, and problems polishes your image as someone this editor wants to work with again.

Be Helpful

If you're like most writers, you've come up with great ideas for articles that, for whatever reason, just aren't right for you. Maybe you don't have the time or the contacts to do the reporting, or maybe it's something that doesn't interest you enough that you want to pursue it. But that doesn't mean those ideas should just wither on the vine. You can share them with editors you work with, at the same time making it clear that you don't want the assignment yourself. Generosity in sharing ideas adds another dimension to your relationship with your editor, one that cannot help but reflect favorably on you the next time this editor has an idea that would be perfect for you.

Any business owner will tell you that the key to building a successful enterprise is repeat business, and this is as true for writers as it is for restaurants. It's easier and less expensive to keep the customers you have than it is to attract new ones. Give every editor your best work and the best customer service, and they'll keep coming back to you.

chapter 7
Book Publishing

For most writers, getting a book published is the holy grail of their career. According to one survey, four of every five American adults feel they have a book inside them, and, according to another study, there are some six million book manuscripts making the rounds at any given time. Small wonder that the world of book publishing seems so daunting to the newcomer. But, if you understand the business, you'll find that this mysterious industry is much like any other.

Types of Publishers

Traditional publishers can be divided into four main categories: major conglomerates, mid-sized houses, small presses, and university presses. (Self-publishers and e-publishing are discussed in Chapter 15.) All told, there are an estimated 80,000 publishers in the United States, and between 8,000 and 11,000 new publishing houses are established in an average year.

Major Conglomerates

The six largest publishers all are headquartered in New York City: HarperCollins, Holtzbrinck Publishing Holdings, Penguin Putnam, Random House, Simon & Schuster, and Time Warner. Of these, Random House is the largest. Together, the conglomerates account for about half of all book sales in the United States. These houses are the most difficult for new writers to break into, in part because they tend to be more interested in commercial titles—that is, titles that are likely to sell 100,000 copies or more. The big publishers also prefer to work with agents rather than unagented writers; four out of five titles they purchase are represented by an agent.

FACT

Whenever you read of a seven-figure advance, the publisher involved is almost certainly one of the so-called Big Six. But a huge advance doesn't necessarily mean a book will become a blockbuster. According to the trade journal *Bookselling This Week*, Random House, Simon & Schuster, and Penguin Putnam accounted for some $100 million in unearned advances in 1996.

Each of the conglomerates has a number of separate divisions, and, in many cases, these divisions act as independent publishing houses. Random House, for example, has at least eleven divisions, and each of these divisions has its own list of imprints. The Ballantine Publishing Group falls under the Random House umbrella, and Ballantine in turn publishes at least eight imprints, among them Fawcett, Ivy, Columbine, and, of course, Ballantine Books.

Divisions and imprints usually have their own unique specialties, and they are typically listed independently in market directories. Doubleday, another Random House imprint, has four listings in *Writer's Market*—one for the Doubleday Broadway Publishing Group, which publishes both non-fiction and fiction (it published *The Da Vinci Code* by Dan Brown); one for Doubleday Religious Publishing, which focuses on spiritual and religious fiction and nonfiction; one for Doubleday/Image, a strictly nonfiction religious/spiritual house; and one for Doubleday Books for Young Readers, which publishes picture books for preschoolers to eight-year-olds.

Mid-Sized Houses

There are several hundred medium-sized publishers in the United States, and these tend to be more open than the conglomerates to new writers. You can thank the growth of major booksellers for the proliferation of mid-sized and small publishers: The rapid expansion of shelf space that must be filled has given new opportunities to these smaller outfits to get their titles into the hands of the reading public.

A study by the Authors Guild, an advocacy group for writers, defines a successful fiction book as one that sells 5,000 copies. A successful non-fiction book sells 7,500 copies. In general, the major publishers have to sell 10,000 copies of a given title to break even. According to some estimates, only three books in ten sell enough copies to earn back the advance.

Like the major houses, most medium-sized publishers prefer to work with agents, although they generally are not closed to unagented writers. Agents serve several important functions for editors. They act as prescreeners, winnowing the masses of submissions to those that are marketable; an agent puts her own reputation on the line every time she submits a proposal to an editor, so she is unlikely to submit material that isn't appropriate. Agents also are familiar with the publishing process; they know which contract items are negotiable and which aren't, how the approval process works in the publishing house, and the industry standards for such things as advances, royalty rates, rights for sale, and so on.

Royalty rates at the mid-sized publishers are similar to those at the conglomerates, but the advances are significantly smaller. These houses simply don't have the financial resources to offer huge advances, and they can't afford to lose the millions of dollars the big houses routinely write off every year. Like the big houses, mid-sized publishers always are on the alert for potential break-out books, but their bread and butter is the broad midlist— books that will sell reasonably well and make a profit, but that are unlikely to hit the bestseller lists.

Small Presses

Small presses often are the easiest markets for new writers to approach. Most of them do not require authors to have agents. You won't be able to quit your day job with a contract from a small press; in fact, in many cases you'll be fortunate if a small press offers even a tiny advance. Initial press runs often are smaller with these houses, too. The average first run is 5,000 copies. With a small press, the initial print run might be as few as 1,000 copies.

That said, novice writers should give full consideration to working with small presses. As with any other publishing credit, a book with a small press can be the first rung of the ladder to larger publishers, who will want to see a book credit among your credentials. Larger houses also routinely review the lists of the smaller presses, looking for promising titles to add to their own catalogs.

University Presses

There was a time when university presses were strictly limited to academic works. However, in recent years, and in response to shrinking financial support from their parent universities, many of them have expanded their lists to include fiction and nonfiction with a broader appeal. University presses rarely offer advances, but they do pay royalties and, like the small presses, they often prefer to work directly with writers rather than with agents. If you can make the right match between your work and a university press, you may have found the launching point for your career as an author.

Behind the Scenes at a Publishing House

Most writers, even seasoned pros, have only a vague idea of what the inside of a publishing house is like. There's much more to the business than just reviewing submissions and deciding whether to offer a contract. In truth, so many people have a hand in deciding the fate of a given submission that it can be difficult to keep them all straight.

The Acquisitions Process

The days when a lone editor fell in love with a manuscript and convinced his boss to buy it are long gone (if, indeed, they ever existed). Today's publishers make decisions by committee, and very often the editor you contact is only one voice among a dozen or more that will weigh in on your idea. The editor's colleagues, the sales staff, the marketing department, and the publicity department all play a role in the process.

Here's what happens at most houses. When an editor receives a proposal or manuscript she likes, she takes it to the editorial meeting, often known informally as the pub board. This committee consists of representatives from all the departments listed above, plus the publisher or editor in chief. The editor will be given a few minutes to make a pitch about the idea she likes. She may ask some of her colleagues to review the submission, or, in some cases, she may recommend acquiring the title.

FACT

At most houses, advances are based on the expected sales performance of the book. Larger houses generally offer larger advances, while smaller publishers may offer only a token advance. As a first-time book author, you can expect your advance to fall between $1,000 and $7,500, although certain types of book will fetch more.

At this point, the others in the room speak their minds, and what they have to say can lift or kill a project. If the sales staff is gloomy about the prospects of interesting booksellers in the title, it probably won't get approved. The publicity rep can deliver a mortal blow by complaining that reviewers don't like this kind of book. Another editor may point out that the publisher already has a similar title, or that a similar title hasn't sold well.

What if the response in the editorial meeting is positive? Most likely, the editor won't rush to the telephone to make an offer. Instead, she'll get approval to research expenses and sales numbers for similar titles. This has to be done in between all her other daily obligations, so it may be several weeks before she has the information to take back to the pub board. If the numbers look good, and if the mood in the house is still positive, the editor will be authorized to offer a contract. If the numbers are poor or other factors have changed, she'll send out a rejection.

Developing the Manuscript

You'll work with the acquiring editor—the one who did all the research and pitching in the pub board meeting—as you write your nonfiction manuscript or polish your fiction manuscript. Once you've delivered the complete product and the acquiring editor has had a chance to read it and suggest changes, she'll turn it over to a new editor, usually called a development editor or project editor. This person concentrates on things like the work's structure and organization, as well as content. You probably will get a new set of questions and suggestions from the development or project editor.

Finally, your work will be turned over to a copy editor, who will go through the text line by line to check for spelling, grammar, punctuation, and style errors; he also may be responsible for fact-checking. Chances are you'll have yet another set of questions and suggestions from the copy editor.

While all of this is going on, other people (whom you most likely will never meet, or even hear of) are busy working on the page layouts of your manuscript, cover designs, illustrations, and copy for the dust jacket or back cover. Although many aspiring writers ask for control over these details, very few authors are even consulted about these things. Publishers spend a lot of money to determine the format, cover design, and page layout that will appeal to the greatest number of readers, and, in nearly all instances, they insist on being able to use their expertise without interference from the author.

The development process can take several months. It culminates in the manuscript being sent to the printer, who creates proofs of the pages. Depending on the publisher and the terms of your contract, you may get to review a copy of the proofs. At this point, though, you are expected to make only minor corrections to the text; all major issues should have been dealt with much earlier in the process.

The Final Product

After the proofs have been corrected, the whole bundle gets sent out for printing and binding. The initial print run usually is determined by preorders for the book—that is, how many copies booksellers have ordered from the publisher's sales staff. Most publishers would rather have too many than too few copies of a book, but even the big houses now base their first print runs on their reading of the market. A few weeks before the book is due to appear in stores, you'll receive a box containing your free copies.

Marketing Support

Most new titles are midlist books. That means they don't get a full-press marketing effort from the publisher; instead, they are placed on the appropriate shelves in stores, and potential readers have to search for them. Only a highly select few titles will get an advertising campaign and a big display at the front of the bookstore. These things are very expensive, and publishers will reserve those tactics for books that are likely to be big commercial successes.

The Publishing Climate

Publishing always has been a competitive business, but never more so than now. The escalating costs of putting out a new title combined with the shrinking popularity of reading as a pastime place increasing pressure on publishers of all sizes to control costs and maximize profits. More and more these days, publishers want big-name authors with big-idea books that are likely to set the reading world on fire right out of the gate.

If you find this picture discouraging, you're not alone. But it's important to understand the factors that influence the decision-makers in publishing. The more you know about the business side of the industry, the better equipped you are to create salable ideas for your own books.

Follow the Money

Publishers make a huge dollar investment in every title they purchase, knowing that, in seven cases out of ten, the odds are against them making a substantial profit. The cost of acquiring, printing, distributing, and marketing a book is at least $50,000, and many observers put the minimum cost at closer to $100,000. The profit margin at most publishing houses, even the conglomerates, is around 5 to 10 percent.

There are standard costs associated with every book. Printing expenses for a hardcover book average at least 8 percent of the retail price. Distribution expenses can range from 1.5 percent to around 15 percent—on the lower end if the publisher has its own warehouse for storing and shipping copies, and on the higher end if these functions are outsourced to other companies. Booksellers usually get a steep discount, usually at least 40 percent and sometimes as much as 50 percent, on the copies they buy, and royalties for the author average just under 11 percent of the retail price.

FACT

Even with all the pressures on publishers, the number of new titles released each year continues to grow, according to *Publishers Weekly*, an industry news magazine. In 2002, U.S. publishers released 150,000 new titles, an increase of nearly 6 percent over 2001, despite a sluggish economy and the aftermath of the September 11, 2001, terrorist attacks.

When all these costs are taken into account, a publisher might see net revenues of $60,000 on a hardcover title that sells 10,000 copies. But the publisher has other expenses, as well: salaries and benefits for staff, insurance, legal services, general office expenses, marketing costs, and the like. The net revenues from all books have to cover not only their own unique expenses, but also the aggregate expenses of being in business.

Fewer Readers

A series of reports in the late 1990s and early twenty-first century painted a grim portrait of reading in the United States. According to a survey by The Jenkins Group, nearly 60 percent of U.S. adults never read another book after high school, more than four in ten college graduates never read another book, and most readers don't get past page eighteen when they do buy a book. A Harris Poll showed that only 30 percent of Americans rank reading a book as their favorite activity.

Those who do read are getting older, and the time they spend reading is shrinking. Meanwhile, *Publishers Weekly* reported that the average person had reduced his reading time to just over two hours a month by 2001, and a separate study showed that the average American spends four hours a day watching television, three hours a day listening to the radio, and a mere fourteen minutes a day reading magazines.

Fiction Markets

Most writers dream of writing fiction. After all, that's what most people read (53 percent, according to *Publishers Weekly*), and that is where the writer's talent for creating compelling plots, well-rounded characters, and descriptive settings is given the most freedom to shine. Unfortunately, it's also one of the hardest markets for new writers to crack. This is partly because so many people want to write fiction; more than half the writers who belong to the Writer's Digest Book Club are writing fiction, and more than a quarter of those who think they'd like to write a book someday would prefer to write a novel. Publishers purchase an average of about 5,500 fiction titles a year. Of these, only about 200—less than 4 percent—are first novels, which just adds to the competitiveness of the field.

ALERT!

For your first novel, probably your second, and maybe even your third, you will have to complete your manuscript before you can expect a contract offer. Even if you've had nonfiction titles published, agents and editors will want proof that you can carry through an entire novel before signing you up.

Adult fiction accounts for more than half of all books sold in the United States each year. The most popular fiction category is mystery and suspense, but every genre has its loyal base of readers. Broadly speaking, fiction can be divided into two categories: mass-appeal, which tends to attract a wide array of readers, and targeted fiction, which tends to have stricter rules about characters and story lines.

Mass-appeal Fiction

Mass-appeal fiction draws readers of both genders and most education and income groups. Because of this broad base, these categories also tend to have the most "break-out" titles, or books that, often unexpectedly, hit the bestseller lists. Such genres generally include action/adventure, horror, mainstream, mystery and suspense, romance, and science fiction and fantasy. Think of authors like Stephen King, Amy Tan, John Grisham, and Danielle Steel.

Each of these genres has its own set of rules for characters and plot, which new writers sometimes find confining. In reality, these rules are based on what readers want and expect when they pick up a book in their favorite genre.

Targeted Fiction

The rules in targeted fiction tend to be more hard and fast than those in mass-appeal fiction. Targeted fiction appeals to a narrower section of the reading public, and those readers usually demand certain elements from their genres. Espionage stories and thrillers, for example, usually emphasize plot over character and almost always involve a race between good and evil. Gothic fiction always must be told from the heroine's point of view, and she must find true love by the end of the story. Historical novels have to include accurate portrayals of life in the period in which the story takes place, right down to clothing, food, and leisure activities.

New fiction writers should expect to write at least two novels in the same genre before switching categories. Readers who love your first book will expect your second book to be similar, and publishers will want to tap into that base of fans. If you want to write in more than one genre, consider using different pen names for each.

Children's Books

The immense popularity of J.K. Rowling's Harry Potter books has given many would-be writers the impression that the children's market is an easy place to launch a career. In one sense, that may be true, assuming you have a top-notch idea that you've executed flawlessly. The truth is that the children's market, both for fiction and nonfiction, is perhaps even more intensely competitive than the adult markets. One observer estimated that out of 10,000 submissions, a dismal three children's books will get published.

This could be because the quality of submissions is generally poor. Writing for children is not like writing for adults, and many aspiring children's authors make the mistake of talking down or preaching to their readers. However, if you truly understand your audience and can write at an appropriate level for the age group you want to reach, there are opportunities for you in this market. No one can promise that you'll be the next Judy Blume or Lemony Snicket, but children are extremely loyal to the authors they like, and you could make a respectable income writing for them.

Nonfiction Markets

Nonfiction is easier for new writers to break into than fiction, in part because there are fewer hopeful writers who aspire to writing nonfiction. But even fiction writers can benefit from exploring nonfiction opportunities, because a nonfiction credit stamps you as a professional author when you're marketing your novel. In addition, nonfiction is a relatively open field, covering everything from self-help and inspirational books to true crime and biographies, with a host of categories in between.

FACT

Fiction and nonfiction sales peak at different times of the year. Fiction is most popular in July; think about your "summer reading" list. Nonfiction reaches almost 50 percent of all sales in December; think Christmas gifts. Overall, fiction accounts for about 60 percent of all sales, and nonfiction accounts for 40 percent.

Of the nine broad categories of books, seven are nonfiction categories. Adult popular fiction (as opposed to literary fiction and poetry) tops the list in sales, but the next five categories are all nonfiction: religious/inspirational, crafts and cooking, general nonfiction (biographies, true crime, history, etc.), self-help or psychology/recovery, and education and technical topics. The other two main nonfiction categories are reference materials, such as study guides and dictionaries, and travel. The demand for these last two is quite small, and the houses that publish these kinds of books generally have stables of writers they deal with, making them difficult targets for newcomers.

FACT

Genres or categories developed over time as a marketing convenience. When they evaluate a book idea, editors think in terms of where it will fit on the bookstore shelves. Manuscripts that don't fit neatly into established categories sometimes have a hard time finding a buyer because the editor doesn't know where to place it.

Identifying the Audience

More so than in fiction, nonfiction writers must provide potential agents and editors with detailed information about who will read their books. If your book is a home-repair guide for first-time homebuyers, you'll need to provide information on how many people buy their first homes in a given year, as well as ideas on how to reach those potential readers. (Chapter 8 has more information on identifying and researching readerships.) Remember that a successful nonfiction book will sell 7,500 copies, and that actual sales reflect only about 1 percent of a book's potential audience. That means you should be able to identify a potential market of at least 750,000 people to convince a publisher that your book can be profitable.

Evaluating the Competition

The beauty of the nonfiction market is that you don't always have to come up with a completely new idea; you just have to come up with an angle no one else has thought of. There are lots of home-repair books out there, for example, but perhaps there aren't any that specifically target lower-income home buyers, or single women homeowners, or people who want to restore historic homes.

An important piece of marketing your nonfiction idea to potential publishers is convincing them that your book will stand out from the crowd by filling a niche that hasn't been exploited.

Matching Ideas and Publishers

Because book publishing is so competitive, writers have to do their homework to match their material with appropriate houses. A small press that focuses on all things South Carolina won't be interested in your international spy thriller, and a romance imprint won't be interested in your biography of John Adams. Fortunately, figuring out where your book might fit in the publishing world is easier than ever. Unfortunately, it still takes time and legwork. Here are the basic steps to get you started in your search:

- **Read the listings in the market directories.** Be sure to check the most current editions, available at your library or bookstore.
- **Check publishers' Web sites.** These usually include writer's guidelines, submission procedures, and catalogues of in-print and upcoming books.
- **Browse the appropriate sections of your library or bookstore.** This is an easy way to find out which publishers are printing your kind of book.
- **Pay attention to the writer's guidelines.** Some publishers have set rules about plot, character, and topics to be avoided.
- **Follow submission procedures.** The best way to create a favorable impression is to give editors exactly what they ask for, nothing more and nothing less.

Most publishers are in business to make a profit (although there are many nonprofit presses), and they don't have the time, the financial wherewithal, or the inclination to take on half-formed or amateur proposals. If your ambition is to write a book, whether it's fiction or nonfiction, you need to offer what publishers are looking for. This is only a brief glimpse at the world as seen through a publisher's eyes, but it should help you understand why your success as a writer depends so heavily on presenting a professional, marketable idea.

chapter 8

Book Proposal Basics

Thanks in large part to the untold thousands of submissions they get every month, most literary agents and many book publishers prefer to see book proposals rather than completed manuscripts, at least at the beginning of the process. Complete proposals, prepared in a professional manner, give most agents and editors everything they need to decide whether they want to pursue an idea. If you know how to put together a strong proposal, you have a better chance of catching an agent's or editor's eye.

Targeting Your Submission

Some writers have dreams of landing a fat contract from one of the big-name publishers and overlook the realities of the publishing business, not to mention genuine opportunities elsewhere. Just as you have to study the magazine markets to find a good fit for your articles and short stories, you have to study the needs of agents and editors to find those who are most likely to be interested in your book. But matching your material is only part of the process. Ultimately, you want a good publishing experience, and that goes beyond mere dollars-and-cents issues.

What Do You Want to Accomplish?

One of your goals, of course, is to see your name on the cover of a book. But there are other considerations that are just as important, such as working with an agent or editor who shares your vision and enthusiasm for your work. If this is your first book, it might be important for you to find an agent or editor who is willing to be a mentor or coach of sorts, helping you learn the ropes and get over any rough spots. If your novel is more literary than commercial in nature, finding a publisher who will preserve the integrity of your story and style may be more important to you than one who will organize a twenty-city book tour and a major ad campaign.

FACT

Most writers have both business projects and personal projects. Business projects are those that you don't necessarily have a passion for, but which will help you attain short- or long-term goals. Personal projects are those you feel strongly about. Your priorities likely will be different for business and personal projects.

Thinking beyond the simple fact of getting published takes some soul-searching because you have to identify your priorities. The good news is that you have complete control over deciding what is most important to you. Once you've figured that out, your search for an agent or publisher actually becomes a little easier, because now you know exactly what you're looking for.

Tiered Marketing

As with any other writing project, your marketing plan for your book proposal should be laid out in phases. Do your research and create a list of possible agents or editors you want to query, and then divide your list into at least two groups. The first group consists of the agents or editors who seem to be the best matches for your material, both in terms of fit and of your own priorities. Limit this group to a maximum of six and see what kind of response you get.

Remember that you can query agents simultaneously, or you can query editors simultaneously, but don't mix the two. Many agents won't consider material that already has been marketed to editors, simply because it's difficult (though not impossible) to get editors to reconsider rejected ideas. Your odds of finding an agent diminish greatly if you've already peppered a long list of editors with your query.

QUESTION?

Should I prepare my proposal before I send out query letters?
Yes. You want to be able to fulfill a request for material as soon as possible. If an agent or editor has to wait weeks or months while you put your proposal together, she probably will forget why she was interested, or, worse, lose interest altogether.

If you don't get any requests for your proposal from your first choices, there are two courses of action open to you. You can move on to your second choices, again limiting your second-tier list to no more than six agents or editors. Or you can re-evaluate your query. A well-written, well-targeted query should get some kind of response, even if it's only a note of encouragement or a suggestion for improvement. If your query isn't generating anything but form rejection letters, chances are you'll get the same results from your second choices if you don't make changes.

You can send out simultaneous queries without announcing to the agents or editors that you are doing so. However, when you get a request for your proposal, be sure to inform the agent or editor in your cover letter that you have queries pending with others. Don't be smug or threatening about it; it's just a courtesy, and it allows you to respond to another request for a proposal with a clear conscience—as long as you tell the second requester that another agent or editor is reviewing your material, too. The disadvantage to sending out simultaneous queries is that an agent or editor may feel pressured to rush consideration of your project, and that can end up shortchanging both of you.

Submitting Your Fiction

Even if you've published short stories or a nonfiction book or two, you'll have to have a complete manuscript before you try to market your novel. Agents and editors generally insist on this, sometimes even for your second or third novel. This is because too many of them have signed contracts with new novelists, only to discover that the writer can't finish the work. In your query, remember to include an exact word count for your manuscript; a phrase like "approximately 125,000 words" will make an agent or editor think that you haven't finished the novel, and they'll be less likely to ask for any other materials.

When you get a request for more material, many agents and editors won't ask for the full manuscript. Instead, they'll ask for a synopsis and perhaps the first fifty pages or the first two or three chapters. Only when they've had a chance to review these will they ask to see the entire manuscript.

The Synopsis

A synopsis is a short overview of your story. It should cover all the major plot points, but it shouldn't delve into too much detail. A good synopsis usually runs two to three pages, single-spaced, but it should never be longer than five pages. It is written in the present tense and, ideally, in the same style as your manuscript.

Writers often feel intimidated by the synopsis, because it can feel like you're shortchanging your hard work by condensing it into a few short pages. But it's an important weapon in your marketing arsenal. A good synopsis hooks the reader—the agent or editor—and makes him feel that he has to read the story. Introduce your main characters and give an idea of the setting, but don't go overboard with subplots and twists.

Try thinking of your synopsis as a brochure for a cruise. The brochure whets your appetite for travel rather than sating it. It offers intriguing glimpses of the overall experience, but it doesn't try to replicate the actual experience. This is your goal when you write your synopsis. You want to paint an accurate and enticing picture of your story, but agents and editors don't expect (or want) all the rich detail of your story until they read the actual manuscript.

Your synopsis must include the ending of your story. Agents and editors will not be tricked into asking for your full manuscript if you omit the ending in your synopsis. On the contrary, they will assume that either you don't know how your story ends or that you are otherwise not ready to be a published author.

The Outline

Agents and editors sometimes, though not always, will request a chapter-by-chapter outline of your novel. It's really a matter of the agent's or editor's personal preference rather than an industry standard. However, it's a good idea to have one prepared in case it is requested.

An outline is really a short synopsis of each chapter, usually two or three sentences long. As in your synopsis, your objective is to highlight the main plot points in each chapter. Write it in the present tense, with chapter numbers and titles, if you elect to use them, in all caps: "In CHAPTER ONE: AT THE AIRPORT, Joe Martin arrives in Los Angeles to spend a weekend with a woman he's been chatting with online but has never met." Your outline should be single-spaced, with an extra line between chapter descriptions.

The Cast of Characters

Like the outline, not all agents and editors expect or ask for a cast of characters. Some do, though, because it can help them keep track of the main players while they're reading your sample chapters. Again, it's useful to have this prepared in case you do get a request for it. All you need is a short paragraph on each of your main characters; you don't need to include minor characters. Give a brief description of each character's motivations and problems that have a direct bearing on your story. Keep each character bio to two or three sentences if possible. Single-space each bio, with an extra line between bios.

Sample Chapters

If an agent or editor likes your query, she'll probably ask for a synopsis and the first two chapters or the first fifty pages of your manuscript. She is not interested in seeing chapters from the middle of your story, or your stirring final chapter. Her goal right now is to see whether your story grabs the reader from the first sentence and keeps him engaged through the opening scenes.

Agents and editors want to see the beginning pages or chapters of novels because first-time novelists often take too long to get to the meat of their stories. By looking at your opening pages, an agent or editor can see whether your manuscript begins where your story really begins.

Submitting Your Nonfiction

Nonfiction books usually are sold on the basis of a proposal rather than a complete manuscript. But, even though you don't have to write the whole book before you begin marketing it, you do have to put substantial time and thought into crafting your proposal. You need to do the same kind of research to find appropriate agents and publishers that you have to do for fiction, and you have to do additional research to show agents and editors that there's a large potential market for your book. You'll find a sample nonfiction proposal in Appendix B. These proposals usually are between thirty-five and fifty pages and consist of the following elements:

- **Cover letter.** Not the same as your query letter. Remind the agent or editor that he asked to see your proposal, include a short paragraph about your book, then close.
- **Table of contents.** For your proposal package, not for your book. It shows the agent or editor what you've included in your package. This will be the last page you prepare for your proposal.

- **Overview.** A broad look at your book in one to three pages. Always written in the present tense. It should also include an approximate word count for your book.
- **Author's bio.** A one-page narrative of who you are and why you're qualified to write this book, including your writing credentials, if any, and other credentials that relate to your topic. Always written in the third person, present tense.
- **Outline.** A chapter-by-chapter look at your book, with one- or two-sentence descriptions of the information covered in each chapter. Should fit on two pages, unless you're planning a very lengthy book.
- **The market for your book.** A one-page look at the potential readership for your book. The more hard numbers you can include here, the better.
- **Competition for your book.** Agents and editors want to see this, because part of your sales pitch is showing how your book is different from the others. Explain how your book is different in terms of target audience, information offered, or the approach.
- **Promotion ideas for your book.** Ideas for what you can do to help promote your book, not what the publisher can or should do. If you have a specific platform you can use to build awareness of and demand for your book, include that here, too.
- **Sample chapter(s).** Submit three sample chapters with your proposal. They don't have to be sequential. Include the chapters that best show off your writing ability and your topic.
- **Endorsements, supporting articles, etc., if applicable.** At the end of your package, include supporting materials that are applicable to this particular project. Don't include other material you've written unless it's related to your book topic. Do include articles from high-profile publications where you were quoted as an expert and endorsements for your book from experts, celebrities, or famous authors.

When considering the market for your book, look for national associations or statistics that correspond to your topic. If your targeted reader is the first-time homebuyer, find out how many people buy their first home in a given year. Assume that only 1 percent of your potential market will actually buy your book. To sell 5,000 copies, your potential readership should be at least 500,000.

ALERT!

Take care to be objective in your discussion of the competition. If you sound mean, petty, or arrogant, you run the risk of turning off an agent or editor. Besides, the agent or editor might have worked on the book you're criticizing.

Don't panic if you don't have endorsements or articles to append to your proposal; most writers don't, and lots of them manage to get publishing contracts from their proposals anyway. In the end, your work has to stand on its own, and even the most gushing blurb from the most famous writer living won't convince an agent or editor to go ahead with a bad proposal.

Required Proposal Elements

Whether you're writing fiction or nonfiction, every proposal package must include a cover letter, an author's bio, and a SASE. You also might want to include a copy of your original query in your proposal package. It helps to remind the agent or editor why she was interested in your material and saves her the trouble of searching for your original query. Put the query right behind the cover letter.

Cover Letter

The cover letter is a short business letter. Your goal is to remind the agent or editor that he requested your proposal and (very briefly) what your book is about. If there are any new developments pertaining to your book's topic, include that information in your cover letter as well. Close by thanking the agent or editor for his time and interest and say you look forward to hearing from him.

Make sure all your contact information is on your cover letter, including your area code and zip code. If you choose to create your own letterhead, select a style and font that is clean and easily readable. Agents and editors who want to contact you don't want to break out the magnifying glass to decipher your telephone number. *Never* handwrite your cover letter.

About the Author

Agents and editors want to know about your qualifications to write your book, so every proposal must include a short narrative about you. (A sample author's bio is included in Appendix B.) Written in the third person, your bio includes your published credits, your expertise on your book's topic, and any awards you have won that relate to your writing or your book topic. Your education and work experience should be included only if they are related to your book topic, or if they give you a platform for promoting your book.

If your book is a collaboration with another author, write an "About the Author" bio for each of you. For nonfiction, if one of you is the expert on the topic and the other is the writer, put the expert's bio first. For fiction, put the authors' bios in the order you want your credit to appear on the book. If you want the credit to read "Jane Smith and Robert Brown," put Jane Smith's bio first.

If you have published credits, put them in the first paragraph; this is the first thing most agents and editors will look for. List book credits first, then magazine and large-circulation newspaper credits. List well-known publications by name. If you don't have credits with big-name periodicals, you can say your "work has been published in several regional and local magazines and newspapers."

If you don't have any published credits to include, do not call attention to that in your bio. Instead, find a way to incorporate your other life experience and accomplishments into a positive reflection of your writing ability.

SASE

Most proposals should fit in a 9 × 12 or 10 × 14 mailer. For your SASE, include the same-sized mailer, with postage affixed, the agent's or editor's name and address in the upper left corner, and your name and address in the center. This is important—and too often forgotten by writers—because some agents and editors separate SASEs from proposal pages. Fold your return mailer in half and place it directly underneath your cover letter.

Some writers prefer to send their proposals via a shipping service like UPS or FedEx because they can track deliveries easily, although the U.S. Postal Service now offers tracking services without requiring the recipient to sign for your package. If you use a service other than the regular mail, don't expect the agent or editor to return your proposal the same way. It's just far too cumbersome, what with special labels and account numbers and finding a drop box or calling for pick-up service. It's easier on everyone if you just include a regular, stamped mailer for returns, no matter which shipping method you use.

Presenting Your Best

When you send out your proposal, you're still in the courting stage of your relationship with an agent or editor. Just as you would be on your best behavior for a first date or a job interview, you need to present your best in your proposal. Of course, the main thing agents and editors look for is outstanding content, but a clean, professional appearance gives your outstanding content the best background possible.

Format and Mechanics

Agents and editors spend many long hours reading thousands and thousands of pages of typescript, and you can imagine how tired their eyes get. You can make their job a little easier by making sure you follow standard formatting practices for your submission. Synopses for fiction and overviews and discussions of market, competition, and promotion ideas can be single-spaced, as can your author's bio. Sample chapters should always be double-spaced, and each chapter should begin on a fresh page with a three-inch top margin. All other pages should have one-inch margins all around.

Don't bind your proposal; agents and editors prefer loose pages. Because of this, you need to take precautions in case your pages get scattered by an accidental bump against the agent's or editor's desk at work or an affectionate pet on the couch at home. Each page of your proposal, beginning with your synopsis or overview, should have a header with the page number in the upper right corner and either your last name or the title of your book in the upper left corner.

> Never send out the only copy of your material, whether it's a query letter, proposal, or manuscript. Keep an extra hard copy for your files and store a backup copy on your computer or a disk. If you have more than one copy, you won't have to insure your proposal when you ship it out or fret about getting it back.

Finally, double-check your spelling, punctuation, and grammar. Remember, you're trying to impress an agent or editor with your writing, so mechanics count. If your word-processing program has a spelling and grammar check, use it, but keep in mind that these programs have limitations when it comes to correct word usage. Complex sentence structure also can confuse these programs. If spelling, punctuation, and grammar aren't your strong suits, find someone who is good at these things to proofread your copy and keep a good dictionary and style guide handy.

Double-Check Your Package

Professional authors often make a checklist for each proposal they send out, just to make sure they don't forget anything. Your checklist might include the elements of your proposal package, discussed above, as well as more mundane things, such as ensuring that you've included your own address on your self-addressed, stamped envelope. Always affix the proper postage to your SASE; don't paperclip it or substitute a check for actual stamps. Make sure your phone number includes the area code.

Common Mistakes

Beginning writers tend to make the same kinds of mistakes when they start to send out their proposals. You can make your proposal stand out from the crowd—and improve your chances of getting a yes from an agent or editor—by taking the time to do a final spit-and-polish before you drop your package in the mail.

Choose the Right Recipients

Probably the most common complaint from agents and editors is that they get too much material that isn't appropriate for them. No matter how many times they say they do not handle romances, for example, they still get dozens of queries and proposals for romance novels every month. It's almost as if these writers don't read the submission guidelines; they seem to just pull names and addresses out of the agents' and publishers' directories at random.

If you want to be successful in your quest for publication, you must give agents and editors what they want. These days, with so many directories that specify what they're looking for and what they're interested in, and often Web sites that give aspiring writers this same essential information, there is really no excuse for wasting your time and theirs by sending stuff they don't want. The good news is that, if you do your homework, you have a much better chance of finding an agent or editor who loves your work and can't wait to get you signed up.

Know Your Purpose

A proposal is a sales tool; your objective is to sell an agent or editor on your book. That means you have to give them enough information to make a decision. Omitting key information, such as a synopsis (complete with the ending) of your novel or the discussion of competing books for your nonfiction book, defeats your purpose. At best, it delays the decision-making process, because the agent or editor has to ask you for the missing information. At worst, the agent or editor may decide to pass on your project because your proposal is incomplete.

You might find it hard to believe, but some hopeful writers forget to include their contact information in their proposals. It's pretty frustrating for an agent or editor to read a proposal that is exactly what she has been looking for, only to find that the writer has given his name but no mailing address, telephone number, or e-mail address.

Stay Positive

Addison Mizner, a flamboyant self-taught architect who designed many of the most extravagant homes in Florida during the early twentieth century, once said that misery loves company, but company does not reciprocate. In other words, even if you've collected several rejections and are feeling discouraged, don't let that color your communications with the people who remain on your marketing list. If you aren't enthusiastic about your proposal, you're going to have trouble generating enthusiasm in publishing professionals.

It can be difficult, but each time you send your proposal to an agent or editor, you have to project an image of cheerful confidence. Don't mention how many times your proposal has been rejected or how you feel about the people who rejected it. After all, even if you haven't gotten an offer yet, you still believe in your work, and each new contact is a clean slate. Let that be the sense you convey every time you send your proposal out.

Follow Directions

Few things are more annoying to agents and editors than hopeful writers who can't or won't follow instructions. Like most of us, agents and editors have particular tastes about what they want to see. If you don't get specific instructions about what to send, follow the guidelines in this chapter; that way, you'll be sure to include everything they need without overloading them.

ALERT!

More is not always better, and inundating an agent or editor with unwanted paper is not the way to win her good graces. Don't send four chapters when she asks for two and never tell her she has to read your entire manuscript to appreciate it. She's a pro; she knows what she needs and will ask for it.

If you do get specific instructions, adhere to them as closely as you can. Some agents and editors want only to see the synopsis and first chapter of your novel. Others might want the synopsis and the first three chapters. A few might request an outline of your novel as well. Be prepared to supply what they ask for, and do it graciously. Even if you've already sent a synopsis, send another copy. Remember that the request is a sign of interest, and that's always a good thing.

chapter 9

Submission Protocol

The old adage that everybody has at least one book in him may or may not be true, but it sure seems true to agents and editors, who spend large portions of their working lives reading queries, proposals, and manuscripts from aspiring authors. And that doesn't even count the writers who are pursuing magazine credits. With all that paper landing on their desks, publishing professionals have been forced to establish rules for authors submitting their work. Following these rules can be frustrating, but it never hurts your cause.

Query First

The query letter is the first line of defense for agents and editors who are trying to stem the flood of paper, or at least maintain some semblance of control over it. Even those who will read unsolicited proposals and manuscripts usually prefer a query first. Queries are convenient for agents and editors to read; well-crafted queries make it easy for them to decide whether they want to see more. In fact, queries are such good prescreening tools that many agents and editors won't accept anything but a query in the first stage of marketing. That way, they don't spend valuable time dealing with stacks of material that isn't right for them.

QUESTION?

When are telephone queries appropriate?
Not until you're well-established with an agent or editor, and even then you shouldn't do it often. A phone call is never appropriate when you're first contacting agents or editors; they are extremely busy with existing clients and works in progress, and phone calls from hopeful unknowns are annoying and intrusive.

Many writers don't like queries and would just as soon skip this step in the process. This may be because writers are impatient to get their work into the hands of the people who can help them get published, or it may be because many writers haven't learned how to write effective query letters. But there are distinct advantages to mastering the query, and it isn't as difficult as you might think.

The Advantage of Queries

There are three good reasons to query before you send out your book proposal, short story, or article.

First, if you read the market listings carefully, you'll notice that response times for queries typically are much shorter than response times for proposals and manuscripts. It's simple logistics: It takes less time to read a one-page letter than it does to read a fifty-page proposal or a four-hundred-page manuscript, and the faster the agent or editor reads your material, the more quickly he can get back to you.

Second, when an agent or editor asks for your material based on your query, it means you've captured his interest. It may seem like a slim advantage, but, in the highly competitive publishing business, it's better to have an agent or editor looking forward to receiving your package rather than glancing through your pages to see if it's worth his time to read it.

Third, querying first saves you money. A one-page query letter with SASE costs you two first-class stamps. A fifty-page proposal with a stamped return mailer will cost you at least a few dollars to mail, and more if you choose to use a shipping service like UPS or FedEx. It may not seem like a huge difference, but it can add up quickly. Mailing ten query letters will cost you less than $10. Mailing ten proposals can cost $40 or more. The extra $30 might be worth it if you were assured of getting more positive responses, but that isn't the way it works. Save your money and save your proposal for the agents and editors who ask to see it.

There's another potential advantage to querying: An agent or editor who isn't interested in your current project may keep your name on file for future projects. It's not a guarantee by any means, but agents and editors often keep notes about the particular qualifications of would-be authors, and they might go through those notes when they need someone with just those qualifications.

Crafting a Good Query

Your query letter may well be the most important piece of writing you ever do, because it's the one thing you can be sure an agent or editor will read, and he will decide whether to request more based solely on your query. Your objective, then, is to convince him that you have the perfect article or book idea for him, one that he would be crazy to pass up, and that you are the perfect person to write your idea. And, as a general rule, you should be able to convince him in one page.

The first paragraph of your query is the hook; you have to interest the agent or editor and make her want to read on. For fiction, you might be able to adapt the opening of your short story or novel. For nonfiction, you can use statistics, summarize an issue, or relate an anecdote to lead into your idea. (Appendix B has sample query letters for fiction and nonfiction projects.) In the second paragraph, expand on your idea. Offer the title of your article, story, or book, and the word count; you can estimate the word count for nonfiction books, but give a precise count for fiction, especially if you're a first-time novelist.

ESSENTIAL

When you query for magazine articles, be sure to specify which rights you're offering for sale. Most magazines purchase first serial rights, which means the work hasn't been published anywhere else, including on the Internet. Some purchase second serial rights, also known as reprint rights. If you have photos or illustrations for your article, mention that in your query, too.

In your third paragraph, explain why you're the right person to write your idea. Be sure to include your published credits if you have them. If you don't have any credits to list, focus on your other qualifications to write your project, such as expertise on the topic.

Close with an acknowledgement of the recipient's time and a call to action. The standard, two-sentence closing that you find in most business letters works perfectly for your query letter: "Thank you for your time and consideration. I look forward to hearing from you."

Remember that you must include a self-addressed, stamped envelope with your query if you hope to get a response. Although agents and editors who are interested in your work might call you to request more material, they are just as likely to write a short letter specifying what they want to see next. However, they can't do that if you neglect to include an SASE.

Know the Guidelines

One of the most common complaints agents and editors have about dealing with hopeful writers is the extraordinary number of inappropriate submissions they receive. On their bad days, agents and editors may feel that writers blindfold themselves, open one of the various directories at random, stab a page with a pushpin and send their materials to whichever name is closest to the pin. Indeed, there seems to be no other explanation for fiction submissions to agents and editors who only handle nonfiction, or pitches for relationship articles to magazines that cover, say, aviation.

Agents and editors include their listings in the directories so writers will know what they're interested in, how they prefer to be contacted, and other essential information. Many of them also publish this information on their Web sites. With these resources at your disposal, there really is no excuse for poorly targeting your submissions.

Genre First

Sometimes writers do their research backward, looking first for agents or editors who will accept unsolicited proposals or manuscripts, for instance, because they don't want to mess around with a query letter. Now that you know the advantages of the query process, though, the first thing you should always look for is an agent or editor who handles your type of work. If a magazine, literary agency, or book publisher doesn't publish what you're writing, nothing else in the directory listing matters.

Methods of Contact

Directory listings usually are quite explicit about how these publishing professionals prefer to be contacted. Some accept queries only and will not open unsolicited submissions. Some accept proposals or partial manuscripts, and some will consider complete manuscripts. When a listing says something like, "Queries preferred, but accepts proposals," you should follow the preferred method.

With the proliferation of home computers and e-mail, listings now usually state whether the agent or editor accepts electronic submissions. Again, pay attention to preferences. Some agents and editors may prefer e-mail queries, but that is by no means universal (and it doesn't necessarily mean a faster response time, since they still have to read through dozens, if not hundreds, of submissions every week). If e-mail is not specifically listed as the preference, use regular mail to submit your material. You won't lose much time, and, since so much submission reading is done after business hours, most agents and editors still prefer to have hard copies.

Cultivate Patience

The picture you have of the publishing world depends on where you're sitting. From the inside, a magazine, literary agency, or publishing house is an insanely busy and active place. Days are crammed with meetings, phone calls, e-mails, questions, crises of varying magnitude to be resolved and decisions of varying importance to be made. There are dozens of tasks to be completed and hundreds of details to be considered, and it all has to be done this month, this week, or this morning.

From the writer's desk, on the other hand, the journey to publication is about as speedy as the flow of sap in February, consisting mainly of long periods of waiting punctuated by tiny drips of activity. You send off your query and wait for a response. You get a request for your proposal, so you send that off, and then you wait for a response. You get a preliminary offer and begin negotiating the terms of the contract, and then you wait for the contract to be approved. Finally, just after you decide your head will explode if you have to wait one more day, you get a phone call saying it's a done deal, and now you have something concrete and specific to work on.

Patience isn't just a virtue for writers. It's a protective shield for your mental health. Especially if you're just starting your writing career, nothing is going to happen quickly from your perspective.

Typical Response Times

Writing is a solitary activity, so it's easy to forget that your work isn't the only thing sitting on an agent's or editor's desk waiting to be reviewed. In fact, your work is among reams of submissions from other writers, each of whom also may be oblivious to the realities of the industry. This is why market directories commonly list average response times.

Note that reporting times vary substantially, depending on the establishment and what has been submitted. Most places respond to queries in two to six weeks. It might take two to three months to respond to a proposal. Complete manuscripts have the longest response times, which can range from three months to a year. Note also that the response times (sometimes called "reporting times") are averages. Any number of things can hold up the response process. Aside from the daily demands that take precedence over considering new submissions, illness, vacations, and personnel changes can create enormous backlogs.

ALERT!

Never call an agent or editor to see if he received your material or what he thinks of it. If you haven't heard anything, it means he either hasn't gotten to it yet or is still considering it. Always assume that no news is good news.

Marking Time

Did you ever collect cereal box tops when you were a kid so you could send off for a free decoder ring or other prize? Remember how it seemed to take eons for that package to arrive? Writers tend to go through similar agonizing periods of waiting after they've mailed their queries or proposal packages. Days suddenly seem to take forty-eight hours instead of the standard twenty-four, and weeks feel like ten to twelve days.

You can put time back in perspective by keeping track of when you actually mail your submission and when you can reasonably expect to get a response. Keep a calendar especially for this purpose, whether it's in the form of an appointment book, a desk or wall calendar, or the calendar function on your computer. Mark down what you send, where you sent it, and the average response time for that market. When you find yourself getting antsy because you haven't heard anything, a glance at your calendar can tell you whether your anxiousness is premature.

When to Follow Up

What if it's been three months since you sent your query, and you still haven't heard anything? Should you call, e-mail, or write? This can be a tough decision, because you don't want to come across as a pest to the agent or editor. Sometimes—not often, but sometimes—queries and other materials do get lost in the bustle of busy offices. Chances are, though, that the writer made some mistake when sending the material. Check your records and see if any of the following apply.

- **Did you forget to include a SASE?** This is the most common reason writers don't hear back on their submissions.
- **Did you send your query by e-mail?** Even valid, nonspam e-mail sometimes doesn't make it to its intended destination. One study indicated that as much as 40 percent of valid e-mail gets lost in transmission, another reason why regular mail is often preferable.
- **Did you address your query to the right person?** Agents and editors often are responsible for specific types of books or articles, and if you don't send your material to the right person, it may never get passed along.

When you haven't heard back on your query, you have two options. You can assume that the agent or editor isn't interested and move on to the next phase of marketing, or you can resubmit your query along with a short, polite letter explaining that you didn't receive a response the first time. Don't toss accusations or jump to conclusions about why you didn't receive a response; the polite, professional thing to do is to assume that your original submission was lost, without blaming anyone for it. If you choose this route, make sure you include a SASE and double-check the name and address of the person you want to contact. If you sent your first query by e-mail, send your follow-up by regular mail.

FACT

Queries for short stories and magazine articles sometimes will get filed in the slush pile for weeks or even months while editors decide whether a piece is right for them. Book queries generally get a yes or no as soon as the agent or editor has time to read it; it's quite rare for agencies or publishers to have a "maybe" pile for books.

Multiple Submissions

When you make multiple or simultaneous submissions, you send your article, short story, or book idea to two or more magazines, agents, or publishers at the same time. Directory listings usually specify whether this practice is acceptable, and many markets will consider multiple submissions. Writers often like the efficiency of sending out batches of material and seeing who responds. But, before you get into the habit of doing this, consider all the ramifications.

First Come, First Served

Most writers choose to make multiple submissions because they can reach all their preferred markets at one time, rather than waiting for one market to respond before moving on to the next one. Some envision being in the middle of a bidding war, with two or more potential markets vying for the same material. This sometimes happens with book manuscripts, but only through agents, for the simple reason that the publishers who get involved in book auctions don't accept unagented material.

Multiple submissions for magazine articles are different, because, in most cases, there are only a few publications that are appropriate for a particular topic and slant, and they are usually fiercely competitive, with overlapping readership and advertising markets. Each wants to scoop the others by having an exclusive. These editors typically are not pleased to be part of a simultaneous submission and may reject it on that basis alone.

If your market research indicates that more than half a dozen magazines are appropriate for a particular article, it is likely that you haven't defined the slant and target audience sharply enough. With such a small universe of potential buyers, it is not too much to ask that they be approached one at a time and that you wait an appropriate period before going to the next on the list.

You should indicate in your query or cover letter that you are making simultaneous submissions. However, don't insist that an agent or editor rush his decision; chances are you'll simply encourage her to pass on your idea. Even with multiple submissions, expect to wait at least the listed time for a response.

If you do make simultaneous submissions for any piece of your writing, you should adopt a first-come, first-served policy. Agents and editors will expect this, since you've already told them you're making multiple submissions. If you get a positive response from Publisher X and tell him you want to wait until you hear from Publisher Y, chances are you'll lose the sale. You might even earn yourself a little black mark with that particular editor, who won't be eager to consider your next submission.

The Second Buyer

What if you sell your article to Magazine X and get a call the following week from Magazine Y? Chances are that the editor at Magazine Y is going to be pretty annoyed, because you didn't inform him that the article had been picked up elsewhere. If you're going to make multiple submissions, it's your responsibility to let other markets know when your submission is no longer available. All it takes is a quick letter or e-mail to notify them that you've sold your article and are withdrawing it from their consideration. You don't have to give details, but you should not allow them to waste time chasing an article that you've sold to someone else.

Make your materials professional. Use a good-quality white paper, a 12-point readable font like Courier or Times New Roman, and black ink. Agents and editors spend much of their waking hours reading, so it's important that your materials be as easy on the eyes as possible.

What if Magazine Y offers you more money than Magazine X? You're out of luck if you've agreed to sell your article to Magazine X. Even if you've only made a verbal agreement, it's important that you keep your word. If you don't, you'll irrevocably burn bridges, and not necessarily just with the editor you stiff. The publishing world is a small community, and word travels quickly. You would be surprised at how fast you can get a bad reputation, and it can follow you for the rest of your career.

When you come up with a good idea for a magazine article, try to think of at least two possible approaches. That way, you'll be prepared when you have two markets interested in your idea; you can sell each nonoverlapping market first serial rights by writing your article twice, each time with a different slant.

When the Answer Is Yes

A successful submission is one that advances you to the next step on the road to publication. For article queries, it means the editor wants to assign your proposed article, and it's time to talk terms. For book queries, that means an agent or editor asks to see more—usually a proposal or partial manuscript, or sometimes the complete manuscript.

For Magazine Articles

Magazine editors usually will call you to discuss your proposed article and the terms of the sale. He may have suggestions for sources or requests for specific information to be included, and he may want to discuss other elements like sidebars and illustrations. He may even want to tweak the slant you proposed. Your responsibility during this conversation is to listen to the editor's needs and make sure you understand what he's looking for. You also should talk about deadlines, delivery methods, and payment arrangements during this phone call. Keep notes about what you discuss and find out how the editor prefers to be contacted with progress reports or problems.

For Book Queries

Positive responses to book queries usually come in the form of a letter or an e-mail, rarely via telephone. Most likely, an agent or editor will ask you to send a synopsis and the beginning pages or chapters of your novel, or a proposal, including sample chapters, for your nonfiction book. (See Chapter 8 for more on book proposals.) Fulfill the request as closely as you can and don't send more than the agent or editor asks for. Remember that these people are professionals, and they have developed their own efficient systems for determining whether material is right for them. What they ask for is all they need. Remember, too, that a request for more material is not a guarantee of anything. All it means is that the agent or editor is interested enough to see more. Don't jump ahead to contract negotiations or book-signing schedules. Take the process one step at a time.

When the Answer Is No

The only writer who never receives a rejection is the one who never submits his material to agents or editors. Considered in their proper light, rejection slips really are medals for bravery; they prove that you have the courage and confidence to let publishing professionals tell you what they think of your work. The more courage and confidence you have—that is, the more aggressively you pursue publication—the more likely you are to run into the word no.

Whys and Wherefores

Nine times out of ten, you'll receive a standard rejection letter, which says only that your submission "doesn't suit our needs at this time." If you're like most writers, you'll feel frustrated at the lack of specific criticism or information, and you may wonder whether the agent or editor even bothered to read your stuff. It's impossible to know for sure when the only thing that connects a boilerplate rejection letter to you is your name at the top.

Standard rejection letters are frustrating because many of us have a nagging fear that our writing isn't really any good. Sometimes, we think, it almost would be better if an agent or editor came right out and said our writing stinks; then, at least, we would know what to defend. But one-size-fits-all rejections don't even give us that meager comfort, and we're left to imagine all sorts of horrible reasons for that cold, curt "no."

You can improve your odds of acceptance by doing your homework on business considerations. Study the markets. Come up with a strong slant or unique approach to make your article or book idea stand out. Pitch your material to agents and editors who are most likely to be interested in it. The extra work you put in on these factors will pay off in fewer rejections.

You may never learn why your material was rejected, but most often it has more to do with the business needs of the agent or editor than with the quality of your work. Maybe the magazine you're pitching already has a similar article in the hopper, or the topic has grown stale from too much coverage. The agent you approached might have heard from publishers that interest in your particular type of book is ebbing. Perhaps the publisher has a related title in its catalog and doesn't want a new book that would compete with it.

These all are business issues that you might not even be aware of and that are beyond your control. When you get a standard rejection, assume these kinds of business reasons constitute the "why and wherefore" of the rejection and focus your energies on what you can control—the quality of your work.

Responding to Rejections

The only time it is appropriate to respond to a rejection is when the agent or editor has offered you suggestions on how to improve your project. You certainly aren't required to respond. But, if you do choose to respond, the only appropriate method is with a short, polite note thanking the agent or editor for his time and advice.

It is never appropriate to respond with anger or insults. In the first place, such a response is unprofessional, and you don't want to make a name for yourself as being difficult to work with. Keep in mind, too, that editors tend to move around within the industry, and they have little difficulty remembering writers who gave them a hard time. Before you fire off a sheet of invective, ask yourself this: Will you be embarrassed to encounter this same agent or editor a year or two from now when you're marketing a new project?

FACT

Agents and editors use form rejection letters because, too often, they've received nasty responses from writers whose work they've turned down. Most people prefer to avoid confrontations if possible, and bland, non-specific rejections offer agents and editors some protection because they provide the least fodder for an irate letter or phone call.

Angry responses to rejections also are ungracious. When agents and editors take the time to even consider your work, they are often doing so during their own free time. If they make specific comments, they are sharing their expertise with you, free of charge. Even if you disagree with the suggestions, you should recognize the spirit of generosity behind them.

The steps for submitting written works have been developed to help agents and editors cope with the volume of material they receive. Perceived shortcuts really are unnecessary detours. You can help the process move along smoothly by understanding and following the protocol, even if it isn't quite as fast as you would like.

chapter 10

Borrowing from Others

Plagiarism used to be, at least to all appearances, confined mainly to scholarly works, punctuated by the occasional lawsuit or scandal involving novelists or movie screenwriters accused of stealing someone else's plot, characters, and setting. More recently, though, plagiarism has spawned ugly headlines in business, journalism, and other professional circles, raising eyebrows and ruining careers. Aspiring writers, and even seasoned professionals now more than ever must be extraordinarily vigilant to make sure that even the slightest sniff of stealing material doesn't taint their output or their futures.

Giving Credit Where It's Due

Plagiarism is just about the worst accusation that can be made against a writer. It's the equivalent of an accountant being charged with embezzlement; it is dishonest, and it is theft. It can be, and often is, a career killer; even if unproven, it can cloud your reputation and make editors leery of taking a chance on you. Your best protection—really, your only protection—is to be so scrupulously careful in your research and writing procedures that there is no room for error.

One of the reasons agents and editors dislike cookie-cutter query letters so much is because they indicate either laziness or dishonesty. Lifting the structure or wording from a how-to-write-a-query book is, in fact, plagiarism, and that turns agents and editors off from the outset, no matter how great your idea is.

Plagiarism is a serious issue, and the consequences can be dire if you're caught stealing someone else's work, even unintentionally. The time and effort you invest in protecting your reputation also will protect your career.

Lessons from School

Remember when you had to write papers in high school and college? Your teachers and professors undoubtedly advised you to read the material, then close the book and write, in your own words, what you read. This is still a good method to use in your writing, but as a professional, you need to take it a step or two further. After you've paraphrased what you've read, go back to the source and make sure you haven't lifted any phrases or sentences verbatim. If you find you have, flag those passages so you'll know that you either need to change the wording or provide a citation of the source.

Double-check the structure of what you're writing, too. You can't take the outline of someone else's work (or even your own, discussed in detail below), convert it to your own words, and pass it off as original. Everything about your work, even the way it's organized, must be your own.

Citation Methods

When you do use direct quotations, make sure you include citations of the sources. There are several ways to do this, and the appropriate method depends in large part on what you're writing. For magazine and newspaper articles, for example, you generally just have to attribute quotes to the source, whether it's an interviewee, a report, a statement, or what have you. Sometimes you can use this method in books, as well. Other options include footnotes or end notes, or a bibliography. Your publisher may have a preference, as well as a specific style for you to follow. In any case, you should have a style guide such as Strunk and White's *The Elements of Style* or another resource on hand to help you make sure your citations are complete.

It's possible to go overboard with citations. When you're using generally accepted facts, your own opinions, or observations that fall under the heading of common sense, you don't have to provide a citation. For your own purposes, however, you might want to make a habit of noting which ideas are yours and which you've gleaned from other sources.

Fair Use

There are circumstances in which it is permissible to use another's work without seeking authorization. However, those circumstances are quite limited, and there is no guarantee that your use will be considered fair use by a court. According to the U.S. Copyright Office, there are four main factors in determining whether a specific use of material is fair.

1. **The nature of the use.** Brief quotes for noncommercial, educational, and commentary uses, such as for reviews or rebuttals, generally are considered fair use.
2. **The nature of the work being used.** Unpublished works are protected by copyright laws as soon as they are in fixed form (see below), and unauthorized use of unpublished work is less likely to be considered a fair use.
3. **The amount and "substantiality" of the work used.** Unless you're doing a parody of a well-known book or movie—think of Mel Brooks' *Space*

Balls, which was a send-up of George Lucas' *Star Wars*—you generally cannot lift the heart of a work without infringing copyright.

4. **The effect on the value or potential market for the work.** In general, if your use costs the copyright owner money, it won't be considered a fair use.

Remember, these are only guidelines. There is no prescribed number of words, phrases, or sentences that marks the threshold between fair use and infringement. And, because there is no such defined boundary, there is no way to predict how a court will rule in any given claim of copyright infringement.

What Is Copyrightable?

Nearly any form of expression that can be put in a fixed format is copyrightable. That covers all forms of writing, as well as music, art, photography, and even dance, if the choreography is notated. Under U.S. copyright law, a work is protected as soon as it is produced in fixed form, regardless of whether it has been, or ever is, published. Your private journal, letters to friends, jottings on the notepad next to the phone—all these are protected by copyright as soon as they are written down. In fact, unpublished works have enhanced protection, because the law recognizes that the author has the right to determine where and when his work will first be published, or to decide that his works cannot be published at all.

Just because a work doesn't have a copyright notice doesn't mean it isn't protected. Works published after March 1, 1989, do not need to display a copyright notice to enjoy full protection. Some works published before then, even without a copyright notice, might still be protected.

What Is Not Copyrightable?

You cannot copyright titles, slogans, names, or short phrases. These sometimes can be protected by trademark laws, but they cannot be copyrighted. That's why you so often find movies and books with the same titles, even though they tell different stories. You also cannot copyright ideas, facts, discoveries, procedures, or devices. Procedures and devices can be

protected by patent law (the requirements for which are much more strenu-
ous than for copyright protection), but they don't fall under copyright laws.
Your description of a procedure or a device can be copyrighted, of course,
but that protection only extends to your expression, not to the subject of
your expression. If you write an article describing a new process for catching mice, no one can publish that article without your permission. But if you
post the article on your Web site, somebody else can use the process you
describe—or build the device you describe—without paying or owing you
anything (unless you have a patent for the procedure or device).

QUESTION?

Should I include a copyright notice on my Web site?
Yes. Such a notice won't guarantee that your copyright won't be
infringed, but a reasonably prominent notice makes it harder for someone to claim ignorance about your copyright if they do use your material without permission.

In general, you also cannot copyright anything until it has been "fixed"
in a tangible form. That is, the short story that has been bouncing around
in your imagination isn't copyrightable until you actually write it down or
record it in some way. A poem you recite off the top of your head isn't protected by copyright until you write it down or record it. There are some
exceptions to this rule, mainly relating to bootleg recordings of concerts
and the like, but the central issue concerning you as a writer is that copyright protection doesn't start until the paper meets the pen, so to speak.

Getting Permission

The safest way to preserve your professional integrity is to always get permission any time you wish to quote another's work. First, look up the copyright
information on the material you want to use. Then, contact the copyright
owner and ask for written permission to use the material. If you make this
your standard operating procedure, you'll be less likely to run into problems.

Look It Up

The Information Age has made it easier than ever to find out whether something is protected by copyright or whether it's in the public domain. Everything published in the United States before 1923 is now in the public domain. Under U.S. copyright law, any work created on or after January 1, 1978, is protected for the life of the author, plus seventy years. This also applies to works that were created before 1978 but not published until after January 1 of that year.

FACT

Thanks to a number of international treaties, including the Berne Convention, copyright laws are more or less the same worldwide. Protection lasts for at least fifty years after the author's death, as long as the author is a citizen of any of the 100-plus member countries, and the protection is automatic. Most industrialized countries are signatories to these treaties, so your work should be well-protected.

So what about works published between 1923 and 1977? It depends on whether the author, or the author's heirs, properly renewed the copyright. If the copyright was not renewed, the work is in the public domain, and you can use it freely. This doesn't mean you can pass off a plot or characters as your own; that's still considered plagiarism. But you can quote from a public domain work (giving the proper attribution, of course) without seeking permission to use it. If the copyright was renewed, and is still in force, you'll have to get permission from the author or the author's estate to use the material.

The most reliable place to find out whether copyrights are still in force is the U.S. Copyright Office. The staff there will check renewal information for you for an hourly fee, which was $75 as of this writing; call the office's Reference & Bibliography Section at (202) 707-6850 for current information. You also can hire a private copyright research firm to find this information for you.

For works published from 1950 on, you can find copyright renewal records online at *www.copyright.gov/records*.

Permission Forms

Many publishers provide their own permission forms, which have been drawn up by their legal departments. Indeed, these publishers likely will require you to use their forms in the event you want or need to use copyrighted material in your work. These forms usually have to be completed and turned in with your final manuscript; publication of your work will not proceed unless these forms are on file.

If your publisher doesn't have permission forms for you to use, you can draw up your own. They can be relatively simple and general or complex and highly specific. If you want to use an unpublished poem your friend wrote, for instance, your permission form might read as follows:

"I, _____, am the author of the poem titled _____, and I authorize its publication in the (book/magazine article/short story) titled _____ written by _____. I certify that I am the owner of all rights in the above-named poem and am free to grant said rights."

The form should include signature and date lines, as well as any restrictions or requirements that go along with the permission being granted. If your friend wants credit for the poem, you can include that in your permission form, for example. If you're publishing the poem on a Web site, the permission form might include a time limit on how long the work will be posted.

If you have any doubts about whether your permission form is adequate to cover your needs, consult a copyright attorney or check out one of the numerous reputable Web sites covering copyright law, such as the U.S. Copyright Office (*www.copyright.gov*), Bitlaw (*www.bitlaw.com*), the Stanford University Libraries site on copyright law (*http://fairuse.stanford.edu*), or the Electronic Frontier Foundation (*www.eff.org*).

Many writers assume that information posted on Web sites automatically is in the public domain. This isn't true. Even when a copyright notice isn't prominently displayed, chances are good that the material is under copyright protection, and you should assume that it is before using it.

Model Releases

If you use photos of people—and sometimes of things—you may need to get signed releases to use the images in your work. This is true whether you're writing magazine articles, short stories with photos, or books, and whether you're going through traditional publishing routes or publishing online or electronically.

As with permission forms for using written work, your magazine, book, or Web site editor may have a model release form for you to use. These grant the publisher permission to use the image, with or without payment to the person or people in the photograph (which will be specified in the form). If the person in the photo is a minor, his or her parents usually have to sign the release.

ALERT!

Merely acknowledging the source of material is not the same as getting permission, and acknowledgement, while it might help your case, doesn't necessarily protect you from claims of copyright infringement. It always is better to attribute material to the source, but the best course of action is to get specific permission in writing.

Release forms are not the same as credit lines, which name the photographer and sometimes the company or news outlet the photographer works for. Photographs are copyright-protected the same way words are. That's why you'll often see something like "Photo used with permission from The Smithsonian Institution" under the photos in books and magazines.

Borrowing from Yourself

There's a popular idea among writers that you can't steal your own ideas and you can't plagiarize yourself. In fact, it's possible to do both, and either one can cause massive headaches—or worse damage—for you, your agent, your editor, and your publisher. Much depends on the terms of your contract, whether for a magazine piece or a book, but, unless you're selling reprint rights (see Chapter 12 for more on contract terms), you generally will be expected to provide fresh material every time you accept a writing assignment, even if it's on a topic you've written about before.

Original Material vs. Expertise

Let's say you've had a bunch of articles published about financial planning, enough that you're considered something of an expert on the subject. Maybe you even have a well-read and well-respected Web site on the topic, filled with useful articles, calculators, and so on. Based on your portfolio, a book publisher is interested in your idea for a financial planning workbook aimed at twenty- and thirty-somethings. The publisher wants you to use the information you've used in your articles, but he also wants the workbook to be original work—that is, different in structure, style, and presentation. You feel stuck, because you think the material you presented in your online articles already is the clearest it can be, and it would be much easier if you could just use the articles you wrote and add a few examples here and there.

Undoubtedly it would be easier. But, in the intensely competitive publishing world, this almost always will be unacceptable, unless you have express permission from the publisher to do so. The fact is, most publishing contracts will require you to create entirely new material, right down to the structure. In other words, you can't lift the outline of a piece of your already-published work, whether it's an article, a book, or even a chapter from another book, and count it as new work.

You also need to be careful about the use of jargon. In some fields, it's almost impossible to write coherently about the topic without using the lingo associated with it. Most publishers won't have a problem with this, as long as you haven't also lifted the substance of the words surrounding the jargon. If the gist of the text around the lingo is too similar to already-published work, you'll probably be accused of plagiarism.

Recycling Ideas

If you stick with the writing game for any length of time, you are likely to reach a point where you're tempted to recycle ideas, either from others or from yourself. There's nothing wrong with this; indeed, some people believe that all ideas are recycled, and have been from the beginning of time. The trick with recycling is ensuring that you come up not just with new packaging for your idea, but different ways of presenting it. In fact, this is an essential skill to develop if you want to avoid problems with your editors and publishers.

This book is a good example of how ideas can be recycled. We wrote *The Everything Guide to Writing a Book Proposal* before we accepted the contract to write this book, and our contract for this book specifies that we will supply original material. However, we also are obligated to cover book proposals in this book, and there are other topics that overlap between the two volumes. Because of the originality requirement, we can't just lift chapters, sections, or even paragraphs from the "Book Proposal" book and insert them in this one. Our responsibility, then, is to find different ways to convey the information you need.

FACT

Recycling ideas is nothing more than fine-tuning an angle or slant to appeal to a specific readership that you haven't reached before. It's another way of squeezing potential opportunities for publication out of one or two strong concepts. Don't be shy about recycling ideas; just be careful that you aren't trying to sell your ideas as one-size-fits-all.

Sometimes, differences in structure will solve this problem for you. For instance, the "Book Proposal" book has separate chapters on fiction and nonfiction book proposals, and goes into great detail about markets for different genres, dealing with rejection, collaborative arrangements, and other facets of book publishing. This book also covers much of the same information, but in different contexts and under a different structure. Chapter 8 covers the basics of creating a book proposal, but because of the structure of this book, we couldn't just plug the information from "Book Proposal" in here; we had to rework and reword it to make it pertinent for this book.

Whose Idea Is It?

Beginning writers often fret needlessly about someone else stealing their ideas. Professional writers don't worry much about this, for two reasons. First, no two writers will take the same idea and go the same way with it. Second, professional writers know that the real problem most writers grapple with is having too many, as opposed to not enough, ideas. When your head is flooded with thirteen different plot lines or topics, and you can't decide which one you want to pursue now and which you want to save for later, the last thing you're motivated to do is take someone else's idea.

Every once in a while, movies or books will be released at about the same time with roughly the same plot line. The movies *Volcano* and *Dante's Peak*, for example, both dealt with undetected volcanic activity that threatened communities. Both featured experts whose warnings went unheeded until the lava began to flow and people could see the danger for themselves. Likewise, the movies *Armageddon* and *Deep Impact* both envisioned the Earth on a collision course with an enormous asteroid capable of destroying all life on our planet, and, in both movies, at least part of the plot revolved around heroic efforts to destroy the asteroid before it intersected with the Earth's orbit.

In both these cases, although the storylines were eerily similar, the ways they played out diverged significantly, as did the characters and the numberless details involved in the stories and their structures. This illustrates the point we made earlier, that no two writers will develop the same story idea in the same way. This is true for nonfiction, too. Even when the topic is identical, no two writers will approach it from exactly the same angle or present it in exactly the same way.

Owning Up

In the old days, plagiarism—intentional or not—was fairly difficult to detect. There was no easy way to compare writings word for word, especially if the original source was some obscure publication; most cases came to light not because an editor spotted it, but because the person whose work was used without permission complained. Today, technology has made it much easier to track and compare phrases, structure, and other elements from a vast library of sources, and most publishers use this technology religiously to ferret out problems before they end up in court.

All this is to give you fair warning that, if you do use someone else's words and pass them off as your own, you will eventually get caught. Much depends, of course, on the extent of the plagiarism and whether it was inadvertent or intentional. But how you respond in such an instance also plays a role in determining whether the problem is a minor bump in your writing career or a brick wall that will bring it to a crashing halt.

The use of plagiarism detection software isn't limited to academia any more. High-profile plagiarism cases have created increased demand for commercial programs like iThenticate to compare, in minute detail, writing from literally billions of digitally stored sources. These programs can find suspicious similarities even in short phrases and are now regularly used in business, law, and, of course, publishing.

Talk to Your Editor

When a question of plagiarism arises, the first thing your editor will do is contact you (or your agent, if you have one) to discuss it. It's a serious issue, and even minor lifting of a phrase or two has been enough, in some cases, to suspend publication of the work. However, regardless of the extent of the problem, it is essential that you talk it over with your editor.

Sometimes, especially if the problem is minor and it happened inadvertently, you'll be asked to fix the text. Publication usually will go forward, as long as you can alter the text to suit the publisher. In these cases, the writer is essentially given a second chance to make good—a rare occurrence in publishing these days, when competition is stiffer than ever and there is a virtually unlimited supply of talented writers just waiting for an opportunity to prove themselves. If you find yourself in this situation, count your blessings and be as gracious and cooperative as you know how to be in fixing the problem. If the mistake happened through carelessness or inattention, explain it to your editor and have a plan in place to prevent such errors in the future. Aside from resolving the immediate issue, the most important thing an editor will need from you is a firm assurance that it won't happen again.

Plagiarism does sometimes happen inadvertently. Alex Haley omitted to give proper credit for a paragraph in his masterpiece *Roots*; he or a research assistant had failed to make a proper notation about the source of the passage, so there was no way to know it wasn't his own work when it came time to insert it in his text.

Refine Your Tracking Methods

Except for magazine and newspaper writing, direct quotes from other sources are frowned upon in commercial publishing. If you do want to use direct quotes, make sure your notes are clear so you can make the proper attribution. You may find it helpful even to note which ideas and phrases are your own by marking them with a large "Me" in the margin. And, as an extra precaution, get into the habit of double-checking your phrasing as you write; this can help you avoid accidentally presenting as your own a phrase or sentence that you remember from your research.

chapter 11

Revising Your Submission

Writers generally fall into one of two camps when it comes to revising their work. Some writers simply hate the idea of rewriting anything; once they've finished their first draft, they would prefer never to deal with it again. Others take revising so seriously that it's hard to get them to stop tinkering and send their work out. If you receive one rejection after another for your queries, proposals, or manuscripts, it's time to sit down and seriously consider making changes in your material.

Serving the Client

Publishing works on the principles of supply and demand, just like any other business, and sometimes it's easier to tackle revisions if you think of your relationship with the publishing business this way. Potential markets are your clients, and you are the supplier of goods. Your responsibility is to understand the demands of your clients and give them what they need so they can serve their clients (i.e., their readers, advertisers, etc.). It's like selling fabric to a sewing store. If none of the store's customers buy corduroy, the store isn't going to carry corduroy in its inventory, and it's pointless for you to try to convince the store owner to purchase your corduroy, even if it's of the best quality ever known.

Thinking of your writing this way has several advantages. First, it requires you to think like an editor (see Chapter 4 for more on this) and develop your ideas with that perspective in mind. Second, it puts rejections on a business, rather than a personal, basis. An editor who can't use your idea is no longer saying you aren't good enough as a writer; he's simply saying that your article or story or book proposal is not in demand at his particular company. Finally, this approach permits you to remove the blinders many writers wear during the submission process, freeing you from the futile task of trying to jam a square peg into a round hole and allowing you instead to look for square holes or ways to shape your idea so it's round, too.

FACT

This advice applies to your search for an agent, too. Although your goal is to become an agent's client, you'll be more successful in your wooing if you think of a potential agent as the client and work to give her exactly what her market demands.

Serving the client doesn't mean you have to subjugate or abandon your own style of writing. It does mean, however, that it is your responsibility to match your goods with the market, and that sometimes means setting your ego and style preferences aside. If your goal is build your clip file, establish long-term relationships with editors, or simply get paid for doing something you love, your primary consideration should be to craft pieces that suit a particular market. Once you make a name for yourself, you'll have more slack to give rein to your own style.

Coping with Criticism

Hard as this might be for many writers to believe, constructive criticism in a rejection actually is cause for optimism. When an agent or editor gives you specific reasons for rejecting your work, it usually means that you have interested him but not met his market needs. More important, in most cases like this, it's a rare chance at a do-over, because there is an implicit invitation to revise and resubmit your work, or to submit other pieces to this market.

To take advantage of these opportunities when they arise, you have to be able to put a healthy emotional distance between you and your writing so you can look at it as objectively as possible. Part of doing this involves learning how to weigh and measure criticism. You should be able to discern between helpful and unhelpful comments; helpful ones cite specific issues or problems to be addressed (though not necessarily how to address them), while unhelpful ones are vague and sometimes unkind.

There is no need to respond to a form rejection letter unless the agent or editor has taken the time to jot a personal note at the end of it. Even when you do get such notes, you aren't required to respond. If you choose to respond, though, the appropriate and professional thing to do is to write a brief note or e-mail, thanking the agent or editor for his comments. Never berate him for offering advice, and don't argue about the merits of his comments. You may want to submit work to this person again, and you don't want to tarnish your image. Remember, too, that such comments are a generous donation of the agent's or editor's time and expertise; accept them in a like spirit.

Keep in mind that agents and editors generally won't give specific comments when material just isn't right for them. If you haven't done your market research—that is, if you're sending a techno-thriller to an agent who only handles women's fiction, or a skydiving article to a cycling magazine—chances are you'll get a standard "doesn't suit our needs" rejection letter.

Common Nonfiction Criticisms

Nonfiction criticisms tend to fall into three broad categories: stale ideas, lack of authority, and lack of human interest. The problem, especially for new writers, is that agents and editors don't always define what they mean by these comments. And you can't fix it if you don't really understand what's broken.

Staleness

One of the most common complaints agents and editors have about the submissions they receive is that there's nothing new, fresh, or original. This can be intimidating to new writers, who wonder nervously how they can possibly come up with fresh ideas when people have been exchanging and publishing ideas for thousands of years. If there really is nothing new under the sun, why do agents and editors keep demanding something new?

QUESTION?

How do I get new information for an article?
Start by contacting the sources you find in already-published articles. If you have questions that those articles didn't answer, ask those questions of the original source. Also ask who else you could contact. Very often, experts will direct you to colleagues who might add another dimension to your coverage.

Here's what these "demanding" agents and editors really mean: They want a fresh perspective on well-worn topics. As discussed in Chapter 4, the quickest way to an agent's or editor's yes file is to find and fill a hole in the market. Say you want to write a piece for a travel magazine on the increasing popularity of heritage tourism. This trend has been covered extensively in both trade and consumer magazines, and they aren't likely to be interested in yet another bland look at it. But, if the coverage has overlooked how smaller, lesser-known attractions have been affected by the trend, you've got a brand-new approach to a not-at-all-new topic.

Lacking Authority

Another common complaint for nonfiction articles and book proposals is that they lack authority. This could mean several things. It may mean that it relies too heavily on one or two experts, or that it doesn't distinguish between opinion and established fact. It also may mean that there are unsupported leaps of logic. These deficiencies almost always are fixable, but it takes some work in the form of additional research and, often, reorganizing the piece to accommodate the changes.

Lack of Human Interest

Finally, agents and editors often complain a nonfiction piece is "flat" or "dry." This usually happens when writers fail to put a human face on an issue. For example, if you're writing an article about the National Flood Insurance Program and delays in getting flood aid to stricken communities, you risk boring your readers to death unless you include the stories of people who actually are affected by the delays. Unless your target publication is aimed at bureaucrats, a process-y article that quotes only government officials and ignores what most editors call "real people" isn't going to interest anybody.

Common Fiction Criticisms

In fiction, rejection is sometimes as much a matter of taste as of objective standards, and it is especially important for fiction writers to remember that a rejection reflects just one person's opinion. The editor at Magazine G might not like your short story, but the editor at Magazine H might think it's the best thing she has read since Hemingway. That said, there are some common problems agents and editors run across in fiction of any length.

Characterization Issues

Lots of unpublished fiction suffers from one-dimensional characterization. This is a particularly challenging problem for short story writers, because you're limited in the space you have to develop your characters. But agents and editors typically will reject stories with characters who are either too good or too bad to be true. Everyone, even your hero and villain, has both admirable traits and flaws, and your job as a writer is to craft word portraits that reveal the shades of gray among the black-and-white outlines.

So-called "wooden characters" also seriously damage a good story, usually by speaking in stilted, awkward dialogue. Train your writing ear to pick up on and replicate natural patterns of speech, and understand your characters well enough to know what kind of phrasing and vocabulary they would use.

Plot Issues

If an agent or editor advises you to scrap the first three or four chapters of your novel, or says you've included too much "back story," it means your story doesn't begin where your manuscript begins. New writers especially tend to ease into their stories as if they were testing the water in the swimming pool with a shrinking toe, but agents and editors—and readers, for that matter—want you to just dive in and get on with it. The back story is useful to the writer to figure out his characters and the build-up of events to the main story, but it almost always is deadly dull to the reader.

There's another pretty good tip-off that you haven't begun your story in the right place. If you feel compelled to tell an agent or editor to be sure to read up to Chapter 12 because that's where it gets really good, you need to seriously edit your manuscript. The real message in a statement like that is that the first eleven chapters are boring, which is sure to put you in the rejection pile.

Agents and editors commonly advise new fiction writers to "bring the plot to the foreground." This means you've allowed too much extraneous material to creep into your story. Remember that every scene in a short story, and every chapter in a novel, must advance the plot. Otherwise, you risk losing your reader and earning a rejection slip.

Before submitting your work, take a hard look at the beginning chapters and ask yourself what would happen if you eliminated them. Would the reader still understand what's going on? Would it help build suspense if you doled out the information contained in the early chapters later on? If the answer is yes (and it often is), you can strengthen your writing immeasurably by taking the time to make these changes before you begin your marketing.

Your stories always should have a motif or theme that weaves through your plot, and your plot progression must make logical sense. If you have to resort to coincidence or other contrivances to bring your story to a climax, consider reworking your plot; readers generally dislike these kinds of stories, and editors won't buy them. Keep narration and exposition to a minimum, and allow your characters to advance your plot through action and dialogue.

Style and Tone Issues

Every writer who has ever taken an English class has been admonished to "show, don't tell" what happens in a story. If your story sounds more like a report on the evening news, you've fallen back on telling readers what they need to know rather than showing them. Think in terms of mystery stories here. The writer knows who committed the crime, but the characters in the story don't know until the end. Readers want to go along with the characters to find out what happens, and they want to make their own judgments along the way by paying attention to the clues you provide in plot and character.

Another common criticism fiction writers hear is that their work is too preachy. This doesn't mean your stories can't take on social or political issues, or that you should shy away from plots that involve controversial topics. However, whatever the lesson, moral, or point of view you're trying to present, you have to allow the reader to absorb it from the momentum of your story. Don't stop the action to expound on your own views. Let your characters and plot work together to get the message across.

Melodrama also often will earn a rejection, unless it's an integral part of the story concept. Even then, stories that blatantly attempt to draw readers in with an exaggerated play on emotion turn off many readers—and therefore many agents and editors. If your work is being described as too sentimental, saccharine, or heavy-handed, this may be why.

Refining Your Angle

"Angle" and "slant" are used interchangeably to describe the unique premise or thesis of an article or book idea. These terms apply almost exclusively to nonfiction. As noted earlier, agents and editors receive thousands of submissions that offer only stale rehashes of topics that already have been done many times over. The thing that keeps them reading is the enticing possibility of finding something fresh and invigorating in their submission piles.

The good news is that it's almost always possible to come up with a new angle. It just takes some practice in asking yourself the right kinds of questions. A general curiosity and desire to know everything there is to know (within reason) about a given subject helps, too.

Detective Work

If finding a unique approach to a topic were easy, writers wouldn't feel so discouraged about coming up with salable ideas. The unfortunate fact is that, whenever you arrive at an idea for an article or book, somebody else most likely has gotten there before you. The onus now falls on you to discover the angle everybody else missed, and that takes time, thought, and persistent researching.

The first step is to find out how other people have approached your subject and search for clues that can lead to new ideas. Study published articles and books, and make a list of questions that occur to you as you read. Sometimes another writer will make an intriguing statement or offer a tantalizing fact that gives you an idea for a new slant. A profile on a sculptor well known for his realistic animal sculptures might mention in passing that his "fun" sculpting work involves mythical creatures like unicorns and dragons, for instance, and that might be a worthwhile clue to follow up. Once you have a potential angle in hand, you'll have to do another round of research to make sure it truly is unique and to find potential markets.

The Unexpected

Keep an eye open for news items, research findings, or facts that surprise you. Awareness of the unexpected can lead to great ideas, because surprise often makes us start asking questions that we otherwise wouldn't think to ask. Recently, there was a national news story about a city that made the world's largest birthday cake, then shipped thousands of pounds of leftovers to a nearby hog farm, where it was used as feed. After seeing this story on television or in your local newspaper, you might begin to wonder whether birthday cake is a good source of nutrition for hogs, or how other cities and organizations have disposed of their leftovers when they made the world's largest pizza or cookie or Thanksgiving dinner, or whether competition to build the "world's largest" anything has increased in recent years.

FACT

The unexpected can make a great hook for an article or book idea by piquing the reader's interest and compelling him to continue reading. This applies to your query letters as well as to your manuscripts. A lead like, "Most people expect to have leftovers at Thanksgiving, but few have enough Tupperware to store 30,000 pounds of sage-and-onion stuffing," can give a refreshing spin to the perennial story on post-holiday menu planning.

Connecting Unrelated Ideas

Most writers are voracious readers, and it's not just because they love words. The more you read, and the more varied your reading material, the better your chances of connecting two or more ideas in a creative way. The news story you read today about self-replicating robots and a blurb about the theory of intelligent design in an education journal might lead to a great story idea about sentient machines. Flipping through the latest camping equipment catalog might spark a story idea about the luxury camping market, leading you to investigate upscale campgrounds that offer everything from satellite television hookups to wireless Internet service.

Changing Your Focus

Focus applies both to the parameters of your article or manuscript and to your target markets. Consumer magazines and trade paperback publishers strive to appeal to a mass audience. Trade journals and niche publishers aim for much more specific audiences. How well the focus of your own work matches the market's needs has a significant impact on the success of your submission.

Think Relevance

A key part of focusing your work, especially for nonfiction, is figuring out what information is relevant for the readers you hope to attract. The topic of federal regulations for day care centers may be relevant to parents, center owners, and staff, but not all these groups need the same information. Parents likely will be most interested in what they should look for in selecting a good day care center and what laws or regulations are in place to protect them and their children. Day care center owners will need to know how the laws and regulations apply to them, how much they cost to implement, and what their obligations are for licensing and the like. Staff members also need to know these things, as well as the processes for obtaining licenses, requirements for continuing education, and so on.

Relevance also applies to your fiction, both in terms of your audience and of the structure and content of your story. If you're writing for the children's market, for instance, you need to understand that young readers usually don't want to read about characters who are younger than they are. Your story about a six-year-old learning how to ride a bike will have no relevance to a ten-year-old reader.

Nearly all fiction benefits from efficient structure and economical writing. Particularly in short stories, you simply don't have the space to include every detail you've thought of. You have to choose which details are most relevant to your story and trust your readers to fill in the rest.

Consider All Potential Audiences

It's rare for an idea to appeal only to one segment of readers. Most of us are interested in more than what comprises our daily lives. We have hobbies, political views, passing interests, and curiosity about a variety of subjects. Many of us just enjoy learning something new, even if it isn't something we would go out and research ourselves. In this sense, then, writers serve an essential function in society by providing the material that entertains, educates, enlightens, and elevates readers.

Beginning writers tend to make one of two mistakes in thinking about who will want to read their material: They try to appeal to everyone (and therefore appeal to no one), or they pare their potential audience down to a tiny sliver of its real size. For most pieces, your audience really is somewhere in the middle—not everybody, but not nobody, either.

What you leave out of your writing is just as important as what you include when you alter the focus of your article or manuscript. For general audiences, you may have to include explanations of key terms or common practices. But, if you include such explanations in a piece targeted to professionals or practitioners in the industry, you'll come across as condescending.

Your writing style, as well as your vocabulary, plays a role in changing your focus. Generally, you'll have better luck with a more relaxed, informal writing style; formal writing is typically limited to scientific and academic publishing. For consumer and even trade magazines, studying several issues will help you get a feel for the writing style the editors favor. Even highly technical topics can be written in everyday language to reach a lay audience, and broad topics can be refined to provide essential information to particular sectors of the population. In fact, professional writers do this regularly, parlaying one idea into pieces for two or more potential markets and finding ways to make the idea relevant to all the target audiences. This takes some careful thought, of course. Readers of a hunting magazine probably wouldn't be interested in your story about natural gardening, but maybe you could recast that story to discuss creating backyard habitats to attract and support game animals.

Likewise, a story about health insurance in the workplace can be written to appeal to several audiences, depending on the focus: working parents, people nearing retirement, or compensation and benefits managers, for instance. Each piece will require different information, which means more research for you, but the extra time you put into preparation can easily pay off in multiple sales to appropriate (but not overlapping) markets.

Broadening Your Appeal

Sometimes a nonfiction idea will be too narrow to suit the markets you want to reach, and you'll need to explore ways to expand the idea for a broader readership. One way to do this is to look for trends. A national magazine is unlikely to be interested in a profile of the new Brazilian restaurant in your city, but it may well be interested in a story about how such restaurants are popping up in major metropolitan areas across the country.

Personal experience and inspirational pieces in particular can suffer from limited-appeal syndrome. Sometimes you can overcome this by marketing your idea as an exception to the rule, but more often you'll have to recast the premise of your article to cover more material. Your memoir about working on a swordfish boat, for example, most likely needs to be more than a simple diary of your experience to find a buyer. Unless you're a celebrity or otherwise well known, you'll have to provide other elements, such as adventure, insight into the character of a swordfish boat captain, and information about the commercial fishing industry, to capture a wider potential readership.

ALERT!

Sidebars—short pieces that amplify a point in your main article or provide additional information—are an easy way to give your magazine article a broader appeal without interrupting the flow or focus of the main story. Editors often look for these kinds of packages when considering submissions, especially for feature-length articles.

Similarly, a magazine piece about flying under the new Homeland Security rules probably will have more appeal if you include the experiences and opinions of several people, from passengers to security personnel to flight attendants to government officials. Even if you envision this piece as a first-person essay, including the observations of others can add texture and color to your writing.

Here are a few techniques for making sure you don't put too many restrictions on your idea's appeal:

- List characteristics of people who should be interested in your story or article. Start with gender, age, occupation, education level, geographic location, income, hobbies, and personality traits.
- Check the readership profiles provided in most publishing directories to see whether you've overlooked potential readers.
- Do a search on the Internet for keywords related to your topic. Study other articles and the markets in which they appeared, as well as any results for associations and organizations related to your topic.
- Look for profiles of people—experts, researchers, participants, etc.—related to your topic. You might gain a deeper understanding of what motivates them.
- Organize your research results into main points and side issues. Play with different combinations of essential and nonessential information to see if something new emerges.

Expanding the appeal of an idea has two main advantages for the beginning writer. First, it stimulates your creativity by forcing you to look at your idea in ways you ordinarily wouldn't consider, sometimes even opening your mental eye to new angles. Second, it keeps you from unduly restricting the potential markets for your idea, because you're always thinking of new readers to reach.

Accepting the Challenge

In Chapter 9, we called rejection slips medals for bravery because they prove you have the courage to submit your work and let others tell you whether it has any market value. Just as important as that medal, however, is what you do after you receive it. In that context, a rejection slip is really a challenge to you to try again.

Assuming that you don't want to stick your work in a drawer and give up your dream of becoming a published writer, you have essentially two options in responding to such a challenge. You can shrug off the rejection from one market and send the material out to the next one on your "possibles" list. Or you can rework your submission to make it more appealing to the markets you want to reach.

New Markets

Many writers elect to move on to the next market on their list, waving a rejection aside with a philosophical, "Oh, well." There's nothing wrong with that approach. In fact, the more philosophical you can be in dealing with rejection, the less stressful your writing career will be. Besides, it's fairly common for your first choice to turn you down, especially if you're aiming at the big markets; they are notoriously difficult to break into.

If an agent or editor rejects your current submission but invites you to submit to her in the future, take it seriously. Agents and editors never include this sort of note out of the goodness of their hearts. When they do, it means that they see talent and potential in you, and they want to see more of your work.

If you're collecting rejections further down your marketing list, however, it's likely that there's a serious flaw in your submission. A fistful of form rejections with no personal notes from an agent or editor indicates that your material isn't properly slanted for the markets you're targeting. If you are getting personalized comments, pay attention to them. These are free, professional opinions, and, even if they sting a little, you should treasure them because few writers ever receive them.

Making Changes

The first thing to remember when you're wavering over whether to revise your material is that it is always your decision. Even if a dozen agents or editors have suggested the same changes, you never have to make them if you don't want to. Of course, if you don't make changes, you may not see this particular piece published, but it's your work, and only you can decide whether the cost of making changes outweighs the benefits.

If you do decide to make changes, and if the changes are inspired by comments you received from agents or editors, you should resubmit your revised material to those people first. It's professional courtesy, because these people gave you the benefit of their expertise and experience at no charge, and they most likely did it on their own time. In addition, an agent or editor who is interested enough to offer you advice gives you a subtle advantage over the dozens or even hundreds of other submissions on his desk.

When you do accept the challenge, keep your expectations realistic. If you get a positive response to your query or proposal—that is, an agent or editor asks to see more—don't expect detailed feedback on the material you first submitted. The fact that an agent or editor wants to see more is a good thing. It means your material shows promise; if it didn't, they wouldn't ask for anything else. Demanding an evaluation or critique before you send more material is no way to endear yourself to the professionals in publishing. Keep an open mind and an optimistic outlook, but don't expect to rule the world.

chapter 12

Reading the Contract

Whenever you sell a piece of writing to someone, you're selling specific rights to use your work in specific ways. Your contract will spell out which rights are being transferred to the publisher, how long the publisher has those rights, and how much the publisher will pay you for them. There are lots of different ways your work can be used, so it's important to look beyond the money when you're offered a contract.

Types of Rights

A copyright is really a generic umbrella covering a broad spectrum of individual rights. In your contract, you transfer to the publisher some or all of the rights covered under your copyright. The rights you grant will vary depending on the type of work you're selling and who is purchasing it. They can be limited by language, geography, or time, and sometimes by all three.

Serial Rights

Serial rights are sold to periodicals—i.e., newspapers and magazines. Many periodicals purchase only first serial rights, meaning they want to be the first to publish the material. Serial rights can be given on a worldwide basis or restricted to a certain region. Many magazines purchase first North American serial rights, which cover the United States, Canada, and Mexico; some purchase first U.S. serial rights. If the first serial rights aren't specifically limited to a particular geographic area, they cover the world. If first serial rights are limited to the United States or North America, you can sell foreign serial rights to publishers in other countries (except Canada and Mexico, if you've already sold first North American serial rights).

To qualify for first serial rights, including syndicated first serial rights, book excerpts must be published before the book itself is published. Excerpts that are published after the book is on the market can only be sold as second serial rights.

Second serial rights, also known as reprint rights, are for subsequent publishers of the same material. If your book on parenting is excerpted in *Parenting* magazine, for example, the magazine is buying second serial rights—also called excerpt or reprint rights. In this case, the excerpt will include a notice about your book, which often helps promote sales. Pay rates for second serial rights are lower than for first serial rights and are often based on a percentage, usually 50 percent, of the rate for first serial rights.

Newspapers sometimes purchase syndication rights, which are a special breed of serial rights. Major U.S. newspaper publishers own papers in several markets and usually have their own wire services through which they distribute articles and features among the member papers. Gannett, for example, owns *USA Today*, as well as dozens of local and regional newspapers around the country. Gannett might purchase syndicated serial rights for excerpts of a book to be published in all its newspapers.

Simultaneous Rights

It's possible to sell the same piece at the same time to two noncompeting markets, although it isn't very common. Because the publishing industry is so competitive, editors rarely are interested in publishing an article or short story that will appear in another publication. And, if you've slanted your article precisely enough, chances are slim that you'll find two markets that want to publish exactly the same piece. However, sometimes a publisher that owns several magazines will purchase one article or short story to appear in more than one of those publications. As noted in Chapter 9, make sure you notify editors that you are making simultaneous submissions when you're marketing your work.

Subsidiary Rights

When you sell a book to a publisher, the contract usually will discuss subsidiary rights as well as book-publishing rights. These can include serial and foreign rights, translation rights, movie and television rights, commercial licensing rights, audio books, and special formats, such as Braille or large-print books, or book-club editions. The contract will spell out which rights you give to the publisher and how you and the publisher will split the proceeds.

Some writers want to hang on to all subsidiary rights, thinking they are protecting their future earnings. But major publishers may be in a better position to exploit these rights, and they may insist on the ability to do so, particularly with an unknown author. As long as the earning splits are reasonable, there's no reason why you shouldn't grant these rights to the publisher, provided the publisher intends to actively pursue them.

Splits for these rights will differ depending on the type of right. According to the Authors Guild, an advocacy group for writers, authors should expect to receive 50 percent of the earnings for book club sales and for paperback sales, if the publisher is first publishing the book as a hardcover. The split on movie and television rights can range from a straight fifty-fifty arrangement to a division that heavily favors the author. For nonfiction, foreign rights usually aren't very lucrative; for fiction, though, foreign sales can bring you a lot of money, and you or your agent should try to retain them if you can.

FACT

There's a difference between foreign rights and translation rights. A publisher may sell your English-language book in France, for instance. The publisher also may sell French translation rights to another company. You should receive 75 percent of the proceeds when your publisher sells translation rights.

Movie, television, and dramatic rights—i.e., for a play—often are sold as an option first, which is a guarantee that no one else can purchase those rights for a specified period. Options fetch a percentage of the total price of the right being optioned; if the movie rights are worth $100,000, for instance, a six-month option might be sold for 25 percent, or $25,000. At the end of the six months (or whatever period is agreed to), the rights revert to the author or publisher, unless the purchaser pays the balance ($75,000 in this example) or renews the option. Whatever the case, the up-front money paid for the option is nonrefundable; the buyer is paying you to "hold" the project, or take it off the market, while he tries to set up deals with producers, etc. If he decides not to pick up the option, you keep whatever he originally paid for it.

The Authors Guild argues that authors should receive 90 percent of earnings from the sale of television and movie rights. However, many publishers insist on a fifty-fifty split, reasoning that strong sales of the book add significant value to such rights. You should always receive at least 50 percent of such earnings.

What's for Sale?

Which rights are for sale depends on the type of work you're selling and who you're selling to. Magazines generally purchase limited rights, such as first serial rights or one-time rights, but occasionally you'll run across one that purchases all rights. As discussed above, book publishers typically purchase a range of rights, with the advance and royalties for the book itself spelled out and a split between author and publisher specified for subsidiary rights. If you're a stringer for a newspaper, your contributions generally are considered "work made for hire," and the newspaper retains all rights to the material.

Any contract for publishing of your work must include the following:

- A description of the work being purchased.
- A specific listing of which rights are being licensed to, or purchased by, the publisher.
- A definition of the rights license period, i.e., how long the publisher owns the rights you are selling and when those rights revert to you.
- Delivery dates for all or portions of the work.
- Terms of payment for the work.

Most publishing contracts will include several other clauses covering such things as acceptability standards, noncompete agreements, and which state laws come into play in the event of a legal dispute between you and the publisher. These clauses usually are part of a publisher's boilerplate, or standard, contract and are not negotiable. Nearly every publisher these days insists on an acceptability or satisfactory clause, which in essence gives them the right not to publish work that doesn't live up to the promises made by the writer.

Noncompete clauses also are the norm; publishers want to make sure their writers don't sell other pieces (articles, short stories, or books) to competing publishers, because such sales could diminish the value of the material they're buying. The "governing law" clause also is a non-negotiable item, because it has to be the state in which the contract is generated—that is, the home state of the publisher or agent.

Description of the Work

The description of the work being purchased can be quite broad or quite specific. In book contracts, the description may be just one sentence, citing the book's working title and its overall focus. Some publishers include the author's outline in the contract, but many don't. Nearly all publishers will include a minimum word count for the manuscript, and some will include a maximum.

Magazine contracts differ, depending on whether you're selling an article or short story that already has been written or being assigned an article that you pitched to an editor. For outright purchases, most magazines offer a simple contract that includes the terms of payment—how much, and when it is to be paid—as well as the title of the piece and the rights being purchased. Such contracts also usually require you to supply your name, contact information, and Social Security number.

In addition to these things, contracts for assigned articles usually will specify the length of the piece and sometimes will even spell out the types of sources to be used. The contract also will have a deadline for completing and delivering the article.

Rights Being Purchased

Unless you agree otherwise in writing, U.S. copyright law states that you are selling only one-time rights to any publisher. This is why even small magazines issue a contract spelling out precisely which rights are being sold and all the other terms of the sale. When you submit your work, whether in a query or with a complete manuscript, you always should specify which rights you are offering for sale.

When you read through the contract, pay close attention to the rights being purchased, because it has a serious impact on how much money you can make from your writing. If you sell all rights to an article or short story, for instance, you cannot resell that piece to anyone else until the rights license period expires. Because of that limitation, you should get more money from a magazine that purchases all rights than a magazine that purchases only first serial rights.

Rights License Period

In book publishing, the rights license period generally lasts as long as the book is in print, and the period covers both the book publishing rights and the subsidiary rights specified in the contract. When the book goes out of print, you usually can regain the rights you transferred by notifying the publisher in writing. To do this, make sure the contract defines "out of print," either by the number of printed copies in stock or the number of sales per year.

QUESTION?

Why is it important to have a reversion of rights clause?
There may be more money in it for you down the road. If your fourth book becomes a bestseller, it could create demand for your earlier books, and a reprinter might be interested in publishing those books again. That means another advance and more royalties on those earlier books for you.

In magazine publishing, you can sell first serial rights only once, unless those rights are limited by geography, language, or other factors. As noted earlier, you can sell first North American or first U.S. serial rights, and then sell first foreign serial rights for the same piece.

Sometimes you can negotiate a set limit on the rights license period for magazines. You can offer first serial rights for twelve months, for example, and if the magazine doesn't publish your piece within that year, the rights revert to you and you can shop them to another magazine.

Delivery Dates

Magazine contracts and many book contracts include one delivery date, or deadline, for the entire manuscript. Some book publishers give interim deadlines, when certain percentages of the manuscript are due, although this is more common for nonfiction books. For most nonfiction books, you'll have at least several months to complete the manuscript. However, when interim deadlines are involved, it's not uncommon to reach the first deadline before you receive the executed copy of your contract.

If you're a first-time or even a second-time novelist, the publisher probably won't offer you a contract until your manuscript is complete; too many publishers have signed fiction writers with unfinished manuscripts who, for whatever reason, were unable to deliver the final product. Also, if a publisher wants major changes to your novel, you most likely will have to make those changes before you get a contract. Because of this now-common requirement for new novelists, your delivery date might will be four to six weeks from the signing of the contract. This gives you enough time to put the finishing touches on your manuscript, but not enough to make major changes in your story.

FACT

Book authors usually receive free copies of their books when they're published. Typically, hardcover publishers will give authors ten free copies; paperback publishers usually will give twenty to twenty-five. You also will have the option to purchase more copies from the publisher at a discounted rate, which should be specified in your contract.

Payment Terms

Your contract should spell out how much you'll get paid for your work and when you'll get paid. This will vary depending on the publisher you're dealing with. If you're stringing for a newspaper, you might get a separate check for each piece, or you may get paid once a month for the pieces that were published in the previous thirty days. Magazines generally pay either on acceptance (which is better for the author) or on publication; because of the long lead times most magazines have, the latter arrangement means you may wait several months before you get paid. Book publishers generally split advance payments into two or more checks, with the first payment made when the contract is executed and later payments tied to delivery of part or all of the manuscript.

Keeping Your Promises

Contracts are a series of promises between you and a publisher, and it's critical for your reputation and your career as a writer that you keep your end of the bargain. That means delivering your work to deadline, ensuring that your work is your own, and projecting a professional image.

Delivering to Deadline

Deadlines in publishing are not mere suggestions. They are the backbone of a rigorous and highly structured publishing schedule. Most magazines have lead times of two to six months; that means they may start working on the August issue in March or April and the December issue might be put to bed—sent to the printer—as early as June. When writers miss their magazine deadlines, it leaves a hole of sometimes several printed pages in the issue, forcing the editor to search frantically through the slush pile in hopes of finding something appropriate to fill the space. Chances are that editor will not be inclined to give you a future assignment once you've burned him by missing a deadline.

> If you can't meet a deadline, it is imperative that you let your agent or editor know as soon as possible. If you have an agent, notify her first and let her talk to the editor. Unforeseen circumstances can interfere with your work schedule, and most agents and editors are willing to do what is possible if they are kept abreast of the situation.

Deadlines are just as critical in book publishing. Delivery of the manuscript is just the first step in a hectic process spanning months. (See Chapter 7 for behind-the-scenes details of the book publishing industry.) Delays in delivery to your acquiring editor means she is delayed in forwarding your manuscript to the development editor, which means delays in getting it to the copy editor, which means delays in getting the final version to the printer. That in turn means a hole in the publisher's catalog and havoc among the sales and marketing staff. And, as in magazine publishing, missed deadlines in book publishing earn you black marks and diminish your marketability for future books.

Original Work

Virtually every contract you encounter in publishing will include a warranties and representations clause, in which you assert that the work you submit is your own material, not plagiarized from any other source, and that it doesn't violate anyone's rights of privacy or other civil rights. Publishers can't take this for granted any more; there have been too many high-profile cases of authors lifting others' material. Most publishers also use various software programs to detect plagiarism, and sometimes this practice is included in the contract so authors know what to expect.

Related to the warranties and representations clause is the acceptability or satisfactory clause, which allows a publisher to reject work that isn't acceptable. Again, this now-standard clause resulted from too many cases where what was turned in was not what the publisher expected. The terms "satisfactory" and "acceptable" may or may not be precisely defined in the contract, but the procedure for fixing problems should be. Generally, the publisher should be required to give you specific reasons for deeming your work unacceptable, citing specific problems that need to be addressed. You should have at least thirty days to correct these specific problems. If you are unable or unwilling to do this, the publisher can hire someone else to make the changes and charge the expense to your advance, or cancel the project altogether. If the project is canceled, you may be required to repay any money you've already received from the publisher.

Professional Image

Not surprisingly, agents and editors prefer to work with writers who are both talented and professional. Professionalism goes beyond meeting your contractual obligations, though. It means working with your agent or editor to resolve problems, handling criticism with at least the appearance of aplomb (however you may feel about it privately), and being respectful of the agent's or editor's time. Phone calls should be kept to a minimum, and e-mails should be limited to necessary communications. Professionalism also means understanding and following the agent's or editor's submission guidelines and being sure to include the SASE with appropriate postage.

Working for Hire

Work-for-hire arrangements, also called works made for hire, are common in newspaper publishing and have become more common in book publishing in recent years. Some writer advocacy groups dislike these arrangements because the writer doesn't retain any rights in the material he creates, so profits are limited. However, works for hire can offer good break-in opportunities for new writers who are building their credentials and clip files.

Under U.S. copyright law, work for hire covers material created by an employee when that work is part of the employee's regular duties, such as a staff writer for a newspaper or magazine. Stringers for newspapers—especially those who cover specific beats, like high school sports or local business—usually are considered independent contractors and fall under the same work-for-hire rules, unless there is a written contract stating otherwise. In all other circumstances, courts have ruled that a valid work-for-hire arrangement requires a written contract in which both parties "expressly agree" to these special terms.

ALERT!

Selling "all rights" to an article or story is not the same as doing a work made for hire. U.S. copyright laws allow you to regain your copyright in an "all rights" work after thirty-five years by following established procedures. Rights in a work made for hire stay with the publisher who commissioned the work forever.

In every work made for hire, you'll be paid a flat fee for creating the work. You won't get any royalties, in the case of a work-for-hire book, and you won't be able to sell reprint or any other subsidiary rights, in the case of a magazine or newspaper article. However, if the fee for doing the work is fair, and if you get authorship credit, works for hire can be a lucrative way to build your portfolio and your reputation as a writer.

Getting Credit

From the point of view of most agents and editors, an unpublished author is a liability. You are an unknown quantity, with no name recognition and no demonstrable track record of being able to deliver quality text to deadline. This is why so many publishing professionals insist on published credits. Especially in book publishing, the enormous cost of printing and distributing a new title makes most publishers leery of taking a chance on an untried writer.

There are countless opportunities for freelance writers to earn quite respectable fees for their work—writing advertising and brochure copy, annual reports, speeches, and other pieces for businesses, for example—but these usually don't give you a byline. For new writers who envision careers as book authors or regular contributors to major magazines, the most important factor in getting published—even more important than how much you get paid, or getting paid at all—is getting credit for what you've written. Many magazines and book publishers refuse to work with unpublished writers, so it's critical to your career to build the credentials that will allow you to break into the bigger markets. (See Chapters 2 and 3 for more information on collecting credentials and building a credible platform.)

For most aspiring writers, the path to the big-time in publishing begins at small-circulation newspapers and magazines, with correspondingly small paychecks. Bylined clips from local newspapers can lead to assignments from larger, regional newspapers; those from small trade or literary magazines can be the first rung on the ladder to publication in progressively larger-circulation and higher-profile magazines. And that collection of clips can provide a springboard into book publishing.

Other opportunities for aspiring book authors include works for hire and coauthorship arrangements. As long as you get authorship credit, a work-for-hire book is exactly the same as a royalty-paying book in the eyes of potential publishers; it proves that you are capable of writing and delivering book-length text. The same goes for coauthorship arrangements. Again, as long as your name appears on the book cover, it counts as a credit and carries the same heft as sole authorship.

Payment Arrangements

As noted earlier, the bottom line of any contract is how much you get paid for your work and when you get paid. Obviously, the best arrangement is to get paid when an editor accepts your article or manuscript, but that isn't always the norm, especially among smaller publishing outlets. Before you sign a contract—and before you start spending the money—be clear on when you can expect a check.

FACT

Small magazines, including literary magazines, often pay contributors only in copies of the issue in which your article or story appeared. The number of copies you receive usually is between one and five. Directory listings of magazines will indicate "contributor copies" in the payment section.

"On Acceptance" vs. "On Publication"

Some magazines, and even a few book publishers, delay payment until a piece is actually published, which can leave you hanging for months on end. Most monthly magazines have lead times of two to six months, while it can take up to two years for a book to reach store shelves. The publishers who have payment-on-publication policies usually won't change them, and most established writers choose not to deal with them. Once you've built a respectable clip file, you may want to steer clear of these publishers, too.

Even with payment on acceptance, don't expect a check by return mail. Most publishers will first send out a contract for your signature. You send it back to the publisher, where it is signed by the appropriate person and payment is then authorized, which can take thirty days or longer. You should receive your check with a copy of the executed contract or soon thereafter.

Kill Fees

Many magazines offer kill fees for articles that have been assigned, but which have been pulled from the publishing calendar for some reason (not related to the writer's work). This could happen for a number of reasons: The editor might decide the topic no longer fits the publication's editorial policy, or a new editor may not like the idea, for example. Kill fees usually are a percentage—sometimes as much as 50 percent—of the fee that would have been paid if the article had been published as planned and are meant to compensate writers for the time they've spent on an assignment that fizzles out.

ALERT!

Sometimes writers will be paid for completed articles or short stories that are never published. First send a polite note to the editor, asking when your piece will appear. If it still hasn't been published after a year, advise the editor that you're reclaiming all rights to the piece under the guidelines established by the American Society of Journalists and Authors.

Although the term "kill fee" is rarely used in book publishing, most houses have a similar payment policy when they decide not to publish a manuscript that has been contracted and accepted. Under such circumstances, the author usually is entitled to keep whatever advance payments she has received for the manuscript. All rights in the manuscript should revert to the author once the publisher has decided not to go ahead.

Royalty Payments

The term royalty is hundreds of years old and stems from the practice of monarchs granting special licenses to companies and individuals. These licenses typically transferred control of some natural resource from the king or queen to the licensee, and the licensee often paid the monarch a share of the profits from such resources.

Traditional book publishers, as well as some self-publishing outfits, pay authors royalties, which is a percentage of a book's selling price. Royalties can be based on the list or retail price of a book, or on the wholesale price—typically about half the list price. Advances are paid against future royalty earnings, and advances have to be earned back before the author gets any royalty checks. If the book doesn't sell well enough to cover the advance, you won't get any royalty payments.

Say you've negotiated a 10 percent royalty on the list price for your book, which sells for $25. That means you earn $2.50 for every book sold. If your advance is $5,000, you won't earn any royalties until 2,000 copies of your book have sold ($5,000 divided by $2.50 = 2,000).

Most publishers calculate royalties twice a year, and it can take up to ninety days after the end of the royalty period for you to receive a statement. If you've earned royalties during the period, a check will accompany the statement. If not, you'll simply receive the statement, showing how many copies of your book sold during the covered period.

Many publishers allow their authors to audit their royalty statements once a year. This is done at your own expense and involves hiring an accountant to review the publisher's records. Such audits can be quite costly and usually are not warranted unless there is some major discrepancy in sales reports.

Publishing contracts can be fairly simple or remarkably complex, depending on the type of work and the circumstances surrounding it. If you have an agent (who typically only will work on book contracts), he should be familiar with industry standards and represent your best short- and long-term interests in the negotiations. If you don't have an agent, or if you are selling your work primarily to markets where an agent isn't necessary or appropriate, you should consider hiring an attorney experienced in working with authors to review any contract before you sign it.

chapter 13

Working with
Your Editor

The divide between writers and editors
is akin to the chasm between the sexes,
and it is at least as old as the concept of
the written word. Writers get frustrated
because they don't know what editors
want; editors get frustrated because they
so seldom get what they want; and, eventually, both may come to a point where
they wonder why they even bother. Like
relationships with the opposite sex, dealing effectively with an editor requires
patience, insight, skill, and, sometimes,
a lot of work.

What an Editor Does

Beginning writers often expect editors to be at their beck and call; after all, an editor's job is to support her writers with suggestions and encouragement, right? Well, yes, but that's only a tiny fraction of a typical editor's duties. You might think that your editor is sitting at her desk, idly thumbing through the latest issue of *Cosmo* and waiting anxiously to hear from you, but the truth is that most editors—even the ones who work for *Cosmo*—rarely have time to do anything idly.

Meetings, Meetings, and More Meetings

Most editors spend much of their workdays in meetings of one sort or another. There might be an editorial meeting to discuss upcoming magazine issues or potential book projects. Your editor, whether for a magazine or book publisher, probably will meet with the production department several times a week, and maybe even daily, to go over issues with layout, design, and problems with manuscripts. He might meet with the art director or photographer to finalize a book cover, a center spread, or illustrations. And he probably will meet with his boss to discuss contracts for various projects.

In addition, a typical magazine editor may have off-site meetings with advertisers and public relations folks who are trying to get their clients' products placed in the magazine. There may be trade shows or receptions or product demonstrations to attend. He may even have a lunch meeting sandwiched between all the other meetings that make up his day.

Messages, Lots of Messages

In between all the meetings, the editor likely has a stack of phone and e-mail messages that would choke a pig. Some of them are urgent and require her immediate attention—problems with contracts, writers who won't be able to make their deadlines, or any of scores of other crises that routinely arise in publishing. Some of them are important but not urgent, such as calls from agents who are checking on the status of submissions or who want to pitch new projects or from established writers who want to do the same. The bulk of them, though, are ones she can safely push to the bottom of her to-do list, like unsolicited e-mails from unknown writers. These might even get deleted without being opened, depending on what else the editor has on her plate that day or that week.

FACT

The official workday in most New York publishing offices begins at 9 A.M. and ends at 5 P.M. But most editors put in at least twelve-hour days during the work week, plus significant time on the weekends. They don't make a lot of money for their standard work week, and rarely, if ever, do they get overtime pay.

Reams of Submissions

On top of the meetings and messages, an editor has stacks and stacks of printed material to go through: queries, requested proposals and manuscripts, and all manner of unsolicited packages from hopeful writers. He may try to keep the stacks under control by diligently sorting through the most important ones each day, but it's like trying to hold back a mudslide with a garden hoe. Every day, usually several times a day, drivers from FedEx, UPS, and the U.S. Postal Service dump pound after pound of material on his desk until, by the end of the week, the editor's space looks more like a Mail Boxes Etc. at Christmastime than a professional office.

As part of his job and his efforts at stemming the tide, the editor takes much of this material home with him, with the result that the couch in his living room looks a lot like his desk at work. He spends the bulk of his evening reading through the submissions, deciding which ones will get a rejection letter and which ones merit further consideration. If he's a magazine editor, he may have a third pile, known as the slush pile, for submissions that have him wavering between a yes and a no. Book editors usually don't have slush piles; submissions to them are either rejected immediately or prompt a request for more material. Magazine editors use slush piles as insurance against future problems. If they need to fill a hole in a hurry, they have a ready-made file of possibilities.

What to Expect from Your Editor

Somewhere among all those meetings, messages, and mounds of material, an editor has to find time to actually edit, too. And here's where writers' dreamy expectations are likely to hit the cold wall of reality with a thud. The truth is, the publishing world does not revolve around writers. Publishing does not change according to writers' demands or ideas of what should make it into print. It doesn't alter its schedule for your convenience. As we've mentioned elsewhere, you are the supplier of raw material in a complex manufacturing business. If you can't or won't provide the right material on time, publishers will find other suppliers who can and will.

The Acquisition Process

Whether you're pursuing publication in a magazine or with a book publisher, chances are the editor does not have the final say on offering a contract. Magazine editors may have to pitch story ideas they like to their colleagues, who may have different views about whether a particular piece will fit in with the magazine's theme or mission. Book editors have even more of a sales job; they have to convince their fellow editors, plus the sales, marketing, and publicity departments, that a book project is good for the house.

ALERT!

Don't pester editors to speed up approval of your idea. They are just as likely to issue a rejection in response to such behavior, because they simply don't have time to deal with overly demanding, unknown writers. If you hope to succeed as a professional writer, patience will be one of the most important tools you can master.

The process at both types of publishers can take weeks, or even months. Especially with book publishers, the yes-or-no decision can be made on anything from the reaction of the sales and marketing departments to an analysis of the project's profitability. At magazines, even if editors really like an idea, it might not fit in well with what has been planned for the next few issues, so they could defer a decision until they have an opening for it.

Praise and Criticism

Occasionally, you might run across an editor who loves your work to death and just can't stop telling you how great it is. Most writers' experience is quite different, though. You are more likely to get a quick "Nice work," possibly accompanied by a "Thanks!" and probably sent via e-mail. And, if you're like a lot of writers, this will be profoundly unsatisfying, even though it's a positive response.

Most writers crave detailed feedback on their work. You want to know what an editor liked, what he didn't like, what turn of phrase worked for him and which parts came across as dull and uninspired. Unfortunately, most editors are just too busy to provide that kind of critique on every piece they deal with. "Nice work, thanks" may seem curt and superficial, but, in reality, it's a great compliment. It means the editor didn't have to do a lot of work to your copy, that you fulfilled the assignment, and that the editor is free to devote his attention to other things. Editors love writers who deliver that kind of work; don't mistake lack of time for lack of appreciation.

FACT

Ask editors about their pet peeves, and most of them will cite, among other things, writers who are too attached to their material. Words are only words, after all, and if you fall in love with your own words, it can blind you to their defects. Respect your editor's opinion; she might be seeing something you've missed.

The same holds true for criticism. Editors often don't have time to sugar-coat their criticisms, and they sure don't have time to coddle their writers. Their job is to make the piece work for the market, and every criticism they offer is aimed at making the material better. They are not out to destroy your self-esteem or ruin your work. Handling criticism is tough. You have to be tough and flexible enough to see the editor's point of view.

What Your Editor Expects from You

Every writer wants definitive, inside information about what editors want. It's simpler than you might think, because every editor wants the same thing: something terrific. They want something that will make their pulses quicken, their eyes shine, and their ganglions vibrate. How do you do that? By crafting material with these qualities:

- Talent combined with a strong grasp of mechanics. Good grammar, syntax, punctuation, spelling—all count.
- Information-gathering skills. Provide accurate information in language readers will understand.
- Clear, concise, unpretentious writing. Inject your own style, but stay within the parameters of the editor's needs.
- Details that illustrate and illuminate your topic.
- An angle the editor hasn't thought of, presented in a way she hasn't thought of.

Editors keep reading the submission pile because of the high they get when they find what they're looking for. Combine terrific material with a professional attitude, and you just may be the answer to an editor's prayer.

Act Like a Professional

In publishing, "professional" means more than getting paid for what you do. It is as much about the way you comport yourself in your dealings with other pros. Understand the demands on an editor's time and energy and be respectful of those other demands when you need to claim the editor's attention. Don't call or e-mail without a good and compelling reason and remember that hounding him about your submission doesn't count as a good reason. Accept suggestions and criticisms with courtesy; fight for what's important, but choose your battles with care. Always be civil, even when you disagree.

Follow the Editor's Rules

Submission guidelines are developed to cope efficiently with the enormous volume of material editors receive. Think about the math involved here. The average magazine editor receives 1,500 or more submissions a year. That's 125 a month, nearly thirty a week, or about six every day. And you thought you got a lot of junk mail.

Novice writers sometimes think they can make themselves stand out from the crowd by ignoring the submission guidelines. Even if that's true, standing out doesn't necessarily improve your chances of getting published. All you really call attention to is the fact that you can't or won't follow directions—a red flag for the editors who might work with you.

Perhaps the worst thing about all those submissions, from an editor's standpoint, is that so many of them will be utterly wrong for him. Chances are that even the ones that are right for him will be irritants, because they'll come in a form he doesn't want, and no writer wants an irritated editor reading her stuff. If the editor prefers a query, send a query. If he doesn't want e-mail submissions, don't send him e-mail submissions. Experienced editors can tell within a few sentences whether a piece is right for them; it's a waste of your time and theirs to give them more than they need to make an informed judgment.

Search for the Right Fit

Part of being professional is matching your material to the right markets. Editors lose a lot of precious time dealing with submissions that aren't appropriate for them, and they are inclined to jump with incredulous joy when they find a submission that is perfectly tailored for their target readers. Study the market listings to find out who those target readers are and refine your material to fit the needs of those readers.

There's another element to finding the right fit: approaching the right editor. At magazines, the managing editor, executive editor, or editor in chief isn't necessarily the best person to address your query to. Check the masthead to find out which editors are in charge of which departments, like health and fitness, relationships, food, and so on. If your idea falls within one of those categories, send it to the editor responsible for it.

Likewise, editors at book publishers usually are responsible for specific imprints, series, or categories of books. Don't expect that the wrong editor will pass your material along to the right one. Take the time to find out who the correct recipient is before you drop anything in the mailbox.

Keep in mind that the information in market directories is invaluable, but it isn't infallible. Editors move to other jobs or to new responsibilities within their company. For magazines, pick up a current copy and check the masthead. For book publishers, check out the Web site or call the general phone number and ask if the editor you've targeted is still in charge of the line you want to query.

Solving Problems

In a perfect world, writers would submit spotless, complete copy well before deadline with facts triple-checked, so that all an editor would have to do is pass it along to the next person on the assembly line. In the world we live in, though, this is nothing more than a fantasy. Problems are bound to crop up in a business as complex as publishing. How you work with your editor to resolve those problems can mean the difference between minor aggravation and major headaches.

Respect Deadlines

Editors expect you to deliver what you promise when you promise to have it done. If something comes up that will prevent you from meeting your deadline, contact your editor immediately and explain the problem. (If you're working on a book manuscript and you have an agent, let the agent know about the problem. She can, and should, deal with the editor on your behalf.) Whenever possible, offer a solution to the problem. The main concern for an editor is getting the material she needs when she needs it. In many cases, she'll be willing to do what can be done.

Be Honest

Editors can't afford to work with writers who lie, plagiarize, or otherwise mislead them. Your behavior and performance reflect on your editor. Do good work, and it helps both of you; do poorly, and it hurts both of you. You have to supply original work. If you're writing nonfiction books or articles, you can't make up quotes or describe scenes that you haven't witnessed. When you supply your credentials, you can't lie about your background, experience, or previous credits. When you propose an idea, fiction or non-fiction, your material has to live up to what you promised.

ALERT!

To ensure your reputation doesn't suffer, don't make a habit of making mistakes. Promises to do better next time lose their luster when repeated too often, and even if you're as fast as a jackrabbit in repairing the damage, the smell of unreliability can linger over your name and your work.

Now, everyone knows that mistakes happen, and no one expects you to be perfect. If you make a mistake—attribute a quote to the wrong source, unintentionally lift a phrase or passage from a copyrighted work, or otherwise err—face up to it immediately and work with your editor to correct it as quickly and painlessly as possible. No matter how embarrassed or awkward you may feel, it's your responsibility to identify the problem and fix it. Editors can forgive a lot when their writers are responsive and responsible.

The Editor's Colleagues

As you've figured out by now, editors don't do it all by themselves. There is a whole building full of people whose job it is to get a publication or book out on time, with a minimum of fuss. Depending on how the operation is set up, you may never come in contact with your editor's colleagues, but it's always good to know who they are and what they do.

Whether you're writing for a magazine or a book publisher, you'll deal most often with the editor who acquired your project. She's your main point of contact with the company; she's the one who will send out your contract, negotiate payment and deadlines, and discuss any changes or additions to the project with you. You'll deliver your manuscript to her, and, if any problems arise, she's the one you call.

At magazines, the editor will give your piece a read and then most likely will pass it on to a copy editor. The copy editor will check your work for spelling, punctuation, grammar, and style, and he or an assistant probably will do fact-checking. If questions arise during this phase, the copy editor may contact you directly or may send his questions to your editor, who will forward them to you.

In book publishing, there's an extra person reviewing your work between the editor's desk and the copy editor, called the development or project editor. This editor is responsible for evaluating the content and structure of your manuscript. She might have suggestions for reorganizing the information or adding or eliminating certain elements. Like the copy editor, the development editor may contact you directly with her comments, or she may funnel them through your acquiring editor.

Some writers get frustrated at having to respond to a series of questions about their work. Remember that everyone involved in the process is working to make the best product possible and do your best to be patient with even the small, annoying stuff.

When your work passes muster with all the people who review it, it will go to the layout or composition people, who are responsible for transferring your manuscript to the printed page and making it mesh with graphics, photos, and other design elements. If everything goes well here, you probably will never know anything about the process. On occasion, there might be a problem with copy fitting—making the words fit the space allotted to them—and your editor might ask you to cut something or expand on something. These instances are pretty rare, though. In most cases, the various editors will make those decisions themselves.

Beyond This Project

The key to establishing yourself as a professional writer is building relationships with editors. Burn an editor once, and you probably won't get another assignment from him; he might even warn his colleagues about you. But, if you come through for him on one piece, he's more likely to consider you for other assignments. And when you've built a good relationship with an editor, that will go with him to his next job.

It isn't difficult to establish a good relationship with an editor. Most of it is common sense and professional courtesy. Submit your copy on time and cover the subject you agreed to cover. Make sure your pieces are at least in the ballpark of the promised length. Give your editor the format she asked for. Understand what she needs for readers and tailor your pitches appropriately. Strive to resolve problems and differences of opinion quickly and amicably. Don't be disrespectful to her, her colleagues, or other writers.

Finally, give editors what they want: something wonderful. Excite them. Show them why your idea is important—not to you, but to their readers. Give them a fresh slant. Be a stickler for accuracy. Wrap it all up in writing that is clear, engaging, witty, stylish, and compelling. If you can do that and do it regularly, you'll have a professional ally for life, and you'll be well on your way to a rewarding career as a published writer.

chapter 14

Creating Buzz

Lots of writers imagine that, once they get a book contract, the reading public will instantly become aware of their work and clamor for more, leading to fame, fortune, and pressing demand for their talents. In the real world, though, it can take even more hard work to earn recognition of your name and your work than it did to write your masterpiece—and most of that work will fall to you. That's why it's so important to learn how to build and sustain buzz.

What Others Will Do

Building buzz almost always begins inside the publishing house with your editor. She has almost at much at stake with your book as you do, especially if you're a first-time author, because, if your book does well, she'll look good to her bosses for recognizing your talent and the money-making potential of your book. She's the one who championed your idea to the pub board; her enthusiasm for your project inspired her colleagues. She'll talk up you and your book to the sales staff, who will talk up you and your book to the book-sellers, who, in turn, just might talk up you and your book to their customers. However, important as such enthusiasm is, it goes only so far. The rest, almost always, will be up to you.

FACT

There are such things as "sleeper" books—books that do unexpectedly well and make lots of money for the publisher and the author. In the industry, these are called "break-out" books, and they achieve high sales figures despite a lack of marketing support from the publisher.

Reasonable Expectations

Spend any appreciable time with published writers, either in person or in online chat rooms, and eventually you'll come across a common complaint: Publishers don't spend enough time or money on promoting books. Many authors, disappointed by lackluster sales of their books, tend to blame their publishers; they believe their books would have soared to the top of the bestseller lists if only the publisher had invested more in marketing. But the hard truth is that almost every book published these days is going to appear in the bookstores without a major publicity campaign. They are simply too expensive for publishers to conduct, unless the book is already expected to be a bestseller.

If you expect your publisher to have you scheduled to appear on the *Today* show and *Good Morning America* the day your book hits the stores, or if you walk into your local bookstore expecting to see a giant poster of the cover of your book atop a table filled with dozens of copies right by the entrance, chances are you're going to be bitterly disappointed. The producers at the major networks aren't interested in interviewing new authors unless there's a news or celebrity angle to cover, and those displays at the front of your neighborhood Barnes & Noble or Borders store cost publishers tens of thousands of dollars. Such promotions are strictly reserved for commercial titles by, usually, authors who already have hit the bestseller lists with earlier books. They are extremely rare for new authors, most of whom are writing midlist books that may hit respectable sales figures but probably won't break out.

Promotion Realities

That said, there are things almost all publishers will do for almost all the books they put out. They usually send out press releases and review copies of their books to major newspapers around the country. They usually promote new titles prominently in their catalogs and on their Web sites. And they usually will coordinate media interviews when the media requests them.

ALERT!

Only amateurs demand extravagant marketing support from their publishers. If your book is expected to become a huge commercial success, your publisher may schedule book tours and interviews with the national media. Otherwise, you'll get the same marketing support all other books get—i.e., a press release and a review copy sent to major media, and not much else.

Before you get too excited about even this modest marketing support, remember that it is extremely rare to get a review in a major newspaper, and small- and medium-sized newspapers often don't even have book reviewers on staff (and publishers usually won't send releases or review copies to these smaller markets, anyway). It's nice to have a full page devoted to your book in the publisher's catalog, but remember that those catalogs (and Web sites) are geared mainly toward booksellers, not to the general reading public. Finally, although the publicity department at your publishing house will handle requests for media interviews, the media isn't likely to be pestering them for an interview with a largely unknown author of a largely unknown book. These resources from the publisher are merely the first baby steps in getting your book in front of potential readers.

What You Can Do

As you can see, chances are the bulk of the marketing work for your book will fall on your shoulders, at least until you do become famous (which, for many authors, doesn't happen until the third, fourth, or fifth book, if it happens at all). So, before you begin shopping your proposal or manuscript to an agent or editor, you'll need to think about what you can do to help promote your book. After all, no one else is going to care as much about your book's success as you do. That's the bad news. The good news is that you have more resources at your disposal than you think, no matter where you live and no matter what you write.

Issue Your Own Release

Your publisher likely will send out a general news release about your book, along with a review copy, to a few dozen major newspapers around the country. But this doesn't preclude you from sending out your own release, as long as you coordinate your efforts with your publisher's publicity department. You have a distinct advantage in doing this, because you can target your own local and regional media, using the same research skills you use in figuring out how to tailor your writing to specific markets.

When you're dealing with local media, your hook most likely will be the fact that you're a resident of your community rather than the topic or slant of your book. Everybody likes hometown bragging rights, whether it's the title-winning high school basketball team or having a bona fide author in their midst. Start with the newspapers, television stations, and radio stations that serve your geographic area, and clearly point out that you live in their service areas. Make sure your news release includes the following:

- Your name
- Your city, town, or village
- At least one phone number where you can be reached

- The title of your book
- The name of your publisher and the publication date
- A short paragraph describing your book
- A short bio on you

Keep your release to one page. Think of it as a query letter, only in this case you want to catch the attention of a reporter or an assignment editor. You have to convince him that this is a story worth pursuing and give him the means to pursue it—that is, your contact information and, if applicable, a Web site where he can find out more about you or your book.

Talk to Your Local Bookseller

Even the big chain booksellers have local or regional managers who arrange things like book signings and readings for local authors. Go to your neighborhood bookstore and introduce yourself as the author of your book, and ask for the name and phone number of the person who coordinates these things. Find out what the bookstore will do to promote a signing or reading, such as in-store posters, invitation lists, and press releases about the event. If the store personnel don't usually write press releases, ask if it's all right for you to issue one to local media. Even a small blurb in the "Community Calendar" section of your local newspaper helps spread the word about your book.

Schedule Local Appearances

Many civic, social, and religious organizations regularly schedule guest speakers for their meetings. Get in touch with the YMCA or YWCA, the Rotary or Kiwanis Club, and similar groups and offer to make a short presentation to their members. Reading circles and community book clubs, which seem to be regaining popularity in some areas of the country, also present good opportunities for you; many of them would jump at the chance to read your book and bring you in to discuss it with the group.

Always let an agent or editor know that you are available for book signings, media interviews, and other personal appearances, but expect to schedule these yourself, and expect to do it mainly on a local or regional level. This is where you'll be most effective, anyway, and it will be good practice for your eventual rise to a national stage.

Starting Small

New authors—and even some seasoned professionals—commonly dream of sitting on a stage chatting with Oprah and her audience, discussing their books with Matt Lauer, or exchanging ideas with the amiable host of *Larry King Live*. There's nothing wrong with those dreams, but don't expect them to come true right away. There's a definite value in starting out small and building up to a national audience, both for creating sustainable buzz and for your own self-confidence.

Local Media

Your community newspaper is the perfect place to start your own public relations campaign. Many weeklies and even smaller dailies will print, word for word, a simple news release announcing the publication of your book. Larger newspapers probably won't print your release verbatim, but they might be interested in doing a profile on you as an interesting person in the community. If nothing else, you might end up with a paragraph about your book in the paper, and that, too, helps spread the word.

ESSENTIAL

Press releases aren't always the most effective way to reach the media, especially your local newspaper or broadcast station. You might have better luck if you call the person responsible for book news with a quick pitch about your own book, and ask if he or she is interested in seeing a press release or review copy.

Check out local radio and television stations as well. Many news and talk radio stations have local programming where they profile local residents, and you might be a perfect guest for one of the shows. Likewise, many television stations have locally produced talk shows or segments on some of their newscasts devoted to people and events in the service area.

Depending on what your book covers, you also might be able to interest local or regional specialty publications in your book. If you've written a financial planning guide for college students, for example, the local business magazine might want to profile you and your book. The local entertainment weekly might be interested in your novel.

Go Back to School

Contact the English and journalism teachers in your area school districts and offer to speak to their classes about writing, the writing life, and becoming an author. Prepare a very brief presentation about yourself, no more than five minutes, and open the floor for questions. In case the students are shy, have questions ready to ask them; this will help break the ice. In nearly every class, there are at least one or two students who are passionate about writing and envision becoming writers themselves someday, and they will be eager, as every burgeoning writer is, to learn what you can teach them from your own experience. Just as important, these students (and their teachers) likely will talk about your presentation to parents, friends, and colleagues, which helps spread the word about you and your book.

Get Wired

Did you know that reporters routinely read blogs to find story ideas and sources for stories? A 2005 study sponsored by Columbia University reported that 53 percent of journalists use blogs to find story ideas, and 36 percent use them to find sources for stories. This is a great new promotion opportunity for authors, and you should be prepared to take advantage of it. Search the Internet for blogs that cover topics related to your book, then contact the host. You might be able to do a stint as a guest blogger on the site, or the host might even be interested in receiving a review copy of your book. Either way, it's another venue for you to spread the word about your book.

FACT

As blogs have become more popular, blog directories are cropping up all over the Internet. Use sites like Blogwise (*www.blogwise.com*) and Globe of Blogs (*www.globeofblogs.com*) to search for blogs by topic, geographic region, or author and find out how to get involved to promote your book or your own blog.

So how does this connect with reporters reading blogs? Most reporters have a stock list of experts they go to when they need a quote or other information for a story. At the same time, most of them are always on the lookout for new experts to turn to. Especially for nonfiction writers, having your name and your book on the appropriate blogs can quickly earn you entry into the source files of journalists all over the country, and even around the world.

Using Your Platform

We discussed ways to build a platform for yourself in Chapter 3. After you've been published, you can put that platform to work in promoting your book. This creates a kind of symbiotic relationship, with the benefits flowing both ways: Having a book published helps solidify and even heighten your platform, while your platform gives you unique opportunities to promote your book.

Personal Appearances

Whether you teach, lead conferences and seminars, or do stand-alone speaking engagements, you can turn virtually any personal appearance into a promotion opportunity. If your book is related to the courses you teach, you might be able to use it as a supplemental textbook for the class, or include it on your reading list. You can make copies of your book available to the people who attend your conferences and seminars, either by including it in the registration fee or by setting up a display and sales table at the back of the room. For speaking engagements, update your bio to include the title of your book, so the person who introduces you can inform your audience that you're the author.

Virtual Appearances

If you have a Web site or blog, be sure to update your site to include information about your book. Ideally, you should be able to show the book's cover, along with links to the publisher's Web site and to an online bookseller like Amazon.com or BarnesandNoble.com. And, of course, make sure your Web site includes a way to contact you.

You also might want to consider setting up an RSS (for Really Simple Syndication) feed from your site; this technology allows you to send periodic updates to people who subscribe (for free) to receive such information via e-mail. You can use an RSS feed to let people know what others are saying about your book, when you reach sales milestones, or even other news about you that might not be directly related to your book.

According to Nielsen/Net Ratings, *www.amazon.com* is routinely the second most popular multicategory commerce site on the Internet. It averages nearly 8 million unique visitors a week, each of whom spends an average of just over twelve minutes browsing the site. A link from your site to *www.amazon.com* is an easy way to direct potential sales of your book.

Tout Your Expertise

Once you've written and published a book (particularly nonfiction), you are considered an expert on the topic. Published novelists can be considered experts, too, on their genre and on creative writing in general. However, you probably will have to seek out opportunities to show off your expertise. Start by using search engines to find recent news stories on your topic and contact information for the reporter who wrote the story; many newspapers today include reporters' phone numbers and e-mail addresses at the end of their stories.

ESSENTIAL

Reporters get a lot of spam e-mail, including e-mailed news releases. To bypass spam filters and junk e-mail folders, be as specific as you can in the subject line of your e-mail. Precise subject lines such as "Re: Your June 22 article on fad diets" or "Tips for your 'Cooking Healthy' column" are more likely to be opened and read.

When you find appropriate articles and contacts, send a brief e-mail to the reporter saying that you read his story and enjoyed it. Then tell him that the next time he needs information on that topic, you are available for interviews. You can point out (after you've said you enjoyed his article) an angle that his story didn't cover, interesting facts and figures, and the like. Be sure to do this tactfully; you won't make any friends if you come across as accusatory or arrogant. Finally, be sure to include your contact information so he can get in touch with you for future articles.

You can do the same thing with radio and television journalists. Again, the best way to do this usually is by e-mail, because it's less intrusive than a phone call and gives the reporter a written record for his files. If you decide to call, be sure to ask if the reporter has a few minutes; he may be working on deadline, which means he won't have time to chat.

Accessing Your Network

First-time authors usually have little trouble disposing of their free author's copies. They're so proud and excited to see the fruits of their labors that they hand out autographed copies to every relation and friend they can think of, and the relations and friends gladly accept them, even if they aren't interested in actually reading the book. But this is only the first step in accessing your network.

If you're like most people, your network probably is bigger than you think. It consists of the people you know, and of the people they know as well. The challenge for you is figuring out how to spread the word through the people you know, who will spread it to the people they know, and so on. One simple way to do this is to always keep business cards handy. Make sure they include your name, e-mail address, Web site, and the name of your book; if you want to get fancy, you can even put an image of your book's cover on one side of the card. Give them to business contacts, friends, and relatives, and give them permission to pass them along to their own circle of contacts.

If you belong to a church or civic group, find out if you can put an announcement in the group's newsletter about your book. If you have a day job (other than your own writing), see if the employee newsletter would be interested in doing a short piece on you and your book. If your neighborhood grocery store has a community bulletin board, ask the manager if it's okay to put up a small poster announcing the publication of your book. (Be sure to include on such a poster that you're a resident of the community—bragging rights count here, too.)

Because writing is a solitary activity, many writers feel shy and uncomfortable talking about their books or other publishing successes. Sometimes even fielding compliments can feel uncomfortable. But remember that getting published still is enough of a rarity that most people are genuinely impressed by it, and they genuinely enjoy meeting a bona fide author. It's okay to take pride in your work and to let other people know about it, and it's okay to enjoy the warm glow you get when people praise your ability and congratulate you on your success.

ALERT!

Some authors, especially self-published ones, try to market their books by buying promotional items like pens, bookmarks, mouse pads, and magnets emblazoned with their name, Web site, or the name of their book. But your best weapon isn't advertising. Save your money and concentrate your efforts on publicity, which is both effective and free.

Parlaying Coverage

When it comes to marketing, parlaying coverage means doing the work once and getting two or more pieces of publicity out of it. Businesses do this all the time. When a car dealer gets an award for its service department, or when a hotel is rated four diamonds by AAA, you'll probably see both a news story about the award or rating and then you'll see it in the business' advertising.

You can do the same thing in marketing your writing. If you're getting an award for something, even if it isn't related to your writing, send a news release to your local newspaper announcing it, and be sure to note that you're the author of your book. It doesn't have to be lengthy or complicated. It can be as simple as this:

> *Jim Robinson of West Suburb will receive the Volunteer of the Year award from the Greater Metropolis Chamber of Commerce at the annual meeting May 18. Robinson, who founded the Greater Metropolis Literacy Project, also is the author of* The Great American Novel *(Big City Publishers, September 2005).*

As always, be sure to include your contact information. You never know when a small thing like this might lead to bigger things. Even a small blurb in the local media puts your name (and the title of your book) in the public eye, and there's a possibility that the editors of the local media will think there's a good story in a profile of you, which further promotes you and your book. Think of parlaying coverage as connecting the dots for the folks in the media. They might not be interested in your award alone, and they may not be interested solely in the fact that you've had a book published. But, by putting the two together, you increase the news value of even the shortest blurb, thus improving your chances of getting the coverage you want.

Recognizing Opportunities

Participating in activities that aren't directly related to your writing or your book can nevertheless help promote both, and doing so also helps your efforts to parlay coverage. One author agreed to do a book signing as part of a fundraiser for her local library. She donated her free author's copies of two of her books for the event and wrote a news release for the local newspaper. The hook for the news release was the fundraiser, but the news release also pointed out that the author was a local resident. That led to a profile of the author in the local newspaper, which mentioned all of the author's books, including an upcoming one.

FACT

Nearly all newspapers subscribe to wire services like the Associated Press, and these services are always looking for timeless features that are of interest to other member papers. If you live in Iowa, a profile of you in the *Fort Dodge Messenger* could easily get picked up by AP and run in several other Iowa newspapers.

If people in your community are talking about you and your book, word will get to the people in the next community, who will pass it on to the community further down the road. Do what you can to get that initial splash, regardless of size, and the ripples will take care of themselves.

chapter 15

Other Roads to Getting Published

Today's writers have more options than ever for seeing their work in print (or, in the case of e-publishing, in virtual print). Just like everything else in publishing, some ideas and methods are more viable than others. If you want to strike out on your own, whether from frustration with traditional publishing or from a burning spirit of entrepreneurship, you need to do the same kind of research, planning, and cost-benefit analysis that's required for any successful writing career.

Creating Your Own Publication

Especially when you can't convince a traditional publisher to take on your idea, the concept of starting your own newsletter, blog, or other publication is quite appealing. Many writers in this position envision instant success with a loyal following—and, maybe, enough fame to make the editors who rejected you kick themselves once or twice. The truth is, there's a lot of hard work involved in launching a publication, whether online or in hard copy. There's also a lot of satisfaction to be had, if that's where your passion lies.

Doing your own thing will require even more research than going the traditional route. Not only do you have to figure out who will be interested in what you have to say and how to make them aware of your publication, you also have to know the actual costs of finding, hooking, and keeping your readers. This is where the fantasy falls apart for many writers; they underestimate the time and energy it takes to build and retain a viable base for their product. One survey showed that the average e-zine editor, for instance, spends up to 60 percent of his time marketing—not writing, not thinking up cool new ideas to write about, but marketing.

ESSENTIAL

If you decide to create your own publication, make sure it's something you feel passionate about and that you will continue to feel passionate about for a long time. If you get bored with the topic, your readers will get bored, too, and that's a recipe for failure.

It also takes time to build a following for your book, your newsletter, your blog, or whatever you're creating. There's a lot of competition for readers' attention out there, especially on the Internet. Most experts agree that you have to publish steadily for at least a year to gain a steady readership. That's a huge time investment, even if your newsletter is a weekly. For blogs, which readers often expect to be updated daily, even more of your time will be eaten up.

None of this is meant to discourage you from pursuing your dream. Lots of writers happily pour their energies into these activities, enjoying the freedom and decision-making power that comes from doing it yourself.

Many of them are quite successful, too. But sometimes the things that look the easiest require the most effort, and, if you're not prepared for the realities of striking out on your own, you may end up disillusioned and disappointed.

Self-Publishing

Self-publishing has gained in popularity in recent years, thanks in part to the Internet, which allows authors to more easily promote their products directly to paying customers. Be very clear: Self-publishing means you are hiring a printer to take your material and create physical books, period. A book printer normally does not do all the things that traditional publishers do, like editing, marketing, promotion, distribution, etc.

Some companies call themselves self-publishers, when really they are vanity publishers. The difference? Vanity publishers will print any book, regardless of merit, if the author has the cash, often making the author think that they are being published. In reality, authors usually don't have any control over editing, design, or other quality-assurance issues, and vanity-press books are almost never carried by booksellers or libraries.

FACT

There aren't any guarantees in publishing, no matter which route you take. Generally, self-publishing works best when you have a clear understanding of who your readers are and how to reach them. Only you can decide whether self-publishing is worth your time, money, and energy.

Reputable book printers may offer a range of services to the author interested in creating their own publishing house. In some cases, they might even offer marketing support. You still pay for the services, but, depending on the terms of the contract, you'll be more involved in making decisions about the final look and feel of your book.

One advantage to self-publishing is that overhead costs are lower, and so is the break-even point. Traditional publishers usually need to sell about 10,000 copies to break even, but self-publishers can hit that milestone with far fewer sales. With a strong marketing plan, you can see actual profits sooner rather than later.

What to Look For

To make sure you aren't getting snookered by a less-than-honest company, there are certain things you should look for. First, check the contract for the grant of rights. All rights should stay with you, and you should have complete control over the printed copies unless you have hired the company to do the marketing and distribution, etc. A genuine book printer serving self-published authors allows you to set the retail price of your book, and you should receive all the proceeds from sales of your book. If the "self-publisher" insists on setting the retail price, or giving you only a royalty percentage on your sales, you may be dealing with a vanity press in disguise. Another clue: Self-published authors get their own ISBNs, while vanity-press authors use ISBNs from the "publisher."

Pros and Cons

As with most things in life, there are advantages and disadvantages to self-publishing. On the plus side, you get much more control over the production of your book than you do with a traditional publisher. Your earnings per book may be higher, too, because advances in print-on-demand technology have dramatically lower production costs. You control the copyright and don't have to worry about reversion clauses or procedures, or what happens to your work if the publisher goes out of business.

On the con side, you take on all the responsibility of publishing and marketing your book, which requires investment of significant money and time. There's no guarantee that you'll ever see a return on that investment, either; you don't get an advance through self-publishing, and, as with any book, there's no guarantee of royalty earnings. Finally, you're on your own when it comes to things like copyright infringement and other potential legal issues.

Print on Demand

Print on demand, or POD, is a technology that allows authors or self-publishing companies to order print runs based on actual orders. In traditional publishing, most houses have to order at least 5,000 copies in order to get a discount on the per-copy price; POD drops the minimum print run to as low as 100, and additional copies can be ordered a dozen or two at a time. When it first came on the scene, the lead times for POD were fairly long, but over the past few years the time between ordering and actual printing has shrunk to between a few days and a couple of weeks.

POD publishers usually offer books for sale on their Web sites, and they sometimes will list their books with other online sellers like Amazon. com. When you're investigating PODs, make sure your book will have an ISBN and a barcode; traditional and online booksellers won't sell any book without an ISBN.

For self-publishing authors, the big advantage to PODs is lower up-front costs. In the bad old days, you had to order several thousand copies of your book, which most people ended up storing in their garages or basements. With POD, you can order, say, 500 copies for your first run and then restock smaller amounts as needed. Since the cost per copy is lower, you also can set a reasonable retail price that still allows you a respectable profit margin. Another perceived advantage for some writers: Unlike traditional publishing, your book stays in print as long as you want it to, regardless of sales.

E-Publishing

The digital age has spawned a whole new range of opportunities for aspiring writers. Between personal blogs and desktop publishing, home pages on the Web and the advent even of pod-casting, the do-it-yourself trend has extended well into publishing territory, and many writers are questioning whether they even need the old school any more. Certainly, this generation of writers has opportunities never dreamed of by our ancestors. But, even though the technology has changed, the basic tenets of professional, successful writing remain the same.

E-Books

E-books generated a lot of buzz when they first came out, and Stephen King gave the technology a boost a few years ago when he released one of his own titles exclusively as an e-book. One major hurdle—that of requiring special devices to read an e-book—has been virtually eliminated as more e-book publishers are using widely available formats like Adobe Acrobat for their books. To address concerns about piracy (this happened to King's e-book), some online sites are experimenting with subscription services, where you pay for and download an e-book and have a limited time to read it, say three or four weeks; when the reading period expires, the file won't open.

Even with these advances, the market for e-books remains small. People who love to read tend to also love the feel of a real book in their hands, and many casual readers don't like having to either print out an entire book or read it on their computer screens. Profits from e-books tend to be higher than with traditional publishing, but sales tend to be lower. In short, you're not likely to get rich overnight—or ever—by publishing e-books.

E-Zines, Etc.

New online magazines and Web sites go live every day, and all of them need content. Do a search for online writers, and you'll probably turn up dozens of matches. But, as with other forms of publishing, not all electronic writing gigs are created equal. In the Internet's relatively short life so far, all kinds of dubious sites have caught unsuspecting writers in their traps.

ALERT!

Lots of writers have been duped into writing for pay-per-click sites, where the writer supposedly gets paid each time an Internet user clicks through to read the writer's material. In fact, the promised revenue never materializes, and writers end up giving their work away. If your choice is between pay-per-click and traditional magazine markets, go the old-fashioned route.

At legitimate sites, however, you can earn quite respectable fees for your work, especially if you understand the unique needs of writing for the Web.

Again, it comes down to understanding your target readers. Online, you can lose readers even faster than in the print world; they only have to click the "back" button to escape content that bores, offends, or otherwise fails to serve their needs. The most effective Web content serves up useful information in easily digestible, easy-to-locate chunks.

Marketing Your Product

Whether you're launching a newsletter, starting a blog, or selling your self-published book, you need to have a marketing plan to reach your readers. For most writers, the plan includes a Web site, usually with a mechanism for ordering the product, whether it's a book or an opt-in for an e-mail newsletter. In fact, well-targeted e-mail newsletters can provide an extra boost for sales of your book because you can use it to announce personal appearances, link to articles about you or by you, and so on.

E-mail Lists

E-mail can be an effective marketing tool for you, but be careful that your tactics don't label you as a spammer. Spam works; according to the Pew Internet & American Life Project, more than 5 percent of people who have e-mail accounts have purchased something through a spam offer. That's a better response rate than the typical direct mail campaign, which averages between 1 and 2 percent, and that's why all of us with e-mail accounts continue to receive so much spam. But spamming can get you in trouble with the law and with your Internet Service Provider, which probably will kick you off if you're caught.

FACT

Some Web sites review e-books, but most print media still ignore e-books and self-published books. That may not be a big deal; book reviews tend to be less important in driving sales than other factors, like the topic, the writing quality, and promotional efforts like online chats, mentions on other Web sites and in other newsletters, etc.

You can purchase software programs to help you manage your e-mail lists, or you can use an online service. Some of these are free, like Topica (*http://lists.topica.com/*) or Yahoo! Groups (*http://groups.yahoo.com/*), and some charge. Your Web hosting service also may offer e-mail list hosting. Such a tool is essential for controlling the sending of your messages as well as subscribe and unsubscribe options.

Personal Appearances

A lot of your marketing and promotion campaign for your self-published book will be the same as the ideas you come up with for a traditionally published book. Book signings and readings at area bookstores and libraries, interviews with local and regional media, and speeches and seminars all can be effective ways to build awareness of and interest in your product. The tips in Chapter 14 also can be applied to your marketing plan.

Knowing What You're Paying For

Self-publishing can be a respectable way to get your words into the hands of interested readers. If you choose this route, you'll also have to choose which service providers to hire for the various support you'll need. In selecting a book printer, an editor, a cover designer, a Web site hosting service, a Web designer, or any other services, you'll be responsible for knowing what you're paying for; no one else is going to look out for your best interests.

Perform Due Diligence

There are legitimate editing and design services, and some of them even bill themselves as book doctors or marketing experts. Always check out any firms before you buy or sign a contract. Read the writers' Web sites to see if there are complaints or warnings about the company or person. Assess those complaints to see if they indicate genuine problems or if they seem to be the rants of a disgruntled writer. If the same types of complaints show up in more than one place, from more than one source—the company didn't deliver the editing services it promised, for example, or there were hidden fees added to the final bill—you probably will be better off looking for another company to perform those tasks for you.

Can You Do It Yourself?

Lots of businesses provide, for a fee, services and information that people could do or find on their own. That doesn't make these businesses illegitimate; sometimes it's worth the cash outlay to have someone else do the legwork for you, especially if you don't have the time or interest to do it yourself. The key is understanding your options, so you can make an informed choice.

Avoiding Scams

Unfortunately, the writing community is a tempting target for unscrupulous people who are anxious to dip into your bank account, and they use every means of flattery and manipulation to achieve their ends. Appeals to a writer's vanity are the most common (and most effective) tactic, because the scammers know how frustrating and ego-damaging it can be to enter the publishing game. If you can keep your ego in check, develop a healthy skepticism about offers that seem too good to be true, and be familiar with the hallmarks of a scam, you've got all the defenses you need to protect yourself.

The Usual Suspects

Most of the scams aimed at writers have been around for donkey's years. The perpetrators introduce a new wrinkle now and then, hoping to ensnare some unsuspecting newbies, but the basic methods for separating writers from their money remain the same. The good news is that these age-old scams are pretty easy to spot, if you pay attention to the clues. Devious people are also quite creative, and there are new scams making the rounds all the time. Most of them are variations of the old standbys, but some of them have just enough flair to make them seem different and, well, plausible. You owe it to yourself and your career to proceed with caution and fully investigate any offer.

Up-Front Fees

These go by a number of labels now, since even the newest of writers knows that "reading fees" are a no-no. Questionable agents now call them by a variety of names, including marketing fees, contract fees, expenses, and retainers. The main point always is that you're expected to pay this money before the agent agrees to represent you.

Generic Solicitations

Be wary of any so-called agent or publisher who contacts you with a "we got your name from . . ." opening. These outfits troll writers' Web sites and even the U.S. Copyright Office looking for victims. A genuine agent or editor who saw and liked something you wrote might contact you, but it won't be with a form letter.

Broad Appeals for Writers

You've seen the ads in writer's magazines saying, "We're looking for writers . . ." often followed by a list that covers every imaginable type of writing. Real agents don't need to advertise for writers; they already get more submissions than they can read. Another tip-off: Real agents do not represent short stories, poetry, magazine articles, or children's books, and you don't need an agent to approach publishers for these things.

"Coinvestment" Requirements

These are the same old vanity publishing scams dressed up in a new outfit, and they aim to take advantage of the confusion some writers have about the difference between vanity publishing and self-publishing. With these operations, you'll have no control over the finished product, you typically have to sign over the rights in your work, and chances are you'll never see a finished product.

Contests

Legitimate contests often carry minimal entry fees, which are used to create the prize pool and pay the costs of administering the contest. Scam contests offer huge "prizes," then notify every entrant that, although they didn't win the prize, their work is still worthy of publication. The catch: Your work won't be included in the anthology unless you purchase a copy.

Writers Scamming Writers

Unfortunately, some frustrated writers apparently have abandoned their own dreams and are instead trying to make a living off the hopes of other writers. They may offer "fool-proof" ways of getting your book on the Amazon bestseller list, or of boosting sales at brick-and-mortar stores. They may claim to have a new scheme for getting agents and editors to notice and buy your work.

The usual catch to all these schemes is that they cost you money, and you get nothing of value in return. In fact, some of them can damage your reputation and your writing career beyond repair, like the one to manipulate the system at Amazon so you can claim bestseller status. When you get caught, you not only will lose the gains you were after, but you'll likely be blacklisted as well. Publishers, agents, editors, and booksellers talk to each other. Writers who employ fraudulent or unethical tactics to skew their sales numbers or other credentials quickly earn an unsavory reputation, and they are firmly pushed out of the legitimate publishing business.

ALERT!

Read any contract carefully before you sign it to make sure you aren't giving away your own rights or agreeing to terms that haven't been disclosed in preliminary discussions. If you don't have a good grasp of legal terminology and the implications, hire a lawyer to review the contract for you.

Of course, not all ideas promoted by other writers are scams. Some of them are born of good intentions, but fall far short of accomplishing their intended goal—usually because they don't understand the publishing business. Web sites that purport to link writers and agents, for example, by giving agents a secure place to read work posted by writers (who, often, have paid for the privilege) are more or less useless. The problem for agents is not being unable to find good material; the problem is that they're inundated with so much material, good and bad, every day. A legitimate, established agent is not likely to go to a Web site to read an unknown author's material, something the site owner probably doesn't understand.

chapter 16

Writing Full-Time

Ah, the ubiquitous writer's fantasy: to be so well-known, so in-demand, so well-paid for your *morceaux* that you can quit your boring, soul-destroying day job and devote your full time and attention to your true passion. You'd spend summer afternoons lazing in the hammock with a glass of iced tea, thinking up new plots, fielding calls from Oprah, and debating who should portray you in the movie of your life. Unfortunately, back here on Earth, such fantasies never come true. Prepare yourself for the hard realities of writing full-time.

Great Expectations

Many writers believe they could be the next Hemingway if they could just escape the daily grind most of the world is accustomed to and spend all their time and energy on writing. Words would flow like honey, thick and rich, and there would be no such things as pressure or writer's block. Life would be one grand sweet song if all they had to do all day was write.

Sounds great in theory. In practice, it's an altogether different song. Even the people who don't have other jobs to pay the bills don't spend their days doing nothing but writing. They do the same things all other writers have to do—coming up with ideas, checking the markets, keeping files and records straight, negotiating contracts, coping with deadlines, and, occasionally, battling writer's block. When you make the jump from working for a paycheck to writing full-time, you don't just become a writer. You also become a salesperson, an office manager, a bill collector, a financial analyst, a business planner, a researcher, and your very own crisis counselor. And you do all that without any guarantee of a steady paycheck, or indeed of any kind of pay.

FACT

Writing is a solitary activity, but writers should get out in the world on a regular basis. Real-life experience, even through a part-time job or volunteer work, enriches your writing and keeps it in perspective. The best writing isn't done in a self-imposed vacuum; it incorporates the color, texture, and feelings of life in all its variety and complexity.

This isn't meant to discourage you from pursuing your dream. It's just a reality check, so you know what you're getting into when you decide to go for it. Trying to squeeze in quality writing time around all your other commitments is tough, but being disillusioned and disappointed by your dreams is worse. If you're well-informed and well-prepared for what lies ahead, the unique challenges of becoming a full-time, self-employed writer won't seem quite as daunting.

Preparing the Ground

Financial planners always advise us to save between three and six months' worth of household expenses to avoid calamity in the event of a job loss. That's also what you should plan to have in the bank if you're planning to quit your regular job to write full-time. You'll be losing a steady income, and unless you already have contracts in place for articles, short stories, or books, chances are you won't see any money from your writing for quite a long time. Remember, query to response can take two to six weeks; completing the assignment can take another two weeks to several months; acceptance of the work and authorization of payment can take another one to three months; and, if you don't get paid until publication, it'll be several more months before you see any money. That's a long time to go without groceries or gas money.

One way to prepare for this is to save all the money you can so you have a comfortable amount to live on while your career ramps up. If you're in a domestic partnership or marriage, look for ways to cut expenses so you can live comfortably on one income, and put your paycheck in the savings account until you make the switch. This will give you a larger cushion for emergencies and other unplanned expenses until you begin to receive income from your writing.

Also plan for the loss of benefits, if you have them, when you quit your job. How will you pay for health insurance, for example? Vacations? Retirement savings? Many of us take these things for granted because they're provided by our employers. Once you're on your own, though, you'll be responsible for paying and planning for all these things. Gone will be automatic deductions for such things as 401(k) plans and Christmas clubs, and if you get sick or decide to take a week off to visit your sister in Wyoming, no one will be paying you for the time you spend not working.

Setting Goals

When you set out to write full-time, you're taking responsibility for managing your time and following your vision. To do that effectively, set specific goals for yourself, both short-term and long-term. If your ultimate goal is to become a book author, but you don't have the right platform or credentials to support that effort right now, then your short-term goals should be to build that platform and collect those credentials (discussed in Chapters 2 and 3). Don't be afraid of starting small and building from there; that's the way most careers are made, and not just in publishing. Besides, each small step you take brings you that much closer to your big dream, and it's easier to keep yourself motivated if you can measure your progress rather than focus on how distant your dream still seems.

Make your short-term goals ones that are within your control. A goal of getting published in *GQ* is laudable, but you can't force that to happen. A more realistic goal would be to submit appropriate material to, say, six national magazines. That opens up many more possibilities for you, even if *GQ* isn't the right market for your work.

Making a Schedule

When you're completely on your own, it's easy to fritter your time away in daydreams, household chores, anything but writing and writing-related tasks. Like all self-employed people, successful full-time writers are self-starters, able to set a schedule for their work and stick to it, at least most of the time. They usually have a plan for the day, and maybe even a self-imposed quota for the work they want to get done. They take their self-employment as seriously as any traditional job, knowing that if they don't dedicate their time and energy to what needs to be done, no one else is there to do it for them.

Time has a remarkable illusory quality, which is what makes it slip away so quickly even when we think we have plenty of it. Goals, schedules, and self-imposed deadlines keep time from escaping you and turn it into the valuable tool it is for your writing career.

You can arrange your schedule any way you like; that's part of the freedom of being self-employed. You might prefer to write in the mornings and reserve your afternoons for attending to queries, submissions, and market research; you might prefer to reverse that. You might not feel the need to divide your time that way, instead deciding to be seated at your desk by nine o'clock each morning and prioritizing that day's tasks. Whatever works for you is fine. Just make sure you don't putter along for three months and suddenly discover that you haven't completed a project or sent out a query.

Creating a Business Plan

Once you've decided to become a full-time writer, you've also decided to become a small business owner. And, like any other small business owner, you'll need to have a plan for the success of your enterprise. Setting goals and a schedule will help you do that. But you also have to think like a business person.

Income and Expenses

Always keep copies of checks and receipts. You can use the check copies to check your year-end earnings statements from publishers, and receipts will help you track the expenses associated with your writing. You also should have an expense diary, where you can record the amount and other details of an expense when you don't have a receipt.

If you earn $600 or more from a single publisher, you'll receive IRS Form 1099 at the end of the year, which will state all your earnings from that particular publisher. The $600 threshold is an IRS requirement, but some publishers send out 1099s for earnings of less than $600, too. If you sell your work to more than one publisher during a calendar year, you should receive a 1099 from each of them.

FACT

If you have an agent, he or she will send you a 1099 listing all your earnings that passed through the agent's office. This usually will not include magazine sales, because most agents don't handle such sales. Your 1099 from your agent should reflect only the monies you actually received, not including the agent's commission.

On the expense side, you need to keep track of such things as office supplies, equipment (computers, copiers, fax machines, etc.), postage and shipping costs, book purchases and magazine subscriptions (related to your writing), membership dues to writers' organizations, conference expenses, and travel expenses, including taxi fares, tolls, parking fees, and mileage. As long as these expenses are related to your writing, you can claim them as deductions on your income tax return. If you aren't sure whether an expense is a valid deduction, keep a record of it and ask your tax preparer about it at tax time.

Writing-related deductions, including deductions for a home office, are generally limited to your writing income in any given year. If your expenses exceed your income, you can't deduct the extra expenses, but you might be able to carry them over into the next year, as long as your writing doesn't fall under the IRS "hobby rule." To avoid that, do your best to show a profit from your writing in at least three out of five years.

Business Structures

Most writers, at least at the beginning of their careers, don't bother with setting up a formal business structure. Even when you're self-employed as a writer and have no other job-related income, your writing business is considered a sole proprietorship—the simplest and most basic business structure. As a sole proprietor, you don't have to file separate business income tax returns; you can attach Schedule C to your personal income tax form.

As your career progresses, however, you might want to consider a more formal business arrangement. You can set up a limited liability company, or LLC; bestselling authors sometimes set up separate LLCs for each of their books, which can protect other assets in the event of a lawsuit. Other options include partnerships (you and at least one other person) and corporations. Each state has its own laws regarding each of these structures, and there are pros and cons to each. Do some research and consult an attorney before deciding whether it makes sense for you to go beyond the sole proprietorship structure.

Accessing Markets

Whether you're writing part-time or full-time, a good share of your time and energy will go into researching markets (see Chapter 4 for more on this). Many beginning writers make the mistake of placing imaginary limits on what they can write and what they want to write. But, when you've made the full-time commitment to writing, you'll benefit from expanding your horizons when it comes to searching for places to sell your work.

FACT

Local governments sometimes hire freelance writers to help them apply for grants or get the word out on upcoming special elections or issues affecting residents. Professional grant writers usually charge a flat fee, plus a small percentage of the awarded grant, for their services. Other projects can be written for a flat fee or on an hourly basis, usually with a not-to-exceed maximum.

Try putting your various writing projects into one of two categories: the personal project, and the business project. The personal project is the one that speaks to your writer's soul, the one you can't wait to work on, the one that makes you want to be a writer in the first place. The business project is one that will further your writing career by giving you another clip for your portfolio and, one hopes, a boost to your bank balance. Business projects also can be used to bring you closer to your long-term goals. If you want to write a book eventually for middle-school children about scuba diving, you should try to sell articles on similar topics to magazines aimed at younger readers.

Fiction writers in particular should remain open to nonfiction writing opportunities. In book publishing, it's easier for new writers to break in with a nonfiction book than with a novel, and a nonfiction book credit will help convince an agent or editor that you're capable of writing book-length work. The competition in magazine markets also is stiffer for fiction than for non-fiction, so you might find it easier to break in there, too. You can still relate your nonfiction to your fiction; magazine credits on scuba diving, marine life, and related topics add credibility to your pitch for that middle-school adventure novel set aboard a modern-day cruise ship.

Juggling Projects and Deadlines

One of the biggest challenges facing full-time writers is managing your time. When you don't have a regular day job, it's easy to fool yourself into thinking you have plenty of time to do lots of writing projects; you tend to forget about other obligations of daily life, like running to the grocery store, doing the laundry, attending your children's soccer games or concerts or plays, and spending time with your family and friends. Because your schedule is your own as a full-time writer, it's your responsibility to be realistic about what you can and cannot do.

Keep Track of Your Projects

One of your first priorities should be to devise a system for keeping track of your projects. Professional writers usually have several projects going at once, in various stages of development. They may be working against a deadline for a magazine article on fly fishing, researching another article on the history of jousting, polishing a short story for submission, and working on plot points for a novel, all while waiting for responses to a query about a nonfiction book on herbal medicine.

FACT

Calendars make convenient tracking devices; you can note when you mailed your material, when you should expect a response, when your deadlines are, and professional and personal events. Having all this data in one place also can help you plan your schedule and determine whether you have enough time to do additional projects.

Even if you're not quite that busy yet, you need a way to keep tabs on the details of each of your projects. There's no right or wrong way to do this;

create a system that works and is convenient for you. It should include such things as what you submitted (a query, a completed article, a proposal, etc.), where you submitted it, when you should expect to get a response (based on listings in the market directories), and where you plan to send it next if this market doesn't pick it up.

Your tracking system also should include a to-do list for projects that aren't ready to be marketed yet and an organized filing system to keep the details of each project together. If each of your projects has its own file folder, you can keep all the paperwork associated with that project, such as rejection slips or e-mails, in that folder, and that lets you see at a glance the history and progress of that particular project. Given that months can go by between when you submit something and when you receive a response, such a filing system helps refresh your memory. It also gives you a place to put notes about new developments or ideas relating to that project.

Stagger Deadlines

A common mistake among new writers is bunching up project deadlines. It is possible, and sometimes even desirable, to work on more than one project at a time, but it's also extraordinarily easy to stretch yourself too thin. And, when that happens, chances are you won't be doing your best work on any of your current projects.

Sometimes writers are afraid to say no to assignments, even when the deadlines conflict with prior obligations. Your natural instinct, especially when you're just starting out to live your dream, is to grab every opportunity that comes your way, even if it means that you won't have time to sleep for the next six weeks. But you aren't always stuck in the take-it-or-leave-it trap when it comes to deadlines. If you think you'll have difficulty meeting a deadline, for any reason—other projects, a scheduled vacation, or whatever—ask the agent or editor if the deadline is negotiable. You might be surprised at how willing editors and publishers are to adjust schedules for projects and writers they really want.

There are advantages to working on more than one project at a time. Having several projects in the hopper helps ease the natural worries most writers have about receiving rejections. When you always have another idea to be polished and fitted for the right market, you're less likely to obsess about the fate of one of your other ideas.

Protecting Your Reputation

Perhaps more than any other business, success in publishing depends as much on your professional image and reputation as it does on your talent and ideas. These intangible qualities can influence your career in ways you may never even realize. Editors who have had good experiences with you, or who have heard about what a treat you are to work with, often will seek you out when they have assignments that you're well-suited for. Such instances mean much more than just a warm and fuzzy feeling for your ego; they mean less work for you in market research and querying, because the projects are coming to you. So your reputation is an asset worth investing in and protecting.

Follow Business Etiquette

You project an image in your first contact with an agent or editor, and that image will color, for good or bad, the project you're hoping to sell. This is why following the submission guidelines is important. They aren't designed to exclude you from publishing's paradise. They are designed to separate the desirable grain from the undesirable chaff in the most efficient way possible. Sidestepping or ignoring the guidelines more than likely will flag your material as chaff. Following the guidelines improves your odds of being picked up as grain. Take these steps to establish and protect your reputation on paper:

- Get the name and publication or company of the recipient right, and use courtesy titles (Mr., Ms.) until you're invited to use first names. If you don't know whether the recipient is a man or woman, use the full name in addresses and salutations.
- Make sure your name, address, telephone number (with area code), and e-mail address appears on every piece of correspondence with an agent or editor.
- Double-check your SASEs to make sure they include the proper postage and your own address.

- Use standard business and manuscript formatting—single-spaced for query and cover letters, double-spaced for manuscript pages, with at least one-inch margins all around.
- Print all submissions only on one side of the page. Never handwrite submissions.
- Send all submission materials in one package—cover letter, SASE, sample chapters or completed pieces, etc.

Business etiquette applies to telephone manners, too. Once you get an assignment or build a relationship with an agent or editor, some of your communication will be done over the phone. It's important to remember that this is still a business communication, and you should strive to be on your best professional behavior. Some tips for achieving that:

- Keep your mouth free of gum, pens, food, and other foreign objects when you're on the phone.
- Use your normal speaking voice; don't whisper, and don't shout, even on a cell phone.
- Use professional language. Don't swear or use vulgar expressions.
- Avoid multi-tasking. Don't try to work on your computer, sort the mail, feed the dog, or wash the dishes while you're on the phone.
- Keep the conversation on track. Editors and agents rarely have time for idle chit-chat.
- Don't call unless it's absolutely necessary.
- When it is absolutely necessary to call, always ask first if this is a good time to talk. If it isn't, ask for a more convenient time, and, whenever possible, agree graciously to postpone the call until then.

The prevalence and convenience of e-mail has greatly reduced the amount of time authors have to spend on the phone with agents and editors. E-mail is an efficient and less intrusive method for exchanging information, asking and answering questions, and even scheduling phone dates. If you can't decide whether you should call or e-mail an agent or editor, always e-mail first; it's more respectful of the agent's or editor's time, and usually you can get what you need this way.

Don't call agents or editors with queries, to press for a decision on a submission, to deliver progress updates, or to complain about a rejection. This wastes time and marks you as an amateur. Even when you're established and the rules for submitting ideas relax a little, e-mail and snail mail remain the preferred contact methods for most agents and editors.

Keeping Your Promises

Professional writers are honest in their dealings with agents and editors, and they don't make promises they can't keep. Whenever you submit a query or other material (even before you have a contract, which puts these promises in writing), you are making an implicit promise that you're telling the truth about yourself and your work. That means you don't claim to be a published author if you're not, you don't claim to have endorsements that you don't have, you don't try to pass off someone else's material as your own, and you don't agree to deadlines that you can't meet. Misleading an agent or editor puts a big black mark against your name and, potentially, your future as a writer.

That said, and this being an imperfect world, there may be times when you can't keep some of your promises for reasons that are beyond your control. Accidents, sudden illness, technical problems, and other unforeseen issues might interfere with your ability to meet a deadline, for example. When these things happen, communicate with your agent and editor. Don't make excuses, but do explain the problem and outline a plan for getting back on track. Facing the issue squarely and immediately is the hallmark of a true professional, and it is the only protection you have for your reputation when things don't go as planned.

It's important to always keep the lines of communication open with your agent or editor. Don't ignore e-mails and phone calls. If you don't have time to respond fully right away, at least send a message acknowledging the contact and stating when you'll be free to address it. Then be sure to live up to your promise of following up.

Cooperation

Most agents and editors prefer to see themselves as part of a team with their authors. The team's goal is to provide the best possible content for readers, with each member of the team contributing substantially to the overall success of the project. Unfortunately, too many authors dismiss this model and instead view agents and editors as obstructionist and recalcitrant, or even as enemies. Obviously, the reputation these authors earn isn't one of professionalism.

Rejections and criticism are integral parts of the publishing game. Learn to receive them with aplomb, at least publicly. If you feel the need to rant and rave, do it in private. Defend your point of view, but do it with a civil tongue and an effort to see the other's perspective.

ESSENTIAL

One of the simplest ways to protect your reputation is to make sure you always have a backup of your work. Whether you print a hard copy, make a disk, or e-mail your work to yourself, routinely backing up everything you write is cheap insurance against technical catastrophes. You'll be awfully glad you have it when you need it.

The spirit of cooperation also comes into play when there are the inevitable glitches in the publishing process. Delays, questions, disagreements, and confusion are frustrating for everyone, but they don't always have to be crises. Train yourself to respond quickly and efficiently to such things, and to recognize and accept when the situation is beyond your ability to correct.

The old philosophy, "What goes around comes around," should be your guide here. The more patient, understanding, and cooperative you are when the problem is not your doing or your responsibility, the more likely you are to receive the same treatment when your circumstances require it.

Measuring Your Rewards

A great advantage to being self-employed, whether as a writer or in another profession, is that you get to define your own measures of success. You decide what is most important to you, what trade-offs you're willing to make, and what kind of balance you want. Most of us have several success yardsticks, but they usually can be divided into two broad categories: financial rewards and emotional rewards.

Go for the Money

As a full-time writer, the money will be important to you. You want to be able to support yourself, even if you never see the mega-bucks advances of celebrities and bestselling authors. If you're like most writers, you'll start out working for very small checks. As you gain more experience, the complexity and length of your assignments will rise, as will your per-word rate. You'll make your way into larger markets with a higher profile, which in turn will make you more salable to even bigger markets. Very likely, you'll get to a point where you have to turn down low-paying assignments so you have enough time to devote to the better-paying ones.

This is a natural progression, though it sometimes is a slow one. When you're a rookie, people in publishing will not value your talent or your time as highly. But, if you stick with it and do what's required to establish and maintain your credibility as a writer, the money will come.

Go for the Joy

Throughout this book, we've shown you how to approach writing as a business and a vocation. This is information you need if you want to fulfill your dreams of getting published and reap the rewards that go along with that accomplishment. But, even when it's work, writing should be fun. It should be stimulating and challenging. And that should be what motivates you to sit down and do the work.

But writing, like any other line of work, can grow stale, particularly if you lock yourself into a narrow niche and think you have to stay there for the rest of your career. It's true that writers, especially in fiction, and especially when just starting out, are expected to pick a genre and stick with it for at least their first two books; it helps build your readership and assists in marketing efforts to tap into and expand that base. But, even for novelists, there are ways around that, such as using different pen names for different genres.

FACT

The pay rates listed in the market directories aren't set in stone. As a new, unknown writer, you might be offered less than what is listed; as an established writer with a solid reputation for delivering good material on time, you can negotiate for more. Use the market listings as a ballpark estimate rather than a guarantee.

If you find that your writing career is losing its freshness, think about ways to recapture the joy of writing. This might mean keeping a personal project close at hand and taking periodic breaks from your business projects to work on your labor of love. It might mean taking the risks you had to take at the beginning of your career, stretching your skills and trying different styles and being willing to face rejection in a new format or market. It might even mean taking a break from writing altogether, until you feel the old, familiar itch in your fingertips that signals the formulation of a new and grand idea.

One of the terrific things about writing is that there's no mandatory retirement age. You have a whole lifetime to explore any kind of writing you like, and that's a fringe benefit you won't find in many other vocations. As a full-time writer, always be aware of where your joy is. Sometimes, it's the only thing that makes the trials and tribulations of the writing life truly worthwhile. If you lose track of it, don't be afraid to go looking for it again.

appendix a

Glossary of Terms

AAR
Association of Author's Representatives; professional organization has established codes of conduct for legitimate literary agents to follow.

ABA
American Booksellers Association, a trade organization for publishers and booksellers.

ABI
Advance Book Information form, used to list upcoming books in directories like Books In Print.

Acceptability/satisfactory clause
Found in most publishing contracts; allows the publisher to require changes to or reject unsatisfactory material.

Acknowledgments
An author's thanks to or recognition of the people who helped him with the current book; may include his agent and editor, friends, consultants, etc. Acknowledgments may be part of the front matter or back matter of a book.

Acquiring editor
Also called an acquisitions editor. At a book publishing house, the person who champions a book idea at pub board and gets the okay to offer a contract to the author; usually an author's first point of contact throughout the writing and editing process.

Advance
In book publishing, an up-front payment against future royalty earnings. Advances usually are tied to an author's stature and sales expectations for the book.

Afterword
Part of a book's back matter, in which the author or someone else talks directly to the reader.

Agent
An author's representative, whose job is to market the author's material, negotiate contracts, audit statements, handle subsidiary rights sales, and other business matters. Legitimate agents earn money through commissions on such sales. Also called literary agents or author representatives.

Agented submissions
In book publishing, queries, proposals, and manuscripts that are forwarded to editors through literary agents. The large houses generally do not accept submissions directly from writers; they only accept agented submissions.

ALA
American Library Association, a trade organization for libraries around the United States.

All rights
Writers can sell all rights in a specific work to a publisher for a specified time or indefinitely. You can't sell any other rights to this particular work until the rights license period expires.

Angle
A particular slant or point of view. Often used to describe magazine articles and nonfiction book

proposals; a unique angle that hasn't been explored before is more likely to pique interest.

Anthology
A collection of writings, usually short stories, essays, or poetry, by one or more authors and published as a single book.

Appendix
Part of the back matter in a book containing additional information, usually reference material, such as other resources or glossaries.

Applicable law
Publishing contracts specify which state laws govern the agreement because writers, agents, and publishers often are in different states. The governing law always comes from the state where the contract originated, i.e., where the agent's or publisher's business is located. Also called governing law.

Author
Originator or creator, especially of written works. Originally used to refer to someone who invented or composed something, the word became linked with writing books in the fourteenth century.

Author copies
In book publishing, the number of free copies the author receives (specified in the contract). For hardcover books, most authors receive ten free copies; for paperback, you might receive twenty or twenty-five.

Author's bio
A one-page narrative, written in the third person, describing the author's qualifications to write a book. For magazine pieces, the bio may be one or two sentences.

Back matter
Material that is located at the back of a book. Common back matter items include the afterword, author's bio, glossary, and index.

Backlist
Books that have been in print for a year or more and are still available from the publisher.

Berne Convention
Arguably the most important of several international treaties protecting copyrights of writers, musicians, and other artists. One hundred countries are signatories to the Berne Convention, which automatically protects the copyrights of artists who are citizens of any of the member countries.

Bibliography
A formal citation of resources used in writing a book or paper.

Big Six
The giant international publishing conglomerates, all with U.S. operations based in New York City: HarperCollins, Holtzbrinck, Penguin, Random House, Simon & Schuster, and Time Warner. Also called the Six Sisters.

Blog
Short for Web log, a type of online journal or diary.

Blurb
A brief endorsement, usually by an expert or celebrity, of a book, often found on the back cover.

BOB
Acronym for "back of the book." In magazine publishing, the publication (and sometimes a specific issue of the publication) is called the "book." At many magazines, some departments and features have their regular homes at the back of the book.

Boilerplate
Standard. Most form letters, including form rejection letters, are called boilerplates. Many press releases also include boilerplate paragraphs with brief descriptions of the company issuing the release.

Break-out book
A book that sells unexpectedly well.

Byline
Author's credit in magazines and newspapers.

Clips
An author's published articles and stories; the most valuable clips, in terms of building a writing career, carry your byline.

Coauthor
A collaborator on a book, story, or article who receives byline credit.

Collaboration agreement
A contract defining the responsibilities and revenue splits between coauthors.

Commercial title
A book that is expected to have great sales potential to a broad audience (as opposed to literary or academic titles, which usually don't achieve bestseller status).

Commission
A percentage of earnings. The typical agent's commission for domestic sales is 15 percent.

Competition discussion
In nonfiction book proposals, a one-page examination of similar books already on the market.

Content edit
A review of a manuscript for content, organization, style, and other factors, as opposed to a line or copy edit for spelling, grammar, punctuation, etc.

Contributing writer
In magazine publishing and book anthologies, a writer who contributes an article or chapter but who is not on the magazine's staff or the primary writer for the book.

Contributor copies
Small and literary magazines often pay writers whose work they publish with copies of the issue in which the writer's work appears.

Copublishing
An arrangement in which the author and the publisher split the expenses of producing and publishing a book; sometimes a viable method of self-publishing, but can be open to abuse.

Copy edit
Also called a line edit. Reviewing a manuscript for spelling, grammar, and other mechanics; may also include fact-checking.

Copy editor
The editor who checks material for style, spelling, grammar, punctuation, and other mechanics; often also acts as a fact-checker.

Copyright
An umbrella of rights covering artistic creation and expression and the sale, production, or publication of such work.

Copyright notice
A notice printed on a copyrightable work, including works posted online, that identifies the copyright owner and the date (usually only the year) of the copyright. Most copyright notices are formatted like this: Copyright © 2005 by Jane Doe.

Cover letter
A business letter sent with materials that have been requested by an agent or editor.

Credit line
Generally applicable to photos and other graphics, a notice identifying who took the photo or created the illustration.

Cutline
A brief description of a photo, chart, or illustration. Also called a caption.

Deadline
A due date for material. Originally, a deadline was a line around a prison, beyond which an inmate was liable to be shot.

Deck or dek
In magazine publishing, the sentence or phrase below the headline, which further describes the article's content. Usually printed in text that is smaller than the headline but larger than the body copy. Also called deck copy.

Dedication
Part of the front matter of a book, in which the author dedicates the work to another person or persons.

Department editor
In magazine publishing, the editor who is responsible for specific topics or sections of the publication, e.g., health editor, senior food editor.

Derivative work
Unoriginal; a work that is based on or taken from another existing work.

Development editor
In book publishing, the editor who checks finished manuscripts for structure, content, and layout (how the final printed page will look). Also called a project editor.

Dramatic rights
One of the many rights covered under the copyright umbrella, which includes plays, movies, and television shows derived from a written work.

Dust cover
The decorative paper wrapping around a hardcover book. Also called a dust jacket.

Editor in chief
The person in charge of a magazine or book publisher, ultimately responsible for editorial decisions and the daily operations of the editorial portion of the business.

Editorial meeting
A meeting of editors and, in book publishing, marketing, sales, and publicity staff, to discuss potential books or articles and other issues. Also called the publication board or pub board meeting.

Electronic publishing
Publication of information via the Internet, e-mail, or other electronic means, as opposed to print publishing.

Endorsement
A statement of support, often by an established celebrity of some sort, designed to influence people to purchase something or otherwise take action.

Excerpt rights
Also called first serial rights, excerpt rights are sold to magazines and, more rarely, to newspapers, to publish significant excerpts of soon-to-be-published books. If the excerpts are published after the book is published, the magazine purchases second serial rights.

Executed contract
A contract that is signed by all parties.

Executive editor
The person responsible for overseeing other editors; may report to or take the place of the editor in chief.

E-zine
An online magazine or newsletter.

Fair use
A legal doctrine that allows limited use of copyright material without seeking permission of the copyright owner.

FAQ
Acronym for Frequently Asked Questions, designed to help beginners or novices understand the basics of a topic.

First serial rights
The right to be the first to publish a specific work in periodical form (i.e., magazines, newspapers, newsletters, journals, etc.). These rights can be limited by geography, language, time, and other factors, e.g., first North American serial rights.

Flat fee
One-time payment, regardless of sales levels, as opposed to royalty payments, which are based on actual sales. Also used as opposed to hourly fees for certain freelance work and for work-for-hire arrangements.

FOB
Acronym for "front of the book." In magazine publishing, the publication (and sometimes a specific issue of the publication) is called the "book." At many magazines, some departments and features have their regular homes at the front of the book.

Foreign agent
An agent based in a foreign country who arranges sales to publishers in that country. U.S. agents often contract with foreign agents to handle foreign sales.

Foreign market
Any market outside the United States, or outside the geographic limits of the rights being sold. For North American rights, Canada and Mexico are not considered foreign markets, but Europe, South America, and Asia would be foreign markets.

Foreign rights
A set of rights under the copyright umbrella for publishing or distributing material in foreign markets, i.e., countries other than where the work was originally published.

Foreword
Part of the front matter of a book, often written by someone other than the book's author and sometimes taking the form of commentary on the book or the author's complete body of work.

Freelancer
Independent contractor, as opposed to being a full- or part-time member of a company's or publication's staff.

Front list
Newly published books, usually those expected to sell well.

Front matter
In book publishing, the introductory material printed before the book's main text, such as dedications, acknowledgments, introductions, and forewords.

Galley
Page proof showing the layout of an article, magazine, or book before it is printed and bound.

Genre
The category of a specific work, especially fiction. Genres were developed as a marketing tool to allow readers to easily find the types of books they want. Fiction genres include romance, mystery and suspense, science fiction and fantasy, and action/adventure.

Ghostwriter
A person who does the actual writing of a book or article but does not get author's credit for the work. Celebrities often hire ghostwriters to write autobiographies.

Governing law
Publishing contracts specify which state laws govern the agreement because writers, agents, and publishers often are in different states. The governing law always comes from the state where the contract originated, i.e., where the agent's or publisher's business is located. Also called applicable law.

Grant of rights
Most commonly, a transferal of specific rights in a specific work. The copyright owner grants certain rights to a publisher, which are spelled out in the contract.

Guarantee
In publishing contracts, a promise that a work is original and does not violate anyone's civil or intellectual property rights and that the person granting the rights actually is the legal owner of those rights.

Hard copy
A printed version of a work.

Hardcover
A book whose covers are made of cardboard. Also called hardback, hardbound, and case-bound.

Head or hed
In magazine and newspaper publishing, a headline.

Header
In manuscript formatting, a line or lines at the top of each page, typically indicating the page number and the author's name or the title of the work.

Honorarium
A token payment for services, often smaller than the full market value of the work.

Imprint
A specific line of books, often used by publishers to create brand identities for different genres or broad categories. Large publishers typically have several imprints.

In print
Books currently available from publishers. Also can refer to print-on-demand books.

Index
An alphabetical listing of terms and the page numbers where they can be found in a particular book.

Infringement
Using portions of copyright-protected work without the copyright owner's permission.

IRC
International Reply Coupon. Writers who submit their material overseas must include IRCs to pay for return postage.

ISBN
Acronym for International Standard Book Number, a unique number that identifies the publisher, edition, and type of binding for a particular book.

ISP
Internet Service Provider. America Online (AOL), Earthlink, and AT&T are examples of ISPs.

Joint contract
A contract between two or more collaborators with an agent or publisher.

Keywords
On the Internet, words that search engines look for.

Kill fee
In magazine publishing, the fee paid when an article has been turned in but will not be published. The fee usually is a percentage of the payment initially agreed upon for publication.

Layout
The design of text, photos, and other graphics on a printed page.

Licensing rights
One of many rights covered by copyright, typically covering merchandise like calendars, apparel, toys, and other retail items.

List
For book publishers, all the titles issued by a given publisher that are currently in print.

List price
The suggested selling price of a book. Also called the retail or cover price.

LMP
Literary Market Place, a comprehensive directory of publishers and literary agents available in public libraries and online.

Managing editor
The person responsible for daily editorial operations at a newspaper, magazine, or book publisher; usually reports to the editor in chief or the executive editor.

Manuscript
Copy for a book, short story, or article that has not been edited or typeset.

Market discussion
In nonfiction book proposals, a one-page description of the targeted readership of the book.

Mass-market paperback
A small, paperbound book, usually printed on less expensive paper and often sold in places like grocery stores as well as traditional booksellers.

Masthead
In newspapers and magazines, the section that lists the publication's ownership, publication schedule, subscription information, key staff, and other details.

Midlist
Newly published books that are not expected to and do not achieve bestseller status.

Model release
For photos and some illustrations, a form that authorizes the use of the person's likeness or image.

Ms/mss
Abbreviation for manuscript(s), commonly found in market listings.

Multiple submission
The process of submitting the same material to more than one agent, magazine, or publishing house for consideration. Also called a simultaneous submission.

News release
A written announcement of an event, new product, or other newsworthy items, sent to media outlets for publication. Also called a press release.

Next-book clause
In book publishing, a clause that gives the publisher the first right of refusal on the author's next book project. Definitions of "next-book project" can be open-ended or tightly defined. Sometimes called an option clause.

Number 10 envelope
Standard business-sized envelope, appropriate for mailing up to five 8 ½ x 11 pages, folded in thirds.

On acceptance
In magazine publishing, when payment is authorized. "On acceptance" generally means quicker payment than "on publication."

On publication
In magazine publishing, when payment is authorized. Because of the lengthy lead times for most magazines, authors who are paid on publication often wait several months before they receive a check.

On spec
Short for "on speculation." Magazine editors often will ask unknown writers or writers they haven't worked with before to submit their material on spec before deciding whether to purchase the article or story.

One-time rights
Unless otherwise specified in writing, you sell only one-time rights to any purchaser. This is why contracts specify things like first serial rights or reprint rights.

Option

A guarantee that no one else can purchase specific rights for a specified period. The option buyer pays the rights owner to keep those rights off the market until the option expires or the buyer decides to purchase the optioned right.

Option clause

See next-book clause.

Originality

The quality of newness in the way ideas are expressed and/or the angle explored.

Out of print

A book that is no longer available from the publisher is considered out of print. Contract clauses may include specific definitions of "out of print," based on sales thresholds, for example.

Outline

For fiction and nonfiction books, a chapter-by-chapter description of the material covered in the manuscript.

Over the transom

Slang for unsolicited or unagented material.

Overview

For nonfiction books, a narrative, two- to five-page discussion of the material covered in the proposed book.

Package

In magazines, a collection of related elements, usually including a main article, sidebars, photos, illustrations, and other graphics.

Page proof

A layout of pages, including all text and graphic elements, as they will appear when printed. Also called a galley.

Paperback

A book whose covers are made from paper rather than board. Also called a softcover or paperbound book.

Partial ms

Partial manuscript.

Pen name

Alias or pseudonym, often used by authors who want to write in different genres.

Periodical

Any magazine, newsletter, or other publication that is issued on a regular basis (e.g., daily, weekly, monthly, quarterly).

Permission

Written authorization from a copyright owner to use material from a protected work. Also can refer to the forms used to document such permission.

Personal essay

A narrative piece that relates the author's experience or opinion.

Plagiarism

The act of copying someone else's work and representing it as your own work.

Podcast

Internet-based audio programming that can be downloaded to MP3 players.

Preface

Part of a book's front matter, usually written by the author and often used to tell readers the author's reasons and goals for writing the book.

Press release

See news release.

Press run
The number of copies to be printed. Also called a print run.

Print on demand (POD)
Technology that allows publishers or printers to create only as many copies as needed.

Profile
A narrative article relating the personal experience, opinions, and personality of the subject, often a celebrity or other person of interest.

Project editor
In book publishing, the editor who checks finished manuscripts for structure, content, and layout (how the final printed page will look). Also called a development editor.

Promotion discussion
In nonfiction book proposals, a one-page description of things the author is willing to do to promote his or her book, including any special access the author has to groups that match the target readership.

Proposal
A marketing package that details a book idea, the market and competition for the idea, and the author's credentials for writing the book, designed to persuade an agent or editor to offer a contract.

Pub board
See editorial meeting.

Public domain
Work that is no longer protected by copyright. Public domain work does not require permission for its use, but it must be attributed to the original source to avoid charges of plagiarism.

Pull quote
A sentence or phrase pulled from the main text and set in large type on the printed page.

Quality paperback
A paperback book, printed on higher quality paper and usually with a larger trim size than mass-market paperbacks. Also called trade paperbacks.

Query/query letter
A business letter describing an article, story, or book idea in which the goal is to convince an agent or editor to ask for more material.

Reading fee
One of many descriptions unethical agents use to charge up-front fees to authors. The AAR prohibits members from charging any sort of up-front fees, which also may be called marketing fees or contract fees.

Release form
Authorization for the use of one's likeness or image in a published form.

Remainders
Leftover stocks of books that are sold at deep discounts when sales fall dramatically or stop altogether. Authors usually receive no royalties on remaindered books but can purchase copies at the remainder price.

Reprint
In book publishing, a reprint uses the original material, sometimes in a different format, such as a large print book previously published as a trade paperback. In magazine publishing, a reprint is republishing the original article or story in its entirety.

Reprint rights
Also called second serial rights; generally sold to magazines after an article, story, or book excerpt has been published elsewhere.

Reserve against returns
An accounting practice that allows a publisher to hold back a portion of an author's royalties in anticipation

that a certain percentage of the copies shipped to booksellers will be returned to the publisher.

Residual rights

Rights that remain with the copyright owner, especially rights that are not specifically addressed in a contract.

Response time

The average time it takes agents and editors to respond to submitted materials. Also called reporting time.

Returns

Books that are not sold at booksellers and are returned to the publisher, usually for full credit. Returns are deducted from an author's royalty payments.

Review copy

A free copy of a book sent to major newspapers, magazines, and others who might help promote the book.

Revised edition

A new printing of a book in which substantial changes have been made. Revised editions require new ISBNs; updated editions do not.

Reversion of rights

A mechanism by which rights that have been granted to another return to the original copyright owner, usually after a specified time has elapsed.

Rights license period

A defined time for which a copyright owner grants certain rights to a purchaser. In the case of books, the rights license period usually lasts as long as the book is in print.

Round-up

An article that quotes or relates the experiences of several subjects on a specific topic.

Royalties

The percentage of sales revenue paid to the author. Royalties can be based on list price or wholesale price, as well as on the number of copies sold.

RSS

Acronym for Rich Site Summary or Really Simple Syndication, a computer application that allows Internet users to sign up for e-mail alerts when information on a specific Web site is updated or changed.

SASE

Self-addressed, stamped envelope. Unless you're using IRCs, always stick the stamp(s) to your SASE.

Second serial rights

Also called reprint rights; generally sold to magazines after an article, story, or book excerpt has been published elsewhere.

Self-publishing

An arrangement in which the author takes on all the responsibilities of writing, designing, printing, marketing, and distributing his or her book.

Service piece

A "how-to" article that gives detailed instructions or steps to accomplish a task or goal.

Short run

A print run of less than 10,000 copies.

Sidebar

A short article related to the main piece.

Simultaneous rights

The rights an author sells when he or she offers the same material to nonoverlapping markets at the same time.

Simultaneous submission

See multiple submission.

Six Sisters

The giant international publishing conglomerates, all with U.S. operations based in New York City: Harper-Collins, Holtzbrinck, Penguin, Random House, Simon & Schuster, and Time Warner. Also called the Big Six.

Slant

See angle.

Slug

A word or brief phrase identifying an article or short story. Used to keep track of copy as it moves through the production process.

Slush pile

In magazine offices, material that has not yet been accepted or rejected. Sometimes called the "maybe" pile.

Snail mail

The U.S. Postal Service, so called because of its slow delivery times compared with e-mail.

Solicited

Material that has been requested on the basis of a query letter. Many agents and editors only read solicited material and will return, unopened, unsolicited materials.

Sp.

Abbreviation for spelling, used to note that the correct spelling of a word needs to be verified.

Special sales

In book publishing, special sales can include arrangements with book clubs, reissuing a title in paperback, and other exploitations of subsidiary rights in a work.

Spine

The part of a book that connects the front and back covers. Sometimes called a backbone.

Stet

A proofreader's mark signifying that other editing marks should be ignored. Stet is an abbreviation of the Latin phrase for "let it stand."

Stringer

In newspaper publishing, a freelance reporter or photographer.

Style guide

A manual that describes a publication's rules for style, punctuation, spelling, and other language rules. Common style guides include *The Chicago Manual of Style* and *The Associated Press Stylebook*.

Subagent

An agent hired to handle specific types of sales, such as foreign rights or movie rights. The agent and subagent typically split the commission from such sales.

Subsidiary rights

A range of additional rights covered under the copyright umbrella that, usually, have lower priority and often lower value than actual publication rights. Subsidiary rights include electronic rights, dramatic rights, translation rights, book club rights, etc.

Subsidy press

A publishing house that charges the author to produce a book. Subsidy presses often are scams set up to bilk authors, and subsidy books generally are not considered legitimate publishing credits. Also called subsidy publishing.

Syndication rights

A special form of serial rights that allows the syndicator to provide the same material to two or more publishing outlets at the same time.

Synopsis

In fiction writing, a brief narrative description of a novel's plot, including the ending.

Title page
In book publishing, the page near the front of the book that includes the book's title, author's name, and the name of the publisher.

TOC
Table of contents.

Trade journal
A newspaper, magazine, or newsletter aimed at members of specific professions or industries.

Trade paperback
A paperback book, printed on higher quality paper and usually with a larger trim size than mass-market paperbacks. Also called quality paperbacks.

Translation rights
The right to translate a work into a language other than the one in which it was originally published.

Trim size
The size of a book page after it has been trimmed. Mass-market paperbacks have smaller trim sizes than trade paperbacks.

Unagented writer
A writer who is not represented by a literary agent. Most small presses and some mid-sized publishers work with unagented writers; the larger houses prefer to work with agents.

Unearned advance
An advance that is not earned back through actual sales of the published book.

Unexecuted contract
A contract that has not been signed by all parties. You receive an unexecuted contract to review, sign, and send back to the publisher for their signature, and another copy, with all signatures, is sent to you for your records.

Universal Copyright Convention
One of several international treaties protecting the copyrights of authors, musicians, and other artists who are citizens of the signatory countries.

Unsolicited
Material sent without a query letter first. Many agents and editors won't consider unsolicited material; they will only read material they requested on the basis of a query.

Vanity press
A form of self-publisher, generally considered illegitimate because the quality of the finished product usually is poor and such books are not stocked by booksellers and libraries. Also called a subsidy press.

Wiki
A form of blog that allows multiple authors to contribute to the same Web page.

Wire service
A news service that collects and sells stories and information to its members. The Associated Press, Gannett News Service, and Reuters are all wire services.

Work for hire
Also called "work made for hire." Work in which the writer is paid a flat fee and retains no rights in the work. Except in cases where employees create the work as part of their regular job duties, all valid work-for-hire must be spelled out in writing.

Working title
A tentative or preliminary title or headline, often changed before actual publication.

appendix b

Sample Query Letters and Proposals

The following pages contain sample query letters for both magazine articles and book ideas, as well as a sample nonfiction book proposal and cover letter and a sample fiction synopsis and query letter. You'll notice that the magazine query, which is for an essay rather than a feature article, doesn't talk about market, but it does talk about the magazine's readership. The nonfiction book query, on the other hand, does talk about the market, because part of the pitch is showing the agent or editor that there's a large potential readership for the book.

Meg Schneider
123 North Street
Suburbia, NY 12345
(555) 222-2222
MegSchneider@mye-mailaddress.com

Joseph Brown, Editor
The Best Writing Magazine Ever
P.O. Box 1111
Middle America, KS 45678

April 27, 2005

Dear Mr. Brown,

I am *way* too normal to be a writer. Handicapped by a happy childhood, wise and loving parents, a fun and fulfilling marriage, and no worse addiction than an occasional intense craving for a proper Philly cheese steak, I am doomed to eternal exclusion from that elite class of unhappy souls known the world over as Great Writers.

Or so I have always been told.

It took me nearly two decades of earning my living as a writer to reach an epiphany that, unfortunately, escapes most aspiring writers: There is no rule requiring writers to suffer the tortures of the damned in order to be any good as writers.

To help your readers avoid torturing themselves about not being tortured enough, I have written an essay titled "Too Happy to be a Writer" for your "From the Desk of" department. It is 1,012 words.

I am an award-winning writer with 17 years' experience in television, radio, newspaper, and public relations. My book credits include *The Everything Guide to Writing a Book Proposal* (Adams Media, May 2005), *The Everything Casino Gambling Book* (Adams Media, September 2004), and *The Birth Order Effect for Couples* (Fair Winds Press, January 2004). My contact information is listed above.

Thank you for your time and consideration. I look forward to hearing from you.

Sincerely,
Meg Schneider

Meg Schneider
123 North Street
Suburbia, NY 12345
(555) 222-2222
MegSchneider@mye-mailaddress.com

K.C. Jones, President
Jones Literary Agency
333 E. Washington Street, Suite 201
Big Apple, NY 01010

April 27, 2005

Dear K.C. Jones,

According to a study by the Hobby Industry Association, 60 percent of all U.S. households engaged in some kind of craft-making or hobby activity in the past year, and 77 percent of all households have at least one member who has, at some point, engaged in craft-making. Retail craft and hobby stores now represent a $29-billion-a-year business.

THE BIG BOOK OF CRAFTING: EXPRESS YOUR CREATIVITY THROUGH EASY, INEXPENSIVE HOME CRAFTS solves that problem for would-be crafters. Designed specifically for beginners, THE BIG BOOK OF CRAFTING encourages readers to experiment with a variety of crafts before making a huge investment in equipment and supplies. Indeed, many of the tools and supplies listed in this book can be used for two or more different categories of crafts, adding further value for the reader.

I am a lifelong dabbler in a wide array of home crafts and an award-winning writer with 17 years' experience in television, radio, newspaper, and public relations. My book credits include *The Everything Guide to Writing a Book Proposal* (Adams Media, May 2005), *The Everything Casino Gambling Book* (Adams Media, September 2004), and *The Birth Order Effect for Couples* (Fair Winds Press, January 2004). My contact information is listed above.

Thank you for your time and consideration. I look forward to hearing from you.

Sincerely,
Meg Schneider

Meg Schneider
123 North Street
Suburbia, NY 12345
(555) 222-2222
MegSchneider@mye-mailaddress.com

K.C. Jones, President
Jones Literary Agency
333 E. Washington Street, Suite 201
Big Apple, NY 01010

June 27, 2005

Dear K.C. Jones,

Enclosed is the proposal you requested for THE BIG BOOK OF CRAFTING: EXPRESS YOUR CREATIVITY THROUGH EASY, INEXPENSIVE HOME CRAFTS. It is envisioned as a one-stop shop for aspiring and beginning crafters who want to experiment with different media before making a significant investment in supplies and equipment.

Although there are dozens of craft books on the market, I have been unable to find a comprehensive guide aimed at adults who are just starting their foray into the highly popular and ever-expanding world of home crafts.

Thank you for your interest and your time. I look forward to hearing from you.

Sincerely,
Meg Schneider

THE BIG BOOK OF CRAFTING:

Express Your Creativity Through Easy, Inexpensive Home Crafts

By

Meg Schneider
123 North Street
Suburbia, NY 12345
(555) 222-2222
MegSchneider@mye-mailaddress.com

CONTENTS

OVERVIEW

THE BIG BOOK OF CRAFTING: EXPRESSING YOUR CREATIVITY THROUGH EASY, INEXPENSIVE HOME CRAFTS is the essential beginner's portal into the fast-growing world of home crafts. Whether your affinity is painting, stitching, stenciling, flower arranging or furniture refinishing, THE BIG BOOK OF CRAFTING shows you how to get started and takes you step-by-step through the process from great idea to fabulous finished product.

THE BIG BOOK OF CRAFTING covers twenty of the most popular home crafts, including scrapbooking, beading, home and holiday décor and decorations, and all manner of stitch-and-sew crafts. Each chapter includes a list of materials and suggestions on where to find them, key tips such as how to use a hot-glue gun and how to choose colors, and tricks to make home crafting even easier and more enjoyable. Easy-to-follow instructions are accompanied by photos and illustrations that show the reader exactly how to complete each step. Along the way, readers also will find inspiration for unleashing their own inner creativity.

THE BIG BOOK OF CRAFTING is the first comprehensive beginner's guide to home crafts. It is approximately 80,000 words.

ABOUT THE AUTHOR

Meg Schneider

Meg Schneider is an award-winning writer with more than a decade of experience in television, radio and print journalism, and an avid crafter of long standing. She is the coauthor of *The Birth Order Effect for Couples* (Rockport Publishers, January 2004), author of *The Everything Casino Gambling Book* (Adams Media, 2004), and coauthor of *The Everything Guide to Writing a Book Proposal* (Adams Media, 2005).

When Schneider isn't writing, she is painting, cross-stitching, stenciling, weaving, or refinishing some project destined for her own home, a friend's or relative's home, or the monthly craft fair down the road from her house. Through her community's Adult and Community Education program, she has taught more than a dozen classes on various crafting techniques to more than 300 students. She also has been invited to speak at craft and hobby conventions throughout the Northeast and has been profiled in *Ain't Crafting Grand* magazine.

Her journalism honors include awards from the Iowa Associated Press Managing Editors, Women in Communications, the Maryland-Delaware-DC Press Association, Gannett, the New York State Associated Press, and the William Randolph Hearst Foundation.

A native of Iowa, Schneider now lives in upstate New York with her husband and three dogs.

THE MARKET

According to a study by the Hobby Industry Association, 60 percent of all U.S. households engaged in some kind of craft-making or hobby activity in 2002, and 77 percent of all households have at least one member who has, at some point, engaged in craft-making. Retail craft and hobby stores reported $29 billion in sales in 2002, a 13 percent increase over the previous year.

To reach these consumers, media groups have launched dozens of magazines, some targeted at a general crafting readership and some aimed more precisely at woodworkers, sewers, quilters, knitters, and so on. Three of the largest of the general craft magazines—*Michaels Create!, Creating Keepsakes,* and *Crafts Magazine*— have a combined circulation of approximately 750,000.

General home-and-lifestyle consumer magazines such as *Better Homes and Gardens, Family Circle, Good Housekeeping,* and *Woman's Day* have added regular crafting features to their editorial lineups. The top ten magazines in this category have a combined circulation of approximately 37 million.

In addition to the plethora of craft shows on public and cable television, not to mention regular segments on national morning news programs such as *Today,* major newspapers, including the *Wall Street Journal* and the *New York Times,* have reported extensively on the popularity of crafts and the success of craft businesses.

Craft and cooking books comprise the third-largest category of book sales in the United States, and general nonfiction, including humor, is the fourth-largest category.

THE BIG BOOK OF CRAFTING could capture a respectable portion of the crafting market as a gift idea for the crafter in your home or an idea generator for crafters.

PROMOTION

Aside from the usual bookselling outlets, THE BIG BOOK OF CRAFTING has great potential in the gift market, particularly among crafters and their friends and relatives. It likely would do well in gift stores and other nontraditional retail locations.

CRAFTING's short, snappy prose lends itself to being excerpted in magazines and on Web sites, such as MSNBC.com's *Today's* Book Club.

CRAFTING also can be promoted effectively through personal appearances by the author and her collection of homemade craft items. The author is available for book signings, media interviews, and speaking engagements.

Various crafting organizations, such as the national Craft & Hobby Association, the Home Sewing Association, the National NeedleArts Association, and the Society of Creative Craft Designers, also are excellent promotional vehicles.

CRAFTING also can be promoted on the Internet via the author's Web site and links on scores of craft sites.

COMPETITION

While there are dozens of home craft books on the market, there is no single comprehensive craft book for adults that covers the full range of popular home crafts. THE BIG BOOK OF CRAFTING fills a void left by these other books by providing readers with essential information on all major crafts in one volume. This approach is particularly useful for beginners, who may want to experiment with many different kinds of crafts before they find the medium they most enjoy.

Because it covers the full range of home crafts, THE BIG BOOK OF CRAFTING can be compared with the *Better Homes and Gardens* series of crafting books, including 100 CRAFTS UNDER $10 (2003) and PAINTED CRAFTS (1990) as well as more specific books like CREATIVE FLORAL ARRANGING (Home Decorating Institute, 1997), NEW METAL FOIL CRAFTS (Rockport Publishers, 2002), and SEW SIMPLE SQUARES (Watson-Guptill Publications, 2003).

OUTLINE

The INTRODUCTION discusses the explosion in home crafting and how many crafters are using their hobbies to relieve stress and unleash their creativity, which often spills over into other areas of their lives.

SECTION ONE: A STITCH IN TIME covers the stitching and sewing craft categories, including cross-stitch, macramé, rug hooking, embroidery, knitting, and sewing doll's clothes. Each category includes a list of needed materials, tips on developing your design, timesavers, and add-ons to make your creation unique.

SECTION TWO: PUT IT ON PAPER covers scrapbooking, photo collages, calligraphy, and papermaking. Each category includes a list of needed materials, tips on developing your design, timesavers, and add-ons to make your creation unique.

SECTION THREE: BEADING shows how to make jewelry, photo frames, baskets, dolls and other bric-a-brac using plastic, ceramic, and wooden beads. Each category includes a list of needed materials, tips on developing your design, timesavers, and add-ons to make your creation unique.

SECTION FOUR: SILK AND DRIED FLOWERS covers a variety of home decorating ideas using silk and dried flowers for holiday or everyday display. Each category includes a list of needed materials, tips on developing your design, timesavers, and add-ons to make your creation unique.

SECTION FIVE: PAINTING, STAMPING, AND STENCILING shows simple ways to dress up everything from glassware to old shoes with paints, stamps, and stencils. Each category includes a list of needed materials, tips on developing your design, timesavers, and add-ons to make your creation unique.

SECTION SIX: FURNITURE FIXES covers painting, refinishing, and upholstering chairs, sofas, ottomans, tables, bookcases, and cabinets to create a new and unique feel at a fraction of the cost of purchasing new furniture. Each category includes a list of needed materials, tips on developing your design, timesavers, and add-ons to make your creation unique.

INTRODUCTION

Unleashing Your Inner Creativity

Home crafts are enjoying record popularity these days, whether it's creating cute scrapbooks of photos and mementos as thoughtful gifts for birthdays and holidays or sprucing up a ratty-looking chair or cabinet to give it new life. In fact, there are so many choices out there for the new crafter that it can be intimidating just to decide which medium you want to work in. This book aims to take some of that intimidation out of the world of crafting by showing you simple and inexpensive ways to experiment with the major areas in home crafting.

Why do people like to do crafts? There are lots of reasons.

Meg Schneider
123 North Street
Suburbia, NY 12345
(555) 222-2222
MegSchneider@mye-mailaddress.com

Jane Smith, Acquisitions Editor
ABC Publishers
P.O. Box 1111
Big City, NY 54321

April 27, 2005

Dear Ms. Smith,

At some point in her life, every woman has felt trapped in a mundane existence and wished for a magical transformation. In the modern age, we seek such magic in cosmetics, clothes shops, and fitness clubs. But in another age, a lucky few had much more potent magic at their disposal: benevolent fairies who bestowed favors upon the deserving.

CINDERELLA is a tale of one such young woman, good-hearted and full of inner beauty but trapped in a life of drudgery and ill-treatment from her vain and cruel stepmother and two stepsisters. She has no means to escape her sorrowful lot until her fairy godmother appears and uses her magic to reveal Cinderella's true beauty and worth to the world. Written with humor and poignancy, CINDERELLA weaves current social issues of class distinction, self-image, and self-worth into a timeless fantasy world populated by fallible humans and the supernatural beings who watch over them.

I am an award-winning writer with 17 years' experience in television, radio, newspaper and public relations. My book credits include *The Everything Guide to Writing a Book Proposal* (Adams Media, May 2005), *The Everything Casino Gambling Book* (Adams Media, September 2004), and *The Birth Order Effect for Couples* (Fair Winds Press, January 2004). At 65,342 words, CINDERELLA is my first novel.

Thank you for your time and consideration. I look forward to hearing from you.

Sincerely,
Meg Schneider

CINDERELLA

Synopsis

Cinderella has had a tough life. Her mother died when she was young, and her adoring father, feeling the child needed a mother, marries a woman with two daughters of her own. Cinderella senses an ominous undercurrent from her stepmother and stepsisters, but she is protected from any overt abuse by her father. Unfortunately, her father dies shortly afterward, and Cinderella's status in the blended family disintegrates almost immediately to that of indentured servant.

For a long time, Cinderella is forced to do all the household chores for her vain and wicked stepmother and her equally vain and wicked stepsisters. She sleeps in the smallest, barest room in the house, wears the same tattered, dirty clothes day after day, and endures the cruel taunts of the others as she does her never-ending work.

One day, word comes that the king, whose son is of the age to marry, will hold a magnificent ball to introduce the prince to all the maidens of the land. Cinderella desperately wants to attend the ball, but her stepmother relegates her to the role of lady's maid for her stepsisters and points out that, even if she did complete her chores in time to go to the ball, Cinderella has nothing but rags to wear. "What prince would waste his time on a filthy servant girl like you?" the stepmother snipes.

Cinderella watches her stepmother and stepsisters leave for the ball. When they are well away, she breaks down and cries as if her heart would break, trapped and hopeless. Through her sobs, she hears a tiny sound and looks up, astonished to see a twinkling fairy gazing benevolently upon her. The fairy asks Cinderella why she is so unhappy, and when Cinderella explains that she has no fine clothes to wear to the ball and no way to get to the king's palace, the fairy says, "But you shall go to the ball, my child." Then the fairy uses her magic to clad Cinderella in a beautiful gown and exquisite slippers made of glass; a pumpkin and four mice are transformed into a golden carriage, horses, and footmen. "The magic will last until midnight," the fairy says. "After that, everything must be the way it was." Cinderella, awed and elated, thanks the fairy and promises to be home before the last stroke of midnight.

At the ball, Cinderella's arrival sets tongues whispering about who she could be, for no one, not even her stepmother and stepsisters, recognizes the downtrodden servant in the lovely young woman. The handsome prince is immediately smitten, and soon he is leading Cinderella across the ballroom floor, ignoring all the other maidens. The evening passes quickly, and it seems but a moment before the clock begins to toll the strokes of midnight. So enchanted is Cinderella that she barely hears the clock, and four strokes have already sounded by the time she remembers the fairy's warning. Frightened of being exposed in front of the prince and her wicked stepfamily, Cinderella runs from the palace. As she flies down the steps, one of her glass slippers falls off. She keeps running, and as the clock registers the final toll of midnight, her fine clothing disappears, replaced by her usual rags, and the spectacular carriage, horses and footmen resume their original forms.

Meanwhile, the prince has found the glass slipper on the palace steps. He doesn't understand why the beautiful girl ran away so abruptly, but he knows he is in love with her, and he resolves to find her. The following morning, he begins a methodical search of the kingdom, stopping at every house and hovel and having every woman he encounters try on the mysterious glass slipper. Eventually, he arrives at Cinderella's home and explains his errand to the stepmother. In turn, the two stepsisters and the stepmother try to jam their substantial feet into the tiny slipper, but it clearly fits none of them. The prince prepares to ride away, but he spots Cinderella behind the house, filling a bucket from the well. The stepmother tries to prevent Cinderella from trying on the slipper, but the prince insists. Cinderella, nervous and not sure what will happen, shyly tries the slipper on. Instantly she is transformed into the beautiful maiden of the ball. The prince gathers her into his arms and declares his undying love, and then carries her away to his palace to live happily ever after.

appendix c

Book Publishers

The book publishing landscape is continually in motion. New publishing houses are cropping up all the time; small publishers often merge with or are acquired by larger houses; editors hop from house to house with amazing frequency. The listings here are representative of royalty-paying opportunities available to book authors in the United States, but you still have to do your research to find out which publishers are looking for your kind of material, whether they are open to unagented writers, and how to submit your material to them.

Major Conglomerates

Except for their children's book divisions, the major publishers deal only with literary agents. Check out the main Web sites for information on children's imprints and submitting your children's material.

HarperCollins
10 East Fifty-third Street
New York, NY 10022-5299
212-207-7000
✐*www.harpercollins.com*

Imprints include Access, Amistad, Avon, Caedmon, Collins (covering the former imprints HarperBusiness and HarperResource), Collins Design, Dark Alley, Ecco, Eos, Fourth Estate, HarperAudio, HarperCollins, HarperEntertainment, HarperLargePrint, HarperSanFrancisco, HarperTorch, Harper Perennial, Perennial Currents, PerfectBound, Rayo, ReganBooks, and William Morrow.

Hyperion
77 West Sixty-sixth Street
Eleventh Floor
New York, NY 10023-6298
212-456-0100
✐*www.hyperionbooks.com*

Imprints include Disney Press, ESPN Books, Hyperion East, Miramax, and Wenner Books.

Penguin Group (USA)
375 Hudson Street
New York, NY 10014-3658
212-366-2000
✐*www.penguingroup.com*
✐*www.penguinclassics.com*

Imprints include Ace, Alpha, Avery, Berkley Books, Chamberlain Bros., Dutton, G. P. Putnam's Sons, Gotham, Putnam, HP Books, Hudson Street Press, Jeremy P. Tarcher, Jove, New American Library, Penguin, Perigee, Plume, Portfolio, Riverhead Books, Sentinel, and Viking.

Random House, Inc.
1745 Broadway
Fourth Floor
New York, NY 10019
212-751-2600
www.randomhouse.com

Imprints include Ballantine, Bantam, Bell Tower, Broadway, Clarkson Potter, Crown, Crown Forum, Del Rey, Dell, Doubleday, Fodor's Travel, Harmony, Knopf, The Modern Library, Nan A. Talese, Pantheon, Prima Games, Random House, Random House Audio, Random House Information Group, Random House Large Print, Random House Reference Publishing, Schocken, Shaye Areheart Books, Three Rivers Press, Villard, Vintage, and Waterbrook Press.

Simon & Schuster, Inc.
1230 Avenue of the Americas
New York, NY 10020-1513
212-698-7000
www.simonsays.com
www.simonsayskids.com

Imprints include Atria, Downtown Press, Fireside, The Free Press, Kaplan, Lisa Drew Books, MTV Books, Paraview Pocket, Pocket Books, Pocket Star, Scribner, Scribner Classics, Scribner Paperback Fiction, Simon & Schuster, Simon & Schuster Classic Editions, Simon & Schuster Libros en Espanol, Simon & Schuster Source, Star Trek, Touchstone, VH1 Books, Wall Street Journal Books, Washington Square Press, and World Wrestling Entertainment Books.

Time Warner Book Group
1271 Avenue of the Americas
New York, NY 10020-1300
212-522-7200
www.twbookmark.com
www.lb-kids.com

Imprints include Aspect; Back Bay Books; Bulfinch; Center Street; Little, Brown and Company; Mysterious

Press; Time Warner AudioBooks; Walk Worthy Press; Warner Books; Warner Business; and Warner Faith.

Smaller Publishers

The following publishers have their own policies about dealing with agents and writers; some prefer agents, while many, especially the small houses, prefer to deal with writers directly. Again, this is only a representative list. You can find more detailed information in other resources like *Literary Marketplace, Writer's Market,* or on the publishers' Web sites. As always, do your research to find out if these publishers are appropriate for your material and how they prefer to receive submissions.

Abbeville Press
137 Varick Street
New York, NY 10013
212-366-5585
www.abbeville.com

Harry N. Abrams, Inc.
115 West Eighteenth Street
New York, NY 10011
212-519-1200
www.abramsbooks.com

Adams Media
An F + W Publications Company
57 Littlefield Street
Avon, MA 02322
508-427-7100
www.adamsmedia.com

Algonquin Books of Chapel Hill
P.O. Box 2225
Chapel Hill, NC 27515
919-967-0108
www.algonquin.com

Allworth Press
10 East Twenty-third Street
Suite 510
New York, NY 10010-4402
212-777-8395
www.allworth.com

Alyson Books
6922 Hollywood Boulevard
Suite 1000
Los Angeles, CA 90028
323-860-6070
www.alyson.com

AMACOM Books
Division of American Management Association
1601 Broadway
New York, NY 10019
212-586-8100
www.amacombooks.org

American Psychological Association
750 First Street, Northeast
Washington, DC 20002-4241
202-336-5500
www.apa.org/books

Andrews McMeel Publishing
4520 Main Street
Kansas City, MO 64111-1876
816-932-6700
www.andrewsmcmeel.com

Applause Theatre & Cinema Books
19 West Twenty-first Street
Suite 201
New York, NY 10010
212-575-9265
www.applausepub.com

Arcade Publishing
141 Fifth Avenue
New York, NY 10010
212-475-2633
www.arcadepub.com

Artisan
708 Broadway
New York, NY 10003
212-254-5900
www.artisanbooks.com

Avalon Publishing Group, Inc.
1400 Sixty-fifth Street
Suite 250
Emeryville, CA 94608
510-595-3664
www.avalonpub.com

Baen Books
P.O. Box 1403
Riverdale, NY 10471
718-548-3100
www.baen.com

Baker Publishing Group
6030 Fulton Street
Ada, MI 49301
616-676-9185

Barricade Books
185 Bridge Plaza North
Suite 308-A
Fort Lee, NY 07024
201-944-7600
www.barricadebooks.com

Barron's Educational Series, Inc.
250 Wireless Boulevard
Hauppauge, NY 11788-3924
631-434-3311
www.barronseduc.com

Beacon Press
25 Beacon Street
Boston, MA 02108-2824
617-742-2110
www.beacon.org

BenBella Books
6440 North Central Expressway
#508
Dallas, TX 75206
214-750-3600
www.benbellabooks.com

Berrett-Koehler Publishers
235 Montgomery Street
Suite 650
San Francisco, CA 94104
415-288-0260
www.bkconnection.com

Beyond Words Publishing, Inc.
20827 Northwest Cornell Road
Suite 500
Hillsboro, OR 97124
503-531-8700
www.beyondword.com

Bleak House Books
953 East Johnson Street
Madison, WI 53703
608-259-8370
www.bleakhousebooks.com

Bloomsbury
175 Fifth Avenue
Suite 300
New York, NY 10010
212-780-0115
www.bloomsburyusa.com

Bonus Books, Inc.
Volt Press
1223 Wilshire Boulevard
#597
Santa Monica, CA 90403
310-260-9400
www.bonusbooks.com

Book Publishing Company
415 Farm Road
Summertown, TN 38483
931-964-3571
www.bookpubco.com

Cambridge University Press
40 West Twentieth Street
New York, NY 10011
212-924-3900
www.cambridge.org/us

Career Press
New Page Books
3 Tice Road
Franklin Lakes, NJ 07417
201-848-0310
www.careerpress.com

Carroll & Graf Publishers, Inc.
245 West Seventeenth Street
Eleventh Floor
New York, NY 10011-5300
212-981-9919
www.carrollandgraf.com

Chelsea Green Publishing
85 North Main Street
P.O. Box 428
White River Junction, VT 05001
802-295-6300
www.chelseagreen.com

Chronicle Books
85 Second Street
Sixth Floor
San Francisco, CA 94105-3459
415-537-4200
www.chroniclebooks.com

City Lights Books
261 Columbus Avenue
San Francisco, CA 94133
415-362-1901
www.citylights.com

Cleis Press
P.O. Box 14697
San Francisco, CA 94114
415-575-4700
www.cleispress.com

Coffee House Press
27 North Fourth Street
Suite 400
Minneapolis, MN 55401
612-338-0125
www.coffeehousepress.org

Collectors Press
P.O. Box 230986
Portland, OR 97281
503-684-3030
www.collectorspress.com

Columbia University Press
61 West Sixty-second Street
New York, NY 10023
212-459-0600
www.columbia.edu/cu/cup

Cornell University Press
Sage House
512 East State Street
Ithaca, NY 14850
607-277-2338
www.cornellpress.cornell.edu

Council Oak Books
2105 East Fifteenth Street
Suite B
Tulsa, OK 74104
918-743-2665
www.counciloakbooks.com

Cumberland House Publishing
431 Harding Industrial Drive
Nashville, TN 37211
615-832-1171
www.cumberlandhouse.com

Dana Press
900 Fifteenth Street NW
Washington, DC 20005
202-408-8800
www.dana.org/books/press

David R. Godine, Publisher
9 Hamilton Place
Boston, MA 02108
617-451-9600
www.godine.com

Davies-Black Publishing
1055 Joaquin Road
Suite 200
Mountain View, CA 94043
650-691-9123
www.daviesblack.com

Dearborn Trade Publishing
30 South Wacker Drive
Suite 2500
Chicago, IL 60606-7481
312-836-4400
www.dearborntrade.com

Dorcester Publishing
200 Madison Avenue
Suite 2000
New York, NY 10016
212-725-8811
www.dorchesterpub.com

Dorling Kindersley Publishing Inc.
375 Hudson Street
Second Floor
New York, NY 10014
212-366-2000
www.dk.com

Dover Publications
31 East Second Street
Minneola, NY 11501
516-294-7000
www.doverdirect.com

Duke University Press
905 West Main Street
Suite 18B
Durham, NC 27701
919-687-3600
www.dukepress.edu

Emmis Books
1700 Madison Road
Cincinnati, OH 45206
531-861-4045
www.emmisbooks.com

F+W Publications, Inc.
4700 East Galbraith Road
Cincinnati, OH 45236
513-531-2690
www.fwpublications.com

Fairview Press
2450 Riverside Avenue
Minneapolis, MN 55454
612-672-4180
www.fairviewpress.org

Farrar, Straus and Giroux
19 Union Square West
New York, NY 10003-3304
212-741-6900
www.fsgbooks.com
www.fsgkidsbooks.com

Frederick Fell Publishers, Inc.
2131 Hollywood Boulevard
Suite 305
Hollywood, FL 33020-6759
954-925-5242
www.fellpub.com

Fulcrum Publishing
16100 Table Mountain Parkway
Suite 300
Golden, CO 80403-5093
303-277-1623
www.fulcrum-books.com

GemStone Press
P.O. Box 237
Sunset Farm Offices
Route 4
Woodstock, VT 05091-0237
www.gemstonepress.com

Globe Pequot Press
246 Goose Lane
P.O. Box 480
Guilford, CT 06437
203-458-4500
www.globepequot.com

Grove/Atlantic, Inc.
841 Broadway
Fourth Floor
New York, NY 10003
212-614-7850
www.groveatlantic.com

Hampton Roads Publishing Company, Inc.
1125 Stoney Ridge Road
Charlottesville, VA 22902
434-296-2772
www.hrpub.com

Harbor House
111 Tenth Street
Augusta, GA 30901
706-738-0354
www.harborhousebooks.com

Harcourt Trade Publishers
15 East Twenty-sixth Street
Fifteenth Floor
New York, NY 10010
619-699-6430
www.harcourtbooks.com

Harvard Common Press
535 Albany Street
Boston, MA 02118
617-423-5803
www.harvardcommonpress.com

Haworth Press, Inc.
10 Alice Street
Binghamton, NY 13904-1580
607-722-5857
www.haworthpress.com

Hay House, Inc.
2776 Loker Avenue West
P.O. Box 5100
Carlsbad, CA 92018-5100
760-431-7695
www.hayhouse.com

Health Communications, Inc.
3201 South West Fifteenth Street
Deerfield Beach, FL 33442-8157
954-360-0909
www.hcibooks.com

Henry Holt and Company
175 Fifth Avenue
New York, NY 10010
646-307-5219
www.henryholt.com

Houghton Mifflin Company
222 Berkeley Street
Boston, MA 02116-3748
617-351-5000
www.houghtonmifflinbooks.com

Howard Publishing Co.
3117 North Seventh Street
West Monroe, LA 71291-2227
318-396-3122
www.howardpublishingdealer.com

Hudson Hills Press
74-2 Union Street
P.O. Box 205
Manchester, VT 05254
802-362-6450
www.hudsonhills.com

THE EVERYTHING GET PUBLISHED BOOK

Human Kinetics Publishers, Inc.
1607 North Market Street
P.O. Box 5076
Champaign, IL 61820
217-351-5076
www.humankinetics.com

Hunter House Publishers
1515 ½ Park Street
P.O. Box 2914
Alameda, CA 94501
510-865-5282
wwww.hunterhouse.com

Hylas Publishing
129 Main Street
Irvington, NY 10533
914-478-6425
www.hylaspublishing.com

Indiana University Press
601 North Morton Street
Bloomington, IN 47404
812-855-8817
www.iupress.indiana.edu

Inner Ocean Publishing, Inc.
1037 Makawao Avenue
P.O. Box 1239
Makawao, Maui, HI 96768-1239
808-573-8000
www.innerocean.com

Inner Traditions
One Park Street
Rochester, VT 05767
802-767-3174
www.innertraditions.com

John Wiley & Sons, Inc.
111 River Street
Hoboken, NJ 07030
201-748-6000
www.wiley.com

Johns Hopkins University Press
2715 North Charles Street
Baltimore, MD 21218-4363
410-516-6936
www.press.jhu.edu

Justin, Charles & Co.
20 Park Plaza
Suite 909
Boston, MA 02116
617-426-4406
www.justincharlesbooks.com

Kensington Publishing Corp.
850 Third Avenue
New York, NY 10022-6222
212-407-1500
www.kensingtonbooks.com

Llewellyn Worldwide Ltd.
P.O. Box 64383
Street Paul, MN 55164-0383
651-291-1970
www.llewellyn.com

Lonely Planet
150 Linden Street
Oakland, CA 94607
510-893-8555
www.lonelyplanet.com

MacAdam/Cage Publishing Inc.
155 Sansome Street
Suite 550
San Francisco, CA 94104
415-986-7502
www.macadamcage.com

McFarland & Company, Inc., Publishers
Box 611
Jefferson, NC 28640
336-246-4460
www.mcfarlandpub.com

McGraw-Hill Companies, Inc.
Two Penn Plaza
Twelfth Floor
New York, NY 10121-2298
www.books.mcgraw-hill.com

M.E. Sharpe, Inc.
80 Business Park Drive
Armonk, NY 10504
914-273-1800
www.mesharpe.com

Meadowbrook Press
5451 Smetana Drive
Minnetonka, MN 55343
952-930-1100
www.meadowbrookpress.com

Mercer University Press
1400 Coleman Avenue
Macon, GA 31207
478-301-2880
www.mupress.org

Mercury House
P.O. Box 192850
San Francisco, CA 94119-2850
415-626-7874
www.mercuryhouse.org

Milkweed Editions
1011 Washington Avenue South
Suite 300
Minneapolis, MN 55415
612-332-3192
www.milkweed.org

Monkfish Book Publishing Company
27 Lamoree Road
Rhinebeck, NY 12572
845-876-4861
www.monkfishpublishing.com

Naval Institute Press
291 Wood Road
Annapolis, MD 21402
410-268-6110
www.usni.org

New Harbinger Publications
5674 Shattuck Avenue
Oakland, CA 94609-1662
510-652-0215
www.newharbinger.com

New Horizon Press
34 Church Street
P.O. Box 669
Liberty Corner, NJ 07931
908-604-6311
www.newhorizonpressbooks.com

Newmarket Press
18 East Forty-eighth Street
Fifteenth Floor
New York, NY 10017
212-832-3575
www.newmarketpress.com

New World Library
14 Pamaron Way
Novato, CA 94949
415-884-2100
www.newworldlibrary.com

New York University Press
838 Broadway
Third Floor
New York, NY 10003
212-998-2547
www.nyupress.org

Nolo
950 Parker Street
Berkeley, CA 94710
510-549-1976
✍*www.nolo.com*

Nomad Press
2456 Christian Street
White River Junction, VT 05001
802-649-1995
✍*www.nomadpress.net*

Northwestern University Press
629 Noyes Street
Evanston, IL 60208-4170
847-491-2046
✍*www.nupress.northwestern.edu*

Ohio University Press
The Ridges
Building 19
Athens, OH 45701
740-593-1158
✍*www.ohio.edu/oupress*

Osprey Publishing, Ltd.
443 Park Avenue South
New York, NY 10016
212-685-5560
✍*www.ospreypublishing.com*

The Overlook Press
141 Wooster Street
Suite 4B
New York, NY 10012
212-673-2210
✍*www.overlookpress.com*

Oxford University Press
198 Madison Avenue
New York, NY 10016-4308
212-726-6000
✍*www.oup.com*

Palgrave Macmillan, Ltd.
175 Fifth Avenue
New York, NY 10010
212-982-3900
✍*www.palgrave-usa.com*

Peachtree Publishers, Ltd.
1700 Chattahoochee Avenue
Atlanta, GA 30318-2112
404-876-8761
✍*www.peachtree-online.com*

Pearson Education
800 East Ninety-sixth Street
Indianapolis, IN 46240
317-428-3042
✍*www.pearsoned.com*

Pelican Publishing Company
1000 Burmaster Street
Gretna, LA 70053
504-368-1175
✍*www.pelicanpub.com*

Penn State University Press
820 North University Drive
USB-1, Suite C
University Park, PA 16802
814-865-1327
✍*www.psupress.org*

Persea Books
853 Broadway
New York, NY 10003
212-260-9256
✍*www.perseabooks.com*

The Perseus Books Group
387 Park Avenue South
Twelfth Floor
New York, NY 10016
212-340-8100
✍www.perseusbooksgroup.com
✍www.dacapopress.com
✍www.publicaffairsbooks.com
✍www.basicbooks.com
✍www.westviewpress.com

Pomegranate Communications, Inc.
P.O. Box 808022
Petaluma, CA 94975-8022
707-782-9000
✍www.pomegranate.com

Potomac Books, Inc.
22883 Quicksilver Drive
Dulles, VA 20166
703-661-1512
✍www.potomacbooksinc.com

Prometheus Books
59 John Glenn Drive
Amherst, NY 14228
716-691-0133
✍www.prometheusbooks.com

Quayside Publishing Group
18705 Lake Drive East
Chanhassen, MN 55317
952-936-4700
✍www.quaysidepublishinggroup.com

Red Wheel/Weiser, LLC.
368 Congress Street
Fourth Floor
Boston, MA 02210-0612
617-542-1324
✍www.redwheelweiser.com

Regnery Publishing
One Massachusetts Avenue Northwest
Washington, DC 20001
202-216-0600
✍www.regnery.com

Rizzoli Publications
300 Park Avenue South
New York, NY 10010-5399
212-387-3400
✍www.rizzoliusa.com

Rodale Inc.
400 South Tenth Street
Emmaus, PA 18098-0001
610-967-5171
✍www.rodalepress.com

Routledge
270 Madison Avenue
New York, NY 10016-0602
212-216-7800
✍www.routledge.com

Running Press Book Publishers
125 South Twenty-second Street
Philadelphia, PA 19103-4399
215-567-5080
✍www.runningpress.com

Santa Monica Press
P.O. Box 1076
Santa Monica, CA 90406
310-230-7759
✍www.santamonicapress.com

Sasquatch Books
119 South Main
Suite 400
Seattle, WA 98104
206-467-4300
✍www.sasquatchbooks.com

Self-Counsel Press
1704 North State Street
Bellingham, WA 98225
360-676-4530
www.self-counsel.com

Seven Locks Press
3100 West Warner Avenue
Suite 8
Santa Ana, CA 92704
714-545-2526
www.sevenlockspublishing.com

Seven Stories Press
140 Watts Street
New York, NY 10013
212-226-8760
www.sevenstories.com

Shambhala Publications
Horticultural Hall
300 Massachusetts Avenue
Boston, MA 02115
617-424-0030
www.shambhala.com

Sierra Club Books
85 Second Street
2nd Floor
San Francisco, CA 94105
415-977-5500
www.sierraclub.org/books

Silver Lake Publishing
111 East Wishkah Street
Aberdeen, WA 98520
360-532-5758
www.silverlakepub.com

Soho Press Inc.
853 Broadway
New York, NY 10003
212-260-1900
www.sohopress.com

Sourcebooks, Inc.
1935 Brookdale Road
Suite 139
Naperville, IL 60563
630-961-3900
www.sourcebooks.com

Square One Publishers
115 Herricks Road
Garden City Park, NY 11040
516-535-2010
www.squareonepublishers.com

St. Lynn's Press
438 Livingston Road
West Mifflin, PA 15122
412-466-0790
www.stlynnspress.com

St. Martin's Press
175 Fifth Avenue
New York, NY 10010-7703
212-674-5151
www.stmartins.com

Stackpole Books
5067 Ritter Road
Mechanicsburg, PA 17055
717-796-0411
www.stackpolebooks.com

Stanford University Press
1450 Page Mill Road
Palo Alto, CA 94304-1124
650-723-1593
www.sup.org

State University of New York Press
194 Washington Avenue
Suite 305
Albany, NY 12210
518-472-5000
www.sunypress.edu

Sterling Publishing Co., Inc.
387 Park Avenue South
New York, NY 10016-8810
212-532-7160
www.sterlingpub.com

Storey Publishing
210 Mass Moca Way
North Adams, MA 01247
413-346-2100
www.storey.com

Surrey Books
230 East Ohio Street
Suite 120
Chicago, IL 60611-3265
312-751-7330
www.surreybooks.com

The Taunton Press
63 South Main Street
Newtown, CT 06470
203-270-8171
www.taunton.com

Temple University Press
1601 North Broad Street
Philadelphia, PA 19122
215-204-1108
www.temple.edu/tempress

Ten Speed Press
Celestial Art/Tricycle Press/Crossing Press
P.O. Box 7123
Berkeley, CA 94707-0123
510-559-1600
www.tenspeed.com

Thames & Hudson Inc.
500 Fifth Avenue
New York, NY 10110
212-354-3763
www.thamesandhudsonusa.com

Thomson Delmar Learning
5 Maxwell Drive
Clifton Park, NY 12065
518-348-2300
www.delmarlearning.com

Timber Press Inc.
133 Southwest Second Avenue
Suite 450
Portland, OR 97204
503-227-2878
www.timberpress.com

The Toby Press
P.O. Box 8531
New Milford, CT 06776-8531
203-830-8508
www.tobypress.com

Trinity University Press
One Trinity Place
San Antonio, TX 78212-7200
210-999-8884
www.trinity.edu/tupress

Tuttle Publishing
364 Innovation Drive
North Clarendon, VT 05759-9436
802-773-8930
https://peripluspublishinggroup.com/tuttle/

University of Alabama Press
Box 870380
Tuscaloosa, AL 35487-0380
205-348-5180
www.uapress.ua.edu

University of Arizona Press
355 South Euclid Avenue
Suite 103
Tucson, AZ 86719
520-621-1441
www.uapress.arizona.edu

University of California Press
2120 Berkeley Way
Berkeley, CA 94704-1012
510-642-4247
www.ucpress.edu

University of Chicago Press
1427 East Sixtieth Street
Chicago, IL 60637-1476
773-702-7248
www.press.uchicago.edu

University of Georgia Press
330 Research Drive
Athens, GA 30602-4901
706-369-6158
www.ugapress.org

University of Hawai'i Press
2840 Kolowalu Street
Honolulu, HI 96822
808-956-8255
www.uhpress.hawaii.edu

University of Illinois Press
1325 South Oak Street
Champaign, IL 61820
217-333-0950
www.press.uillinois.edu

University of Michigan Press
839 Greene Street
Ann Arbor, MI 48104
734-764-4388
www.press.umich.edu

University of Missouri Press
2910 LeMone Boulevard
Columbia, MO 65201-8227
573-882-7641
www.umsystem.edu/upress

University of Nebraska Press
111 Lincoln Mall
Lincoln, NE 68588-0630
402-472-3581
www.nebraskapress.unl.edu

University of North Carolina Press
116 South Boundary Street
P.O. Box 2288
Chapel Hill, NC 27515-2288
919-966-3829
www.uncpress.unc.edu

University of Oklahoma Press
2800 Venture Drive
Norman, OK 73069-8216
405-325-2734
www.oupress.com

University of Pennsylvania Press
3905 Spruce Street
Philadelphia, PA 19104-4112
215-898-6261
www.upenn.edu/pennpress

University of South Carolina Press
1600 Hampton Street
Fifth Floor
Columbia, SC 29208
803-777-2021
✍www.sc.edu/uscpress

University of Tennessee Press
110 Conference Center
University of Tennessee
Knoxville, TN 37996-4108
865-974-3321
✍www.utpress.org

University of Virginia Press
210 Sprigg Lane
P.O. Box 400318
Charlottesville, VA 22904
434-924-3468
✍www.upress.virginia.edu

University of Washington Press
P.O. Box 50096
Seattle, WA 98145
206-543-4050
✍www.washington.edu/uwpress

University Press of Kansas
2501 West Fifteenth Street
Lawrence, KS 66049-3905
785-864-4154
✍www.kansaspress.ku.edu

University Press of Kentucky
663 South Limestone Street
Lexington, KY 40508
859-257-8761
✍www.kentuckypress.com

University Press of Mississippi
3825 Ridgewood Road
Jackson, MS 39211-6492
601-432-6205
✍www.upress.state.ms.us

University Press of New England
37 Lafayette Street
Lebanon, NH 03766
603-643-5585
✍www.upne.com

Visible Ink Press
43311 Joy Road
Suite 414
Canton, MI 48187
734-667-3211
✍www.visibleink.com

Voyageur Press
123 North Second Street
P.O. Box 338
Stillwater, MN 55082
651-430-2210
✍www.voyageurpress.com

Walker & Company
104 Fifth Avenue
New York, NY 10011
212-727-8300
✍www.walkerbooks.com

Watson-Guptill Publications
770 Broadway
New York, NY 10003
646-654-5460
www.wgpub.com

Wilderness Press
1200 Fifth Street
Berkeley, CA 94710
510-558-1666
www.wildernesspress.com

Workman Publishing Company
708 Broadway
New York, NY 10003-9508
212-254-5900
www.workman.com

W.W. Norton & Company
500 Fifth Avenue
New York, NY 10110-0020
212-354-5500
www.wwnorton.com
www.countrymanpress.com

Yale University Press
302 Temple Street
P.O. Box 209040
New Haven, CT 06520-2251
203-432-0966
www.yale.edu/yup

Yorkville Press
1202 Lexington Avenue
Suite 315
New York, NY 10028
212-650-9154
www.yorkvillepress.com

appendix d

Literary Agents

This is a representative listing of literary agents in the United States, who either are members of the Association of Author's Representatives or who follow the AAR's code of ethics. You can check out the AAR listings online at *www.aar-online.com* or *Literary Marketplace* (in your local library, or online for a fee) to find out what kind of material individual agents are looking for, whether they're accepting new clients, and what their submission preferences are.

Andree L. Abecassis
Ann Elmo Agency, Inc.
60 East Forty-second Street
New York, NY 10165

Dominick Abel
Dominick Abel Literary Agency, Inc.
146 West Eighty-second Street
#1B
New York, NY 10024

Tracey Adams
Adams Literary
295 Greenwich Street
#260
New York, NY 10007

Linda Allen
Linda Allen Literary Agency
1949 Green Street
#5
San Francisco, CA 94123

Miriam Altshuler
Miriam Altshuler Literary Agency
53 Old Post Road North
Red Hook, NY 12571

Betsy Amster
Betsy Amster Literary Enterprises
2151 Kenilworth Avenue
Los Angeles, CA 90039

Marcia Amsterdam
Marcia Amsterdam Agency
41 West Eighty-second Street
New York, NY 10024

Stein Anna
Donadio & Olson
121 West Twenty-seventh Street
New York, NY 10001

Nicole Diamond Austin
The Creative Culture
72 Spring Street
Suite 304
New York, NY 10012

Steven Axelrod
The Axelrod Agency Inc.
55 Main Street
P.O. Box 357
Chatham, NY 12037

Donna Bagdasarian
Maria Carvainis Agency, Inc.
1350 Avenue of the Americas
Suite 2905
New York, NY 10019

Richard Balkin
The Balkin Agency
P.O. Box 222
Amherst, MA 01004

Paula Balzer
126 Fifth Avenue
Suite 300
New York, NY 10011

Lisa Bankoff
International Creative Management
40 West Fifty-seventh Street
New York, NY 10019

Dave Barbor
Curtis Brown, Ltd.
Ten Astor Place
New York, NY 10003

Julie Barer
Barer Literary, LLC
156 Fifth Avenue
Suite 1134
New York, NY 10010

Loretta Barrett
Loretta Barrett Books Inc.
101 Fifth Avenue
Eleventh Floor
New York, NY 10003

Faye Bender
1841 Broadway
Suite 903
New York, NY 10023

Mel Berger
William Morris Agency, Inc.
1325 Avenue of the Americas
New York, NY 10019

Meredith Bernstein
Meredith Bernstein Literary Agency
2095 Broadway
Suite 505
New York, NY 10023

Daniel Bial
Daniel Bial Agency
41 West Eighty-third Street
Suite 5-C
New York, NY 10024

Vicky Bijur
Vicky Bijur Literary Agency
333 West End Avenue
Apartment 5B
New York, NY 10023
E-mail: vbijur@aol.com

Agnes Birnbaum
Bleecker Street Associates, Inc.
532 LaGuardia Place
#617
New York, NY 10012

David Black
David Black Literary Agency
156 Fifth Avenue
Suite 608
New York, NY 10010-7002

Beth Blickers
Abrams Artists
275 Seventh Avenue
Twenty-sixth Floor
New York, NY 10012

Olivia B. Blumer
The Blumer Literary Agency
350 Seventh Avenue
Suite 2003
New York, NY 10001-5013

William Blumer
The Blumer Literary Agency
350 Seventh Avenue
Suite 2003
New York, NY 10001-5013

Rolph Blythe
Dunow & Carlson Agency
27 West Twentieth Street
Suite 1003
New York, NY 10011
E-mail: rolph@dunowcarlson.com

Judy Boals
Berman, Boals, & Flynn, Inc.
A Talent & Literary Agency
208 West Thirtieth Street
Room 401
New York, NY 10001

Anne Borchardt and Valerie Borchardt
Georges Borchardt, Inc.
136 East Fifty-seventh Street
New York, NY 10022

Katherine Boyle
1157 Valencia
Suite 4
San Francisco, CA 94110
E-mail: kboyle1@mindspring.com

Carl Brandt
Brandt & Hochman Literary Agents, Inc.
1501 Broadway
New York, NY 10036

Helen Brann
The Helen Brann Agency, Inc.
94 Curtis Road
Bridgewater, CT 06752

Nathan Bransford
Curtis Brown, Ltd.
Ten Astor Place
New York, NY 10003
E-mail: nb@cbltd.com

Barbara Braun
Barbara Braun Associates, Inc.
104 Fifth Avenue
Seventh Floor
New York, NY 10011

Gertrude Bregman
Blanche C. Gregory, Inc.
2 Tudor City Place
New York, NY 10017

Helen Breitwieser
Cornerstone Literary, Inc.
4500 Wilshire Boulevard
Third Floor
Los Angeles, CA 90010

Andrea Brown
Andrea Brown Literary Agency, Inc.
1076 Eagle Drive
Salinas, CA 93905

Elliott Brown
Franklin Weinrib Rudell Vassallo
488 Madison Avenue
New York, NY 10022

Knox Burger
Knox Burger Associates Ltd.
10 West Fifteenth Street
#1914
New York, NY 10011

John Buzzetti
The Gersh Agency
41 Madison Avenue
Thirty-third Floor
New York, NY 10010

Sheree Bykofsky
Sheree Bykofsky Associates, Inc.
16 West Thirty-sixth Street
Thirteenth Floor
New York, NY 10018

Ben Camardi
Harold Matson Company, Inc.
276 Fifth Avenue
New York, NY 10001

Kimberley Cameron
Reece Halsey North Literary
    Agency
98 Main Street
#704
Tiburon, CA 94920

Cynthia Cannell
Cynthia Cannell Literary Agency
833 Madison Avenue
New York, NY 10021

Moses Cardona
John Hawkins & Associates
71 West Twenty-third Street
Suite 1600
New York, NY 10010

Jennifer Carlson
Dunow & Carlson Literary Agency
27 West Twentieth Street
Suite 1003
New York, NY 10011

Maria Carvainis
Maria Carvainis Agency, Inc.
1350 Avenue of the Americas
Suite 2905
New York, NY 10019

Julie Castiglia
Julie Castiglia Literary Agency
1155 Camino del Mar
Suite 510
Del Mar, CA 92014

Jane Chelius
Jane Chelius Literary Agency
548 Second Street
Brooklyn, NY 11215

Linda Chester
Linda Chester and Associates
630 Fifth Avenue
Suite 2662
New York, NY 10111

Faith Hampton Childs
Faith Childs Literary Agency, Inc.
915 Broadway
Suite 1009
New York, NY 10010

Lucy Childs
The Aaron M. Priest Literary
    Agency
708 Third Avenue
Twenty-third Floor
New York, NY 10017

Michael Choate
The Choate Agency, LLC
1320 Bolton Road
Pelham, NY 10803

Paul Cirone
The Aaron M. Priest Literary
    Agency
708 Third Avenue
Twenty-third Floor
New York, NY 10017

Ginger Clarke
Writers House
21 West Twenty-sixth Street
New York, NY 10010

William Clark
Wm. Clark Associates
355 West Twenty-second Street
Fourth Floor
New York, NY 10011-2650

Elizabeth Coen
Stuart Krichevsky Literary Agency,
    Inc.
381 Park Avenue South
Suite 914
New York, NY 10016

Nancy Coffey
Literary & Media Representation
240 West Thirty-fifth Street
Suite 500
New York, NY 10001

Ruth Cohen
Ruth Cohen Literary Agency, Inc.
P.O. Box 2244
La Jolla, CA 92038-2244

Shana Cohen
Stuart Krichevsky Literary Agency,
    Inc.
381 Park Avenue South
Suite 914
New York, NY 10016

Susan Cohen
Writers House
21 West Twenty-sixth Street
New York, NY 10010

Talia Cohen
Laura Dail Literary Agency, Inc.
350 Seventh Avenue
Suite 2003
New York, NY 10001

Frances Collin
Literary Agent
P.O. Box 33
Wayne, PA 19087-0033

Nina Collins
Collins McCormick Literary Agency
30 Bond Street
New York, NY 10012

Cristina Concepcion
Don Congdon Associates, Inc.
156 Fifth Avenue
Suite 625
New York, NY 10010

Don Congdon
Don Congdon Associates, Inc.
156 Fifth Avenue
Suite 625
New York, NY 10010

Michael Congdon
Don Congdon Associates, Inc.
156 Fifth Avenue
Suite 625
New York, NY 10010

Bill Contardi
Brandt & Hochman Literary Agents,
    Inc.
1501 Broadway
Suite 2310
New York, NY 10036
E-mail: bill@billcontardi.com

Eileen Cope
Lowenstein-Yost Associates Inc.
121 West Twenty-seventh Street
Suite 601
New York, NY 10001
www.lowensteinyost.com

Claudia Cross
Sterling Lord Literistic, Inc.
65 Bleecker Street
Twelfth Floor
New York, NY 10012

James R. Cypher
The Cypher Agency
816 Wolcott Avenue
Beacon, NY 12508-4261
E-mail: jimcypher@prodigy.net
http://pages.prodigy.net/
    jimcypher

Laura Dail
Laura Dail Literary Agency, Inc
350 Seventh Avenue
Suite 2003
New York, NY 10001
www.ldlainc.com

Leslie Daniels
The Joy Harris Literary Agency, Inc.
156 Fifth Avenue
Suite 617
New York, NY 10010

Liza Dawson
Liza Dawson Associates
240 West Thirty-fifth Street
Suite 500
New York, NY 10001

Brian DeFiore
DeFiore and Company
72 Spring Street
Suite 304
New York, NY 10012

Joëlle Del Bourgo
Joëlle Del Bourgo Associates, Inc.
450 Seventh Avenue
Suite 3004
New York, NY 10123

Sandra Dijkstra
Sandra Dijkstra Literary Agency
PMB 515
1155 Camino Del Mar
Del Mar, CA 92014

Kenneth Dingledine
Samuel French, Inc.
45 West Twenty-fifth Street
New York, NY 10010

Lucienne Diver
Spectrum Literary Agency
320 Central Park West
Suite 1D
New York, NY 10025

Jonathan Dolger
The Jonathan Dolger Agency
49 East Ninety-sixth Street
9B
New York, NY 10128

Janis A. Donnaud
Janis A. Donnaud and Associates,
   Inc.
525 Broadway
2nd Floor
New York, NY 10012

Sarah Douglas
Douglas & Kopelman Artists, Inc.
393 West Forty-ninth Street
Suite 5G
New York, NY 10019

B. J. Doyen
Doyen Literary Services, Inc.
1931 660th Street
Newell, IA 50568

Dick Duane
Pinder Lane & Garon-Brooke
   Associates, Ltd.
159 West Fifty-third Street
New York, NY 10019

Jennie Dunham
Dunham Literary, Inc.
156 Fifth Avenue
Suite 625
New York, NY 10010

Henry Dunow
Dunow & Carlson Literary Agency
27 West Twentieth Street
Suite 1003
New York, NY 10011

Jane Dystel
Dystel & Goderich Literary
   Management
One Union Square West
Suite 904
New York, NY 10003

Arielle Eckstut
Levine Greenberg Literary Agency
112 Auburn Street
San Rafael, CA 94901
E-mail: aeckstut@levinegreenberg.
   com

Anne Edelstein
Anne Edelstein Literary Agency
20 West Twenty-second Street
New York, NY 10010

Danielle Egan-Miller
Browne & Miller Literary Associates
410 South Michigan Avenue
#460
Chicago, IL 60605
✎www.browneandmiller.com

Lisa Ekus
Lisa Ekus Public Relations Co., LLC
57 North Street
Hatfield, MA 01038
E-mail: lcecooks@lisaekus.com

Leigh Ann Eliseo
David Black Literary Agency, Inc.
156 Fifth Avenue
Suite 608
New York, NY 10010

Ethan Ellenberg
The Ethan Ellenberg Literary
   Agency
548 Broadway
#5E
New York, NY 10012
E-mail: Ethan@EthanEllenberg.com

Jake Elwell
Wieser & Elwell
80 Fifth Avenue
#1101
New York, NY 10010

Elaine English
Graybill & English
1875 Connecticut Avenue NW
Suite 712
Washington, DC 20009

Felicia Eth
555 Bryant Street
Suite 350
Palto Alto, CA 94301

Joni Evans
William Morris Agency, Inc.
1325 Avenue of the Americas
New York, NY 10019

Mary Evans
Mary Evans, Inc.
242 East Fifth Street
New York, NY 10003

Stephany Evans
Imprint Agency Inc.
5 West 101st Street
Suite 8B
New York, NY 10025
E-mail: imprintagency@earthlink.
net

Diana Finch
Diana Finch Literary Agency
116 West Twenty-third Street
Suite 500
New York, NY 10011
E-mail: diana.finch@verizon.net

Tracy Fisher
William Morris Agency
1325 Avenue of the Americas
New York, NY 10019

Christy Fletcher
Fletcher & Parry
The Carriage House
121 East Seventeenth Street
New York, NY 10003

Evan M. Fogelman
The Fogelman Literary Agency
7515 Greenville Avenue
Suite 712
Dallas, TX 75231

Emily Forland
Wendy Weil Agency, Inc.
232 Madison Avenue
Suite 1300
New York, NY 10016
E-mail: eforland@wendyweil.com

Peter Franklin
William Morris Agency
1325 Avenue of the Americas
Fifteenth Floor
New York, NY 10019

J. Warren Frazier
John Hawkins & Associates, Inc.
71 West Twenty-third Street
Suite 1600
New York, NY 10010

Jeanne Fredericks
Jeanne Fredericks Literary Agency,
Inc.
221 Benedict Hill Road
New Canaan, CT 06840

Robert Freedman
Robert A. Freedman Dramatic
Agency, Inc.
1501 Broadway
Suite 2310
New York, NY 10036

Molly Friedrich
The Aaron M. Priest Literary
Agency
708 Third Avenue
Twenty-third Floor
New York, NY 10017-4103

Candice Fuhrman
Candice Fuhrman Literary Agency
60 Greenwood Way
Mill Valley, CA 94941

Russell Galen
Scovil Chichak Galen Literary
Agency, Inc.
381 Park Avenue South
Suite 1020
New York, NY 10016

Kate Garrick
DeFiore and Company
72 Spring Street
Suite 304
New York, NY 10012

Ellen Geiger
Curtis Brown, Ltd.
Ten Astor Place
New York, NY 10003

Jane Gelfman
Gelfman Schneider
250 West Fifty-seventh Street
Suite 2515
New York, NY 10107

Jeff Gerecke
Gina Maccoby Literary Agency
P.O. Box 60
Chappaqua, NY 10514
E-mail: jeff.gerecke@verizon.net

Karen Gerwin
William Morris Agency
1325 Avenue of the Americas
New York, NY 10019

Anna Ghosh
Scovil Chichak Galen Literary
    Agency, Inc.
381 Park Avenue South
Suite 1020
New York, NY 10016
✐www.scglit.com

Ted Gideonse
Ann Rittenberg Literary Agency,
    Inc.
30 Bond Street
New York, NY 10012
✐www.rittlit.com

Peter Ginsberg
Curtis Brown, Ltd.
1750 Montgomery Street
San Francisco, CA 94111

Mollie Glick
Jean V. Naggar Literary Agency, Inc.
216 East Seventy-fifth Street
New York, NY 10021

Suzanne Gluck
William Morris Agency
1325 Avenue of the Americas
New York, NY 10019

Barry Goldblatt
Barry Goldblatt Literary Agency,
    Inc.
320 Seventh Avenue
#266
Brooklyn, NY 11215

Frances Goldin
Frances Goldin Literary Agency, Inc.
57 East Eleventh Street
Suite 5B
New York, NY 10003
E-mail: agency@goldinlit.com
✐www.goldinlit.com

Debra Goldstein
The Creative Culture, Inc.
72 Spring Street
Suite 304
New York, NY 10012

Arnold Goodman
Goodman Associates
500 West End Avenue
New York, NY 10024

Elise Simon Goodman
Goodman Associates
500 West End Avenue
New York, NY 10024

Irene Goodman
Irene Goodman Literary Agency
80 Fifth Avenue
Suite 1101
New York, NY 10011

Nina Graybill
Graybill & English
1875 Connecticut Avenue NW
#712
Washington, DC 20009
E-mail: ninagraybill@aol.com

Ashley Grayson
Ashley Grayson Literary Agency
1342 Eighteenth Street
San Pedro, CA 90732

Carolyn Grayson
Ashley Grayson Literary Agency
1342 Eighteenth Street
San Pedro, CA 90732

Daniel Greenberg
Levine Greenberg Literary Agency
307 Seventh Avenue
Suite 1906
New York, NY 10001
E-mail: dgreenberg@levine
    greenberg.com

Maxine Groffsky
Maxine Groffsky Literary Agency
853 Broadway
Suite 708
New York, NY 10003

Ronald Gwiazda
Rosenstone/Wender
38 East Twenty-ninth Street
Tenth Floor
New York, NY 10016

Peter Hagan
The Gersh Agency
41 Madison Avenue
Thirty-third Floor
New York, NY 10010

Faith Hamlin
Sanford J. Greenburger Associates
55 Fifth Avenue
Fifteenth Floor
New York, NY 10003

Jeanne K. Hanson
Jeanne K. Hanson Literary Agency
6708 Cornelia Drive
Edina, MN 55435

Elizabeth Harding
Curtis Brown, Ltd.
Ten Astor Place
New York, NY 10003

Laurie Harper
Sebastian Literary Agency
2160 Kenwood Way
Wayzata, MN 55391

Joy Harris
The Joy Harris Literary Agency, Inc.
156 Fifth Avenue
Suite 617
New York, NY 10010

A.L. Hart
Fox Chase Agency, Inc.
Chesterbrook Corporate Center
701 Lee Road
Suite 102
Chesterbrook, PA 19087

Jo C. Hart
The Fox Chase Agency, Inc.
Chesterbrook Corporate Center
701 Lee Road
Suite 102
Chesterbrook, PA 19087

Pamela Harty
The Knight Agency, Inc.
Madison, GA
E-mail: Knightagent@aol.com
www.knightagency.net

Anne Hawkins
John Hawkins & Associates, Inc.
71 West Twenty-third Street
Suite 1600
New York, NY 10010

John Hawkins
John Hawkins & Associates, Inc.
71 West Twenty-third Street
Suite 1600
New York, NY 10010

Merilee Heifetz
Writers House
21 West Twenty-sixth Street
New York, NY 10010

David Hendin
DH Literary, Inc.
P.O. Box 990
Nyack, NY 10960
E-mail: Dhendin@aol.com

Richard Henshaw
Richard Henshaw Group
127 West Twenty-fourth Street
Fourth Floor
New York, NY 10011-2418
www.rich.henshaw.com

Jeff Herman
The Jeff Herman Agency, LLC
9 South Street
Stockbridge, MA 01262

Patrick Herold
ICM
40 West Fifty-seventh Street
Sixteenth Floor
New York, NY 10019

Gail Hochman
Brandt & Hochman Literary Agents,
   Inc.
1501 Broadway
Suite 2310
New York, NY 10036

Barbara Hogenson
165 West End Avenue
Suite 19-C
New York, NY 10023

Pamela A. Hopkins
Hopkins Literary Associates
2117 Buffalo Road
Suite 327
Rochester, NY 14624

Aileen Hussung
Samuel French, Inc.
45 West Twenty-fifth Street
New York, NY 10010

Jennifer Jackson
Donald Maass Literary Agency
160 West Ninety-fifth Street
Suite 1B
New York, NY 10025
www.jenniferjackson.org

Emilie Jacobson
Curtis Brown, Ltd.
Ten Astor Place
New York, NY 10003

Robin Kaver
Robert A. Freedman Dramatic
    Agency
1501 Broadway
Suite 2310
New York, NY 10036

Mary Alice Kier
Cine/Lit Representation
P.O. Box 802918
Santa Clarita, CA 91380-2918
E-mail: cinelit@msn.com

Jeff Kleinman
The Graybill & English Literary
    Agency
1875 Connecticut Avenue NW
Suite 712
Washington, DC 20009
E-mail: jeff@graybillandenglish.
    com
✑www.graybillandenglish.com

Harvey Klinger
Harvey Klinger, Inc.
301 West Fifty-third Street
New York, NY 10019

Edward Knappman
New England Publishing Associates
P.O. Box 5
Chester, CT 06412
E-mail: ed@nepa.com
✑www.nepa.com

Deidre Knight
The Knight Agency, Inc.
Madison, GA
E-mail: Knightagent@aol.com
✑www.knightagency.net

Ginger Knowlton
Curtis Brown, Ltd.
Ten Astor Place
New York, NY 10003

Timothy Knowlton
Curtis Brown, Ltd.
Ten Astor Place
New York, NY 10003

Linda Konner
Linda Konner Literary Agency
10 West Fifteenth Street
Suite 1918
New York, NY 10011

Charles Kopelman
Douglas & Kopelman Artists, Inc.
393 West Forty-ninth Street
#5G
New York, NY 10019

Elaine Koster
Elaine Koster Literary Agency LLC
55 Central Park West
Suite 6
New York, NY 10023
E-mail: ElaineKost@aol.com

Barbara S. Kouts
Literary Agent
P.O. Box 560
Bellport, NY 11713

Stuart Krichevsky
Stuart Krichevsky Literary Agency,
    Inc.
381 Park Avenue South
Suite 914
New York, NY 10016

Miriam Kriss
Irene Goodman Literary Agency
80 Fifth Avenue
#1101
New York, NY 10011

Raymond Kurman
Rights Unlimited, Inc.
101 West Fifty-fifth Street
Suite 2D
New York, NY 10019

Ronald Laitsch
Authentic Creations Literary
    Agency, Inc.
875 Lawrenceville-Suwanee Road
Suite 310-306
Lawrenceville, GA 30043

Heide Lange
Sanford J. Greenburger Associates
55 Fifth Avenue
Fifteenth Floor
New York, NY 10003

Robert Lantz
The Lantz Office
200 West Fifty-seventh Street
Suite 503
New York, NY 10019

Michael Larsen
Michael Larsen/Elizabeth Pomada
    Literary Agents
1029 Jones Street
San Francisco, CA 94109

Owen Laster
William Morris Agency, Inc.
1325 Avenue of the Americas
New York, NY 10019

Sarah Lazin
Sarah Lazin Books
126 Fifth Avenue
Suite 300
New York, NY 10011

Ned Leavitt
The Ned Leavitt Agency
70 Wooster Street
New York, NY 10012
✍www.nedleavittagency.com

Stephanie Lee
Manus & Associates Literary
    Agency West
425 Sherman Avenue
Suite 200
Palo Alto, CA 94301

Lettie Lee
Ann Elmo Agency, Inc.
60 East Forty-second Street
New York, NY 10165

Robert Lescher
Lescher & Lescher, Ltd.
47 East Nineteenth Street
New York, NY 10003

Susan Lescher
Lescher & Lescher, Ltd.
47 East Nineteenth Street
New York, NY 10003

Donna Levin
Manus & Associates Literary
    Agency
425 Sherman Avenue
Suite 200
Palo Alto, CA 94306
E-mail: donna@manuslit.com

Ellen Levine
Trident Media Group
41 Madison Avenue
New York, NY 10010

James A. Levine
Levine Greenberg Literary Agency,
    Inc.
307 Seventh Avenue
Suite 1906
New York, NY 10001

Wendy Lipkind
Wendy Lipkind Agency
120 East Eighty-first Street
New York, NY 10028

Simon Lipskar
Writers House
21 West Twenty-sixth Street
New York, NY 10010

Laurie Liss
Sterling Lord Literistic Inc.
65 Bleecker Street
New York, NY 10012

Daniel Listwa
Maria Carvainis Agency
1350 Avenue of the Americas
New York, NY 10019

Brad Lohrenz
Samuel French, Inc.
45 West Twenty-fifth Street
New York, NY 10010

Robin London
The Joy Harris Literary Agency
156 Fifth Avenue
Suite 617
New York, NY 10010

Toni Lopopolo
Toni Lopopolo Literary
    Management
8837 School House Lane
Coopersburg, PA 18036

Julia Lord
Julia Lord Literary Management
38th West Ninth Street
#4
New York, NY 10011
E-mail: julialordliterary@nyc.rr.com

Chris Lotts
Ralph M. Vicinanza, Ltd.
303 West Eighteenth Street
New York, NY 10011

Nancy Love
Nancy Love Literary Agency
250 East Sixty-fifth Street
New York, NY 10021

Barbara Lowenstein
Lowenstein-Yost Assoc. Inc.
121 West Twenty-seventh Street
Suite 601
New York, NY 10001

Selma Luttinger
Robert A. Freedman Dramatic
    Agency, Inc.
1501 Broadway
Suite 2310
New York, NY 10036

Jennifer Lyons
Writers House
21 West Twenty-sixth Street
New York, NY 10010

Jonathan Lyons
McIntosh & Otis
353 Lexington Avenue
New York, NY 10016

Donald Maass
Donald Maass Literary Agency
160 West Ninety-fifth Street
Suite 1B
New York, NY 10025

Gina Maccoby
Gina Maccoby Literary Agency
P.O. Box 60
Chappaqua, NY 10514
E-mail: gmaccoby@aol.com

Pamela Malpas
Harold Ober Associates, Inc.
425 Madison Avenue
New York, NY 10017

Daniel Mandel
Sanford J. Greenburger Associates,
    Inc.
55 Fifth Avenue
Fifteenth Floor
New York, NY 10003

Jay Mandel
William Morris Agency
1325 Avenue of the Americas
New York, NY 10019

Kristen Manges
Curtis Brown, Ltd.
Ten Astor Place
New York, NY 10003

Carol Mann
Carol Mann Agency
55 Fifth Avenue
New York, NY 10003

Janet Wilkens Manus
Manus & Associates Literary
    Agency, Inc.
445 Park Avenue
Ninth Floor
New York, NY 10022

Jillian W. Manus
Manus & Associates Literary
    Agency West
425 Sherman Avenue
Suite 200
Palo Alto, CA 94306

Denise Marcil
Denise Marcil Literary Agency, Inc.
156 Fifth Avenue
Suite 625
New York, NY 10010
www.denisemarcilagency.com

Elaine Markson
Elaine Markson Literary Agency,
    Inc.
44 Greenwich Avenue
New York, NY 10011

Mildred Marmur
Mildred Marmur Associates, Ltd.
2005 Palmer Avenue
Suite 127
Larchmont, NY 10538

Evan Marshall
The Evan Marshall Agency
Six Tristam Place
Pine Brook, NJ 07058-9445

Tonda Marton
The Marton Agency, Inc.
One Union Square
Suite 612
New York, NY 10003-3303

Lysna Marzani
Samuel French, Inc.
45 West Twenty-fifth Street
New York, NY 10010

Jonathan Matson
Harold Matson Company, Inc.
276 Fifth Avenue
New York, NY 10001

Margret McBride
Margret McBride Literary Agency
7744 Fay Avenue
Suite 201
La Jolla, CA 92037

Shawna McCarthy
The McCarthy Agency, LLC
7 Allen Street
Rumson, NJ 07660

Gerard McCauley
Gerard McCauley Agency, Inc.
P.O. Box 844
Katonah, NY 10536

Anita McClellan
Anita D. McClellan Associates
50 Stearns Street
Cambridge, MA 02138

Cameron McClure
Donald Maass Literary Agency
165 West Ninety-fifth Street
Suite 1B
New York, NY 10025

Tanya McKinnon
Mary Evans, Inc.
242 East Fifth Street
New York, NY 10003

Patricia McLaughlin
Beacon Artists Agency
208 West Thirtieth Street
Suite 401
New York, NY 10001

Sally Hill McMillan
Sally Hill McMillan & Assocs., Inc.
429 East Kingston Avenue
Charlotte, NC 28203
E-mail: mcmagency@aol.com

Scott Andrew Mendel
Mendel Media Group LLC
254 Canal Street
Suite 4018
New York, NY 10013
E-mail: scott@mendelmedia.com
✍www.mendelmedia.com

Claudia Menza
Claudia Menza Literary Agency
1170 Broadway
New York, NY 10001

Marianne Merola
Brandt & Hochman Literary Agents,
   Inc.
1501 Broadway
Suite 2310
New York, NY 10036
E-mail: mmerola@bromasite.com

Doris S. Michaels
Doris S. Michaels Literary Agency,
   Inc.
1841 Broadway
Suite 903
New York, NY 10023

Martha Millard
Martha Millard Literary Agency
50 West Sixty-seventh Street
1G
New York, NY 10023

Patricia Moosbrugger
Patricia Moosbrugger Literary
   Agency
165 Bennet Avenue
#6M
New York, NY 10040
E-mail: pmrights@aol.com

Howard Morhaim
Howard Morhaim Literary Agency
11 John Street
Suite 407
New York, NY 10038-4067
E-mail: erin@morhaimliterary.com

Gary Morris
David Black Literary Agency
156 Fifth Avenue
Suite 608
New York, NY 10010

Nicholas A. Mullendore
Loretta Barrett Books, Inc.
101 Fifth Avenue
Eleventh Floor
New York, NY 10003

Erin Murphy
Erin Murphy Literary Agency
2700 Woodlands Village
#300-458
Flagstaff, AZ 86001-7127

Jean Naggar
216 East Seventy-fifth Street
Suite 1E
New York, NY 10021

Mary Ann Naples
The Creative Culture, Inc.
72 Spring Street
Suite 304
New York, NY 10012

Muriel Nellis
Literary and Creative Artists, Inc.
3543 Albemarle Street NW
Washington, DC 20008-4213
E-mail: limn@lcadc.com,
   muriel@lcadc.com
✍www.lcadc.com

Craig Nelson
Craig Nelson Company
New York, NY
E-mail: litagnt@aol.com
✍http://members.aol.com/litagnt

Jandy Nelson
Manus & Associates Literary
   Agency West
425 Sherman Avenue
Suite 200
Palo Alto, CA 94306

Kristin Nelson
Nelson Literary Agency
1020 Fifteenth Street
Suite 26L
Denver, CO 80202
🖳www.nelsonagency.com

Penny Nelson
Manus & Associates Literary
   Agency West
425 Sherman Avenue
Suite 200
Palo Alto, CA 94306

Ken Norwick
110 East Fifty-ninth Street
29th Floor
New York, NY 10022

Emily Nurkin
The Carol Mann Agency
55 Fifth Avenue
New York, NY 10003-4301
E-mail: emily@carolmannagency.
   com

Neil Olson
Donadio & Ashworth, Inc.
121 West Twenty-seventh Street
Suite 704
New York, NY 10001

Bruce Ostler
Bret Adams Limited Agency
448 West Forty-fourth Street
New York, NY 10036

Tony Outhwaite
JCA Literary Agency, Inc.
27 West Twentieth Street
Suite 1103
New York, NY 10011

Sonia Pabley
Rosenstone/Wender
38 East Twenty-ninth Street
Tenth Floor
New York, NY 10016
E-mail: spabley@rosenstone
   wender.com

Merry Gregory Pantano
Blanche C. Gregory, Inc.
2 Tudor City Place
New York, NY 10017

Theresa Park
Sanford J. Greenburger Associates,
   Inc.
156 Fifth Avenue
Suite 1134
New York, NY 10010

Richard Parks
The Richard Parks Agency
P.O. Box 693
Salem, NY 12865

Emma Patterson
The Wendy Weil Agency, Inc.
232 Madison Avenue
Suite 1300
New York, NY 10016
E-mail: epatterson@wendyweil.
   com

Laura Blake Peterson
Curtis Brown, Ltd.
Ten Astor Place
New York, NY 10003

Cheryl Pientka
The Joy Harris Literary Agency, Inc.
156 Fifth Avenue
Suite 617
New York, NY 10010

Samuel L. Pinkus
McIntosh and Otis, Inc.
353 Lexington Avenue
New York, NY 10016

Elizabeth Pomada
Michael Larsen/Elizabeth Pomada
   Literary Agents
1029 Jones Street
San Francisco, CA 94109

Marta Praeger
Robert A. Freedman Dramatic
   Agency, Inc.
1501 Broadway
Suite 2310
New York, NY 10036

Helen F. Pratt
1165 Fifth Avenue
New York, NY 10029

Aaron M. Priest
The Aaron M. Priest Literary
    Agency
708 Third Avenue
Twenty-third Floor
New York, NY 10017-4103

Susan Ann Protter
Susan Ann Protter Literary Agent
110 West Fortieth Street
Suite 1408
New York, NY 10018
E-mail: sapla@aol.com

Victoria Gould Pryor
Arcadia
31 Lake Place North
Danbury, CT 06810
E-mail: arcadialit@att.net

Susan Raihofer
David Black Literary Agency
156 Fifth Avenue
Suite 608
New York, NY 10010-7002

Theron Raines
Raines & Raines
103 Kenyon Road
Medusa, NY 12120

Susan Ramer
Don Congdon Associates, Inc.
156 Fifth Avenue
Suite 625
New York, NY 10010

Jodi Reamer
Writers House
21 West Twenty-sixth Street
New York, NY 10010

Helen Rees
Helen Rees Literary Agency
376 North Street
First Floor
Boston, MA 02113-2103

Joseph Regal
Regal Literary
1140 Broadway
Penthouse
New York, NY 10001

Jody Rein
Jody Rein Books, Inc.
7741 South Ash Court
Centennial, CO 80122
www.jodyreinbooks.com

Anne Reingold
The Marton Agency, Inc.
One Union Square West
Suite 612
New York, NY 10003

William Reiss
John Hawkins & Associates, Inc.
71 West Twenty-third Street
Suite 1600
New York, NY 10010

Jodie Rhodes
Jodie Rhodes Literary Agency
8840 Villa La Jolla Drive
Suite 315
La Jolla, CA 92037

Angela Rinaldi
The Angela Rinaldi Literary Agency
2965 Motor Avenue
Los Angeles, CA 90064

Ann Rittenberg
Ann Rittenberg Literary Agency,
    Inc.
30 Bond Street
New York, NY 10012
www.rittlit.com

B.J. Robbins
5130 Bellaire Avenue
North Hollywood, CA 91607
E-mail: robbinsliterary@aol.com

Jane F. Roberts
Literary & Creative Artists, Inc.
3543 Albemarle Street NW
Washington, DC 20008

Linda Roghaar
Linda Roghaar Literary Agency Inc.
133 High Point Drive
Amherst, MA 01002

Barbara Collins Rosenberg
The Rosenberg Group
23 Lincoln Avenue
Marblehead, MA 01945
www.rosenberggroup.com

Rita Rosenkranz
Rita Rosenkranz Literary Agency
440 West End Avenue
Apartment 15D
New York, NY 10024

Howard Rosenstone
Rosenstone/Wender
38 East Twenty-ninth Street
Tenth Floor
New York, NY 10016

Gail Ross
Lichtman, Trister, Singer & Ross
1666 Connecticut Avenue NW
Suite 501
Washington, DC 20009

Stephanie Kip Rostan
Levine Greenberg Literary Agency
307 Seventh Avenue
Suite 1906
New York, NY 10001
E-mail: srostan@levinegreenberg.
com

Jane Rotrosen
Jane Rotrosen Agency
318 East Fifty-first Street
New York, NY 10022

Damaris Rowland
The Damaris Rowland Agency
5 Cooper Road
13H
New York, NY 10010

Peter Rubie
Peter Rubie Literary Agency
240 West Thirty-fifth Street
Suite 500
New York, NY 10001

Jennifer Rudolph Walsh
William Morris Agency
1325 Avenue of the Americas
New York, NY 10019

Robin Rue
Writers House
21 West Twenty-sixth Street
New York, NY 10010

Mark Ryan
New Brand Agency Group
E-mail: queries@literaryagent.net
✍ *www.literaryagent.net*

Raphael Sagalyn
Sagalyn Literary Agency
7201 Wisconsin Avenue
Suite 675
Bethesda, MD 20814

Ben Salmon
Doris S. Michaels Literary Agency,
Inc
1841 Broadway
Suite 903
New York, NY 10023
✍ *www.dsmagency.com*

Victoria Sanders
Victoria Sanders & Associates
241 Avenue of the Americas
Suite 11H
New York, NY 10014

Charles Schlessiger
Brandt & Hochman Literary Agents,
Inc.
1501 Broadway
New York, NY 10036

Wendy Schmalz
Wendy Schmalz Agency
Box 831
Hudson, NY 12534

Harold Schmidt
415 West Twenty-third Street
#6F
New York, NY 10011

Deborah Schneider
Gelfman Schneider
250 West Fifty-seventh Street
Suite 2515
New York, NY 10107

Susan Schulman
Susan Schulman Literary Agency
454 West Forty-fourth Street
New York, NY 10036

Timothy Seldes
Russell & Volkening, Inc.
50 West Twenty-ninth Street
New York, NY 10001

Edythea Ginis Selman
Edythea Ginis Selman Agency
14 Washington Place
New York, NY 10003

Richard Selman
Edythia Ginis Selman Agency
14 Washington Place
New York, NY 10003

Mary Sue Seymour
The Seymour Agency
475 Miner Street Road
Canton, NY 13617
E-mail: marysue@slic.com
✍ *www.theseymouragency.com*

Robert Shepard
The Robert E. Shepard Agency
1608 Dwight Way
Berkeley, CA 94703
✍ *www.shepardagency.com*

Wendy Sherman
Wendy Sherman Associates, Inc.
450 Seventh Avenue
New York, NY 10123

Rosalie Siegel
International Literary Agent, Inc.
One Abey Drive
Pennington, NJ 08543

Ira Silverberg
Donadio & Ashworth, Inc.
121 West Twenty-seventh Street
Suite 704
New York, NY 10001

Irene Skolnick
Irene Skolnick Agency
22 West Twenty-third Street
Fifth Floor
New York, NY 10010

Karen Solem
Spencerhill Associates, Ltd.
P.O. Box 374
Chatham, NY 12037

Philip Spitzer
Philip G. Spitzer Literary Agency
50 Talmage Farm Lane
East Hampton, NY 11937

Pattie Steele-Perkins
Steele-Perkins Literary Agency
26 Island Lane
Canandaigua, NY 14424

Peter Steinberg
Regal Literary
1140 Broadway
Penthouse
New York, NY 10001
✍www.regal-literary.com

Emilie Stewart
Anne Edelstein Literary Agency
20 West Twenty-second Street
Suite 1603
New York, NY 10010
E-mail: emilie@aeliterary.com

Rosemary B. Stimola
Stimola Literary Studio
308 Chase Court
Edgewater, NJ 07020

Sam Stoloff
Frances Goldin Literary Agency
57 East Eleventh Street
Suite 5B
New York, NY 10003

Robin Straus
Robin Straus Agency, Inc.
229 East Seventy-ninth Street
New York, NY 10021

Pamela Dean Strickler
Pam Strickler Author Management
P.O. Box 429
Accord, NY 12404
✍www.pamstrickler.com

Wendy J. Strothman
The Strothman Agency, LLC
One Faneuil Hall Marketplace
Third Floor
Boston, MA 02109

Moira Sullivan
Maria Carvainis Agency, Inc.
1350 Avenue of the Americas
Suite 2905
New York, NY 10019

Emma Sweeney
Harold Ober Associates
425 Madison Avenue
New York, NY 10017

Mary M. Tahan
Mary M Tahan Literary Agency
Gracie Station
P.O. Box 1060
New York, NY 10028
E-mail: querymarytahan@
    earthlink.net
✍www.tahanliterary.com

John Talbot
The John Talbot Literary Agency,
    Inc.
540 West Boston Post Road
PMB 266
Mamaroneck, NY 10543-3437
E-mail: talbotagency@mac.com
✍www.johntalbotagency.com

Roslyn Targ
Roslyn Targ Literary Agency, Inc.
105 West Thirteenth Street
15E
New York, NY 10011
E-mail: Roslyn@RoslynTarg
    Agency.com

Alice Tasman
Jean V. Naggar Literary Agency
216 East Seventy-fifth Street
#1E
New York, NY 10021

Patricia Teal
Patricia Teal Literary Agency
2036 Vista del Rosa
Fullerton, CA 92831

Nephele Tempest
The Knight Agency, Inc.
577 South Main Street
Madison, GA 30650

Craig Tenney
Harold Ober Associates, Inc.
425 Madison Avenue
New York, NY 10017

Michelle Tessler
Tessler Literary Agency, LLC
27 West Twentieth Street
Suite 1003
New York, NY 10011

Robert Thixton
Pinder Lane & Garon-Brooke
    Associates, Ltd.
159 West Fifty-third Street
New York, NY 10019

Geri Thoma
Elaine Markson Literary Agency
44 Greenwich Avenue
New York, NY 10011

Rosalie Grace Thompson
Heacock Literary Agency, Inc.
507 Grand Boulevard
P.O. Box 226
Cloudcroft, NM 88317-0226
E-mail: GraceBooks@aol.com

Scott Treimel
Scott Treimel New York
434 Lafayette Street
New York, NY 10003

Joy E. Tutela
David Black Literary Agency
156 Fifth Avenue
Suite 608
New York, NY 10010

Jennifer Unter
RLR Associates, Ltd.
7 West Fifty-first Street
New York, NY 10019
E-mail: junter@rlrassociates.net
✍www.rlrliterary.net

Michael Valentino
Cambridge Literary
135 Beach Road
Unit C-3
Salisbury, MA 01952

Ralph Valentino
Cambridge Literary
135 Beach Road
Unit C-3
Salisbury, MA 01952

Charles R. Van Nostrand
Samuel French, Inc.
45 West Twenty-fifth Street
New York, NY 10010

Lisa Erbach Vance
The Aaron M. Priest Literary
    Agency
708 Third Avenue
Twenty-third Floor
New York, NY 10017

Rachel Vater
Donald Maass Literary Agency
160 West Ninety-fifth Street
Suite 1B
New York, NY 10025
E-mail: rvater@maassagency.com

Nicole Verity
Barbara Hogenson Agency, Inc.
165 West End Avenue
19C
New York, NY 10012
E-mail: bhogenson@aol.com

Ralph Vicinanza
Ralph Vicinanza, Ltd.
303 West Eighteenth Street
New York, NY 10011

David Vigliano
David Vigliano Agency, Ltd.
584 Broadway
Suite 809
New York, NY 10012

Liza Pulitzer Voges
Kirchoff/Wohlberg, Inc.
866 United Nations Plaza
New York, NY 10017

Alvin Wald
Mary Jack Wald Associates, Inc.
111 East Fourteenth Street
PMB 113
New York, NY 10003

Mary Jack Wald
Mary Jack Wald Associates, Inc.
111 East Fourteenth Street
PMB 113
New York, NY 10003

Elizabeth Wales
Wales Literary Agency, Inc.
P.O. Box 9428
Seattle, WA 98109-0428

Maureen Walters
Curtis Brown, Ltd.
Ten Astor Place
New York, NY 10003

Harriet Wasserman
Harriet Wasserman Literary
    Agency, Inc.
137 East Thirty-sixth Street
New York, NY 10016

Mitchell S. Waters
Curtis Brown, Ltd.
Ten Astor Place
New York, NY 10003

Wendy Weil
The Wendy Weil Agency, Inc.
232 Madison Avenue
Suite 1300
New York, NY 10016

Ted Weinstein
Ted Weinstein Literary
    Management
35 Stillman Street
Suite 203
San Francisco, CA 94107
www.twliterary.com

Amy Berkower Weiss
Writers House
21 West Twenty-sixth Street
New York, NY 10010

Jennifer Weltz
Jean V. Naggar Literary Agency
216 East Seventy-fifth Street
New York, NY 10021

Phyllis Wender
Rosenstone/Wender
38 East Twenty-ninth Street
Tenth Floor
New York, NY 10016

Phyllis Westberg
Harold Ober Associates, Inc.
425 Madison Avenue
New York, NY 10017

Lynn Whittaker
Graybill & English, LLC
1875 Connecticut Avenue NW
Suite 1715
Washington, DC 20009

Elizabeth A. Winick
McIntosh & Otis, Inc.
353 Lexington Avenue
Fifteenth Floor.
New York, NY 10016

Eugene Winick
McIntosh & Otis, Inc.
353 Lexington Avenue
Fifteenth Floor
New York, NY 10016

Edwin John Wintle
Curtis Brown, Ltd.
Ten Astor Place
New York, NY 10003

Sally Wofford-Girand
Brick House Literary Agents
80 Fifth Avenue
Suite 1101
New York, NY 10011
E-mail: woffordgirand@brick
    houselit.com

Audrey A. Wolf
Audrey A. Wolf Literary Agency
2510 Virginia Avenue NW
#702N
Washington, DC 20037

Robert Wolgemuth
Wolgemuth & Associates, Inc.
8600 Crestgate Circle
Orlando, FL 32819

Nancy K. Yost
Lowenstein-Yost Assoc. Inc.
121 West Twenty-seventh Street
Suite 601
New York, NY 10001

Susan Zeckendorf
Susan Zeckendorf Associates, Inc.
171 West Fifty-seventh Street
New York, NY 10019

Albert Zuckerman
Writers House
21 West Twenty-sixth Street
New York, NY 10010

Index

The EVERYTHING Series!

BUSINESS & PERSONAL FINANCE

Everything® Accounting Book
Everything® Budgeting Book
Everything® Business Planning Book
Everything® Coaching and Mentoring Book
Everything® Fundraising Book
Everything® Get Out of Debt Book
Everything® Grant Writing Book
Everything® Home-Based Business Book, 2nd Ed.
Everything® Homebuying Book, 2nd Ed.
Everything® Homeselling Book, 2nd Ed.
Everything® Investing Book, 2nd Ed.
Everything® Landlording Book
Everything® Leadership Book
Everything® Managing People Book, 2nd Ed.
Everything® Negotiating Book
Everything® Online Auctions Book
Everything® Online Business Book
Everything® Personal Finance Book
Everything® Personal Finance in Your 20s and 30s Book
Everything® Project Management Book
Everything® Real Estate Investing Book
Everything® Robert's Rules Book, $7.95
Everything® Selling Book
Everything® Start Your Own Business Book, 2nd Ed.
Everything® Wills & Estate Planning Book

COOKING

Everything® Barbecue Cookbook
Everything® Bartender's Book, $9.95
Everything® Chinese Cookbook
Everything® Classic Recipes Book
Everything® Cocktail Parties and Drinks Book
Everything® College Cookbook
Everything® Cooking for Baby and Toddler Book
Everything® Cooking for Two Cookbook
Everything® Diabetes Cookbook
Everything® Easy Gourmet Cookbook
Everything® Fondue Cookbook
Everything® Fondue Party Book
Everything® Gluten-Free Cookbook
Everything® Glycemic Index Cookbook
Everything® Grilling Cookbook

Everything® Healthy Meals in Minutes Cookbook
Everything® Holiday Cookbook
Everything® Indian Cookbook
Everything® Italian Cookbook
Everything® Low-Carb Cookbook
Everything® Low-Fat High-Flavor Cookbook
Everything® Low-Salt Cookbook
Everything® Meals for a Month Cookbook
Everything® Mediterranean Cookbook
Everything® Mexican Cookbook
Everything® One-Pot Cookbook
Everything® Quick and Easy 30-Minute, 5-Ingredient Cookbook
Everything® Quick Meals Cookbook
Everything® Slow Cooker Cookbook
Everything® Slow Cooking for a Crowd Cookbook
Everything® Soup Cookbook
Everything® Tex-Mex Cookbook
Everything® Thai Cookbook
Everything® Vegetarian Cookbook
Everything® Wild Game Cookbook
Everything® Wine Book, 2nd Ed.

GAMES

Everything® 15-Minute Sudoku Book, $9.95
Everything® 30-Minute Sudoku Book, $9.95
Everything® Blackjack Strategy Book
Everything® Brain Strain Book, $9.95
Everything® Bridge Book
Everything® Card Games Book
Everything® Card Tricks Book, $9.95
Everything® Casino Gambling Book, 2nd Ed.
Everything® Chess Basics Book
Everything® Craps Strategy Book
Everything® Crossword and Puzzle Book
Everything® Crossword Challenge Book
Everything® Cryptograms Book, $9.95
Everything® Easy Crosswords Book
Everything® Easy Kakuro Book, $9.95
Everything® Games Book, 2nd Ed.
Everything® Giant Sudoku Book, $9.95
Everything® Kakuro Challenge Book, $9.95
Everything® Large-Print Crossword Challenge Book
Everything® Large-Print Crosswords Book
Everything® Lateral Thinking Puzzles Book, $9.95
Everything® Mazes Book

Everything® Pencil Puzzles Book, $9.95
Everything® Poker Strategy Book
Everything® Pool & Billiards Book
Everything® Test Your IQ Book, $9.95
Everything® Texas Hold 'Em Book, $9.95
Everything® Travel Crosswords Book, $9.95
Everything® Word Games Challenge Book
Everything® Word Search Book

HEALTH

Everything® Alzheimer's Book
Everything® Diabetes Book
Everything® Health Guide to Adult Bipolar Disorder
Everything® Health Guide to Controlling Anxiety
Everything® Health Guide to Fibromyalgia
Everything® Health Guide to Thyroid Disease
Everything® Hypnosis Book
Everything® Low Cholesterol Book
Everything® Massage Book
Everything® Menopause Book
Everything® Nutrition Book
Everything® Reflexology Book
Everything® Stress Management Book

HISTORY

Everything® American Government Book
Everything® American History Book
Everything® Civil War Book
Everything® Freemasons Book
Everything® Irish History & Heritage Book
Everything® Middle East Book

HOBBIES

Everything® Candlemaking Book
Everything® Cartooning Book
Everything® Coin Collecting Book
Everything® Drawing Book
Everything® Family Tree Book, 2nd Ed.
Everything® Knitting Book
Everything® Knots Book
Everything® Photography Book
Everything® Quilting Book
Everything® Scrapbooking Book
Everything® Sewing Book
Everything® Woodworking Book

Bolded titles are new additions to the series.
All Everything® books are priced at $12.95 or $14.95, unless otherwise stated. Prices subject to change without notice.

HOME IMPROVEMENT

Everything® Feng Shui Book
Everything® Feng Shui Decluttering Book, $9.95
Everything® Fix-It Book
Everything® Home Decorating Book
Everything® Home Storage Solutions Book
Everything® Homebuilding Book
Everything® Lawn Care Book
Everything® Organize Your Home Book

KIDS' BOOKS

All titles are $7.95

Everything® Kids' Animal Puzzle & Activity Book
Everything® Kids' Baseball Book, 4th Ed.
Everything® Kids' Bible Trivia Book
Everything® Kids' Bugs Book
Everything® Kids' Cars and Trucks Puzzle & Activity Book
Everything® Kids' Christmas Puzzle & Activity Book
Everything® Kids' Cookbook
Everything® Kids' Crazy Puzzles Book
Everything® Kids' Dinosaurs Book
Everything® Kids' First Spanish Puzzle and Activity Book
Everything® Kids' Gross Hidden Pictures Book
Everything® Kids' Gross Jokes Book
Everything® Kids' Gross Mazes Book
Everything® Kids' Gross Puzzle and Activity Book
Everything® Kids' Halloween Puzzle & Activity Book
Everything® Kids' Hidden Pictures Book
Everything® Kids' Horses Book
Everything® Kids' Joke Book
Everything® Kids' Knock Knock Book
Everything® Kids' Learning Spanish Book
Everything® Kids' Math Puzzles Book
Everything® Kids' Mazes Book
Everything® Kids' Money Book
Everything® Kids' Nature Book
Everything® Kids' Pirates Puzzle and Activity Book
Everything® Kids' Princess Puzzle and Activity Book
Everything® Kids' Puzzle Book
Everything® Kids' Riddles & Brain Teasers Book
Everything® Kids' Science Experiments Book
Everything® Kids' Sharks Book
Everything® Kids' Soccer Book
Everything® Kids' Travel Activity Book

KIDS' STORY BOOKS

Everything® Fairy Tales Book

LANGUAGE

Everything® Conversational Chinese Book with CD, $19.95
Everything® Conversational Japanese Book with CD, $19.95
Everything® French Grammar Book
Everything® French Phrase Book, $9.95
Everything® French Verb Book, $9.95
Everything® German Practice Book with CD, $19.95
Everything® Inglés Book
Everything® Learning French Book
Everything® Learning German Book
Everything® Learning Italian Book
Everything® Learning Latin Book
Everything® Learning Spanish Book
Everything® Russian Practice Book with CD, $19.95
Everything® Sign Language Book
Everything® Spanish Grammar Book
Everything® Spanish Phrase Book, $9.95
Everything® Spanish Practice Book with CD, $19.95
Everything® Spanish Verb Book, $9.95

MUSIC

Everything® Drums Book with CD, $19.95
Everything® Guitar Book
Everything® Guitar Chords Book with CD, $19.95
Everything® Home Recording Book
Everything® Music Theory Book with CD, $19.95
Everything® Reading Music Book with CD, $19.95
Everything® Rock & Blues Guitar Book (with CD), $19.95
Everything® Songwriting Book

NEW AGE

Everything® Astrology Book, 2nd Ed.
Everything® Birthday Personology Book
Everything® Dreams Book, 2nd Ed.
Everything® Love Signs Book, $9.95
Everything® Numerology Book
Everything® Paganism Book
Everything® Palmistry Book
Everything® Psychic Book
Everything® Reiki Book
Everything® Sex Signs Book, $9.95
Everything® Tarot Book, 2nd Ed.
Everything® Wicca and Witchcraft Book

PARENTING

Everything® Baby Names Book, 2nd Ed.
Everything® Baby Shower Book
Everything® Baby's First Food Book
Everything® Baby's First Year Book
Everything® Birthing Book
Everything® Breastfeeding Book
Everything® Father-to-Be Book
Everything® Father's First Year Book
Everything® Get Ready for Baby Book
Everything® Get Your Baby to Sleep Book, $9.95
Everything® Getting Pregnant Book
Everything® Guide to Raising a One-Year-Old
Everything® Guide to Raising a Two-Year-Old
Everything® Homeschooling Book
Everything® Mother's First Year Book
Everything® Parent's Guide to Children and Divorce
Everything® Parent's Guide to Children with ADD/ADHD
Everything® Parent's Guide to Children with Asperger's Syndrome
Everything® Parent's Guide to Children with Autism
Everything® Parent's Guide to Children with Bipolar Disorder
Everything® Parent's Guide to Children with Dyslexia
Everything® Parent's Guide to Positive Discipline
Everything® Parent's Guide to Raising a Successful Child
Everything® Parent's Guide to Raising Boys
Everything® Parent's Guide to Raising Siblings
Everything® Parent's Guide to Sensory Integration Disorder
Everything® Parent's Guide to Tantrums
Everything® Parent's Guide to the Overweight Child
Everything® Parent's Guide to the Strong-Willed Child
Everything® Parenting a Teenager Book
Everything® Potty Training Book, $9.95
Everything® Pregnancy Book, 2nd Ed.
Everything® Pregnancy Fitness Book
Everything® Pregnancy Nutrition Book
Everything® Pregnancy Organizer, 2nd Ed., $16.95
Everything® Toddler Activities Book
Everything® Toddler Book
Everything® Tween Book
Everything® Twins, Triplets, and More Book

PETS

Everything® **Aquarium Book**
Everything® Boxer Book
Everything® Cat Book, 2nd Ed.
Everything® Chihuahua Book
Everything® Dachshund Book
Everything® Dog Book
Everything® Dog Health Book
Everything® **Dog Owner's Organizer,**
$16.95
Everything® Dog Training and Tricks Book
Everything® German Shepherd Book
Everything® Golden Retriever Book
Everything® Horse Book
Everything® Horse Care Book
Everything® Horseback Riding Book
Everything® Labrador Retriever Book
Everything® Poodle Book
Everything® Pug Book
Everything® Puppy Book
Everything® Rottweiler Book
Everything® Small Dogs Book
Everything® Tropical Fish Book
Everything® Yorkshire Terrier Book

REFERENCE

Everything® Blogging Book
Everything® **Build Your Vocabulary Book**
Everything® Car Care Book
Everything® Classical Mythology Book
Everything® Da Vinci Book
Everything® Divorce Book
Everything® Einstein Book
Everything® Etiquette Book, 2nd Ed.
Everything® Inventions and Patents Book
Everything® Mafia Book
Everything® Philosophy Book
Everything® Psychology Book
Everything® Shakespeare Book

RELIGION

Everything® Angels Book
Everything® Bible Book
Everything® Buddhism Book
Everything® Catholicism Book
Everything® Christianity Book
Everything® History of the Bible Book
Everything® **Jesus Book**
Everything® Jewish History & Heritage Book
Everything® Judaism Book
Everything® Kabbalah Book
Everything® Koran Book
Everything® **Mary Book**

Everything® Mary Magdalene Book
Everything® Prayer Book
Everything® Saints Book
Everything® Torah Book
Everything® Understanding Islam Book
Everything® World's Religions Book
Everything® Zen Book

SCHOOL & CAREERS

Everything® Alternative Careers Book
Everything® **Career Tests Book**
Everything® College Major Test Book
Everything® College Survival Book, 2nd Ed.
Everything® Cover Letter Book, 2nd Ed.
Everything® **Filmmaking Book**
Everything® Get-a-Job Book
Everything® Guide to Being a Paralegal
Everything® Guide to Being a Real Estate
Agent
Everything® **Guide to Being a Sales Rep**
Everything® **Guide to Careers in Health**
Care
Everything® **Guide to Careers in Law**
Enforcement
Everything® **Guide to Government Jobs**
Everything® Guide to Starting and Running
a Restaurant
Everything® Job Interview Book
Everything® New Nurse Book
Everything® New Teacher Book
Everything® Paying for College Book
Everything® Practice Interview Book
Everything® Resume Book, 2nd Ed.
Everything® Study Book

SELF-HELP

Everything® Dating Book, 2nd Ed.
Everything® Great Sex Book
Everything® Kama Sutra Book
Everything® Self-Esteem Book

SPORTS & FITNESS

Everything® **Easy Fitness Book**
Everything® Fishing Book
Everything® Golf Instruction Book
Everything® Pilates Book
Everything® Running Book
Everything® Weight Training Book
Everything® Yoga Book

TRAVEL

Everything® Family Guide to Cruise Vacations
Everything® Family Guide to Hawaii

Everything® Family Guide to Las Vegas,
2nd Ed.
Everything® **Family Guide to Mexico**
Everything® Family Guide to New York City,
2nd Ed.
Everything® Family Guide to RV Travel &
Campgrounds
Everything® Family Guide to the Caribbean
Everything® Family Guide to the Walt Disney
World Resort®, Universal Studios®,
and Greater Orlando, 4th Ed.
Everything® **Family Guide to Timeshares**
Everything® Family Guide to Washington
D.C., 2nd Ed.
Everything® Guide to New England

WEDDINGS

Everything® Bachelorette Party Book, $9.95
Everything® Bridesmaid Book, $9.95
Everything® **Destination Wedding Book**
Everything® Elopement Book, $9.95
Everything® Father of the Bride Book, $9.95
Everything® Groom Book, $9.95
Everything® Mother of the Bride Book, $9.95
Everything® Outdoor Wedding Book
Everything® Wedding Book, 3rd Ed.
Everything® Wedding Checklist, $9.95
Everything® Wedding Etiquette Book, $9.95
Everything® **Wedding Organizer, 2nd Ed.,**
$16.95
Everything® Wedding Shower Book, $9.95
Everything® Wedding Vows Book, $9.95
Everything® **Wedding Workout Book**
Everything® Weddings on a Budget Book,
$9.95

WRITING

Everything® Creative Writing Book
Everything® Get Published Book, 2nd Ed.
Everything® Grammar and Style Book
Everything® Guide to Writing a Book
Proposal
Everything® Guide to Writing a Novel
Everything® Guide to Writing Children's
Books
Everything® Guide to Writing Research
Papers
Everything® Screenwriting Book
Everything® Writing Poetry Book
Everything® Writing Well Book